Underfoot

Underfoot

An Everyday Guide to Exploring
the American Past

David Weitzman

Charles Scribner's Sons
New York

1 3 5 7 9 11 13 15 17 19 M/C 20 18 16 14 12 10 8 6 4 2
1 3 5 7 9 11 13 15 17 19 M/P 20 18 16 14 12 10 8 6 4 2

—•·•—

Printed in the United States of America.
Library of Congress Catalog Card Number 76-11475
ISBN 0-684-14767-X
ISBN 0-684-15066-2 pbk.

This book was edited and prepared for publication
at The Yolla Bolly Press, Covelo, California.
The work was done between September 1975 and April 1976
under the supervision of James and Carolyn Robertson.
Staff members: Colleen Carter, Sharon Miley, Gene Floyd, Richard Wilson.

—•—

Acknowledgement is made to:

Alex Haley for use of excerpts from "My Furthest Back Person—The African," Copyright © 1972 by Alex Haley and reprinted by permission of Paul R. Reynolds, Inc.

The University of Chicago Press for permission to use excerpts from B. A. Botkin (ed.), *Lay My Burden Down: A Folk History of Slavery*, © 1945, The University of Chicago Press.

Ellen C. Masters for her permission to reprint "The Hill" from Edgar Lee Masters' *Spoon River Anthology*, Copyright © 1962 by The Crowell-Collier Publishing Company.

Columbia University Press for permission to use excerpts from *Ozark Superstitions*, by Vance Randolph, Copyright © 1947 by Columbia University Press.

Dover Publications, Inc. for permission to reprint illustrations from *Early New England Gravestone Rubbings* by Edmund Vincent Gillon, Jr. Copyright © 1966 by Dover Publications, Inc.

Doubleday & Company, Inc. for permission to reprint illustrations from *The Primer of American Antiquities* by Carl W. Drepperd. Copyright © 1944 by Carl W. Drepperd.

For My
Mother and Father

Foreword

Among the Cherokee, as among most families everywhere, the elders were by tradition the keepers of tribal history. But instead of beginning their tales "Once upon a time," as we might, they began their retelling of the past by saying, "This is what the old men told me when I was a boy." For those of us seeking a reconciliation with the past, there is in this choice of a beginning a subtle distinction, a lesson, a reminder of what history once meant, indeed all that it has ever meant. Much of our history comes not from the distance of once upon a time but from the memories of those closest to us and with whom we have lived our lives. Beginning a tale of the ancestors as the old Cherokee story-tellers did created from the very first words a comforting sense of continuity. Never is the listener allowed to forget that there have always been elders with lives rich in detail and experience, and that there will always be children to captivate and instruct with the images, the sounds, the textures, the tastes, and the smells of all that has gone before. Nor would the storyteller's opening words, repeated over a lifetime, ever let us forget from where and from whom we've come. For, if our search for roots seems of no avail, and if, despite our most fervent seeking, the answers still elude us, it's not because we are not wise enough, or that the paths to what used to be are such mysterious ones, but perhaps because we are looking in the wrong place. Search as we might in the history-book lives of others we don't know, and have never known, sooner or later we will return to find that the answers to who we are and where we've been are nearby, and many of them are underfoot.

D.W.

Table of Contents

◆◆◆

Table of Illustrations

CHAPTER I

Historian Everyman

Our preoccupation with print sometimes leads us to belittle the spoken word—until we see something in writing we often won't accept it. Still, the voice is capable of tones and colors infinitely more various than any words on any page and, for most of us, is the most natural means of expression. There were times, and there are still places in America too, in which writing was not considered essential to communication. Moreover, thousands of years of history have survived in considerable detail in vocal form—recited, chanted, and sung. The learning and retelling of one's family history, for instance, is seldom done through the printed word and almost never in a deliberate way. To be sure, there are, in every village and town, elders who have mastered centuries of history, but most of us learn our family history as children listening to the stories of parents and relatives—our ancestors—perhaps at a gathering of the clan or perhaps during nothing more than an hour or two of leisure.

My father's store was the only one in Mackerel Cove, a mile from those in Beverly Town and three miles from the one at Beverly Farms. Its miscellaneous stock contained almost everything except liquor, which was a sore deprivation for tipplers who had to go clear to Salem for their grog, for Beverly went dry in 1839.

Kim's store (so-called because my father's name was Andrew Kimball Ober)—the stock fluctuated, much of it depending upon the cargoes of ships coming into Salem or Boston. There were quantities of home products—flour, meal, potatoes, dried apples, peas and, of course, beans, for Beverly was dubbed Beantown from the very first. And Beverly was proud of the distinction of creating the first earthen bean pot in New England in her own pottery. There were big boxes of Boston pilot bread, big, round crackers as tough and dry as chips, the bread supply for fishing vessels. In close proximity to the crackers were great, round cheeses, freely sampled by the men who made the store a rendezvous.

On a counter near the entrance were bales of cloth, homespun, flannel and linsey-woolsey. A large glass case stood nearby containing offerings to feminine vanity—silks, ribbons, laces, buttons, buckles, jewelry, pins, needles, and thread. On the top of this case were large glass jars filled with lollipops, peppermints, sticks of red and white candy, and Gibraltars, a white candy made only in Salem, each piece about three inches long, hard as the rock they were named for. The opposite side of the store most intrigued me. I often lingered there absorbed (my father called me "the little Dreamer"), poring over quaint tea chests covered with Chinese characters, trying to imagine the pig-tailed men who had made them. Boxes of rice made me see broad "paddies" where big-hatted coolies labored, but trays of whole spices interested me the most. I sniffed the fragrance of cinnamon bark, cloves, nutmegs, allspice and mace, all from far Cathay. . . .

As a little girl I had my toys on the broad counter by the front window and could see all the passing on the country road below. When the stage passed twice a day, it was most exciting to hear the fanfare of a bugle sounding a salute to the store, which I took to be a salute to my father. The great stage, gay with bright yellow trimmings, creaked and rumbled as it swayed on broad leather straps. The four high-spirited horses raced and pranced and curveted as though they were fresh from their stable and had not come fifteen miles from Gloucester that morning. Old Cap'n Levi held the ribbons proudly and was resplendent in gray, square-topped beaver, bright blue coat with yellow facings and high-topped boots. The stage passed at nine in the morning, so regularly that clocks were set by it, and returned in the afternoon at half-past two.

There was no tinware in the store, for a tin peddler came along at certain times in the year. It was a great occasion when his big red cart came jingling and rattling along, bristling with brooms, mops, rakes, hoes, and pitchforks, with an occasional tin dishpan rattling among them. Children came running to flock about it and watch him open the great rear doors of the wagon and exhibit fascinating arrays of bright tins, fancy goods, and toys. Then Mother brought out bulging rag bags in which for months were garnered every bit of waste cloth. There were careful weighings and close computations until prices were agreed upon. Mother selected what she needed of kitchenware, always remembering toys for the children and some bit of fancy cloth for her young serving maid. Meanwhile local news was exchanged for the racy information gleaned by the peddler from the wide range of country which he had traversed. [Augustus Peabody Loring, ed., "Kim's Store: Reminiscences of Sarah Endicott Ober," in *Old-Time New England*, Spring, 1951]

Sarah Endicott Ober is a historian, but don't bother trying to place the name; you probably wouldn't know her unless you'd lived in Mack-

erel Cove many years ago. I met her only by accident, a fortuitous acquaintance that began a few months ago in a library and in the bookstall of a county historical museum. We've not really met, of course. Sarah died four years before I was born. Before she died back in 1932, in her eighties, she was known only as Miss Ober who lived with her cousins the Obers at Pride's Crossing, back of Mr. Henry Clay Frick's barn. There is an Ober Street in Mackerel Cove, named for Sarah's great-grandfather, a French Huguenot (the family name was Auger then) who fled to England and then to America in the late 1600s. In recalling a time in her childhood many, many years ago, Sarah probably didn't think of herself as a historian, but she was one nonetheless. Sarah would have said she was merely reminiscing, just looking back over all her years as she had done so often before with brothers and sisters, nieces and nephews, and all the grandchildren and great-grandchildren. After all, she might have said, when you've lived as long as I have, you know a lot of history, and besides I enjoy telling it. Reminiscing, recalling, talking family, just remembering, or whatever she might have called it, her thoughtfulness and sense of history, the pride of a long lifetime fully lived, or whatever it was that prompted her to leave us a record of her life, makes ours all the richer and hers that much longer. Surely historian is an appropriate name for someone who can do that.

I met other such historians in that same library—Rae McGrady Booth, whose recorded reminiscences as an Iowa farm girl go back to the time of her birth in 1889. She too would probably feel strange with the title "historian," and yet hers is the most meaningful kind of history there is, the retelling of personal experience with such vividness that the listener and reader experience it too. In a simple voice she tells of her earliest memories:

My paternal grandparents inherited 160 acres of virgin prairie land in Boone county from an uncle who was given a "land grant" for his services in the Union Army during the Civil War. It was on that farm in 1889 that I was born. Some of my fondest memories of childhood are the hours I spent with my grandparents. Grandpa had a nice white beard and would let me braid it as I sat on his lap in his old rocking chair. He and grandma each had their own rocking chair and I firmly believe they were the first examples of perpetual motion. Grandma used to give me my bath every Saturday night in a large brass kettle behind the pot-bellied stove which stood on a large square of linoleum called "oilcloth" in those days.

Her description of days on a farm near Des Moines is filled with happenings that anyone raised on a farm anywhere in America can remember, little things that after so many years seem so valuable to our sense of who we are:

Threshing days were big events for the children. We looked forward to the day when the big steam engine pulled into the barnyard followed by the horse-drawn water tank. All the neighbors pitched in to help each other. A few men with hayracks brought the sheaves of grain from the fields of oats or barley—wheat was not grown in Iowa at that early date. Several men were required to process the grain through what was called the separator, boys were needed to cut the binder twine with which each sheaf was tied, while others manned the wagons into which the fine grain was loaded and then hauled to the granary where they shoveled it from the wagons by hand. If my grandfather could see one of the modern threshing outfits I believe he would run for his life, scared by such a monster!

And she recalls some of the "buzz" of everyday life:

A few of the things one always saw around the house were: kerosene lamps and lanterns which had to be cleaned daily; a toothpick holder was always found on a well-set table; a lady's dressing table had a hair receiver where she placed her combings which were saved to make a switch later; fly swatters were branches of trees and the whole family chased flies before we could sit down to a meal; there was usually a hammock in the yard made of barrel staves and wire and seldom occupied; there were fancy lamps with glass shades and crystals hanging in the center of the front room; a few Currier & Ives prints were on the walls; a "piddy pot" was under each bed and always frozen solid in wintertime; and most homes were well-supplied with spitoons. Dad preferred to use the stove rather than a spitoon. Fruit was canned in stoneware jars and sealed with wax. Hog's intestines were used for stuffing sausage. Dad would use a short piece of railroad iron to crack walnuts for us on winter nights. Such things as button hooks for fastening the high button shoes and husking pegs for husking the corn were a must to be found in every home. [Rae McGrady Booth, "Memoirs of an Iowa Farm Girl," in *Annals of Iowa*, Fall, 1966]

It all seems so natural, so much of a piece, so familiar that every bit of it could be lost for-

Steam tractor, ca. 1900

ever, just because it has been so taken for granted. In our preoccupation with greatness, with importance, we lose the tiny details, the hammock in the yard, the texture of a grandfather's beard, the fragrance of freshly cut grain, the articles on a mother's dressing table —all of which together constitute a way of life.

It seems strange that while the memories of childhood are often the sweetest and toward the end of a long life the most memorable, history to most of us is the history of adults' lives and almost never of children's. In our scheme of history, children count for so little that they are all but ignored by the historian except when they are mentioned in passing, when they die in large numbers from pestilence or war, or are born in large numbers and thus constitute a baby boom. But I think that in a certain sense children may be the best historians of all, certainly the most sensitive. Perhaps the reason is that for the young everything that happens is an event, more vivid, more memorable because everything is new. The child has not lived long

enough to become jaded and skeptical of life, and having lived so few years has less to forget.

Caroline Cowles Richards began her diary on the occasion of her tenth birthday. That was in 1852, making her about the same age as my great-grandmother. There is little chance that they knew each other, Caroline having grown up in Canandaigua, New York, and my great-grandmother in Pine Bluff, Arkansas, yet I can't help but believe that their lives in village America were quite similar and familiar one to the other. For example, Caroline's husband, like my great-grandfather, fought in the Civil War (albeit on the other side). Both she and my great-grandmother would also, I'm sure, share memories of family gatherings, afternoons on the lake, thoughts of friends and family who returned from the War and those who didn't, birthdays, the gossip about their small towns, and holiday tables.

There's even something about Caroline's experiences that strike me as not much different from mine. One of the entries in her diary re-

My parents were married in 1880. My mother was born near Pleasantville in Marion county and her father was a surgeon in the Union Army. Her mother had a hard time taking care of the family during those years and consequently she died when my mother was only 10 years old. She was 20 when she and my father were married and they lived with my grandparents at 909 Ninth street, Des Moines, where my eldest brother was born.

The family moved to our Boone county farm in the fall of 1881 and lived in the new barn until they could build a house. The land was bare, virgin soil, and there was not a tree in sight. They set out a grove of lovely willow trees north of the house for a windbrake, and planted maples, cottonwoods and box-elders in the houseyard, in addition to an orchard of apple, cherry and plum trees.

I don't think my father was ever cut out to be a farmer, having lived to the age of 23 in the "city" of Des Moines. He had been reared in a religious atmosphere; grandmother, he said, was a "rock-ribbed and rubber-coated" Methodist. There

was no card-playing, dancing, smoking or profanity permitted when she was around. She read her Bible every day and family prayers were held at night. Both she and grandpa refused to attend my commencement exercises when I graduated from Perry High School in 1907 because the event was held in the opera house, that "den of iniquity!" [Rae Mc-Grady Booth, "Memoirs of an Iowa Farm Girl," in *Annals of Iowa*, Fall, 1966]

August 17 [*1858*] — There was a celebration in town today because the Queen's message was received on the Atlantic cable. Guns were fired and church bells rung and flags were waving everywhere. In the evening there was a torchlight procession and the town was all lighted up. . . .

November 19 [*1863*] — We wish we were at Gettysburg to-day to hear President Lincoln's and Edward Everett's addresses at the dedication of the National Cemetery. We will read them in to-morrow's papers, but it will not be like hearing them.

April 15 [*1865*] — The news came this morning that our dear president,

Abraham Lincoln, was assassinated yesterday, on the day appointed for thanksgiving for Union victories. I have felt sick over it all day and so has every one that I have seen. All seem to feel as though they had lost a personal friend, and tears flow plenteously. How soon has sorrow followed upon the heels of joy! One week ago to-night we were celebrating our victories with loud acclamations of mirth and good cheer. Now every one is silent and sad and the earth and heavens seem clothed in sack-cloth. The bells have been tolling this afternoon. The flags are all at half mast, draped with mourning, and on every store and dwelling-house some sign of the nation's loss is visible. Just after breakfast this morning, I looked out of the window and saw a group of men listening to the reading of a morning paper, and I feared from their silent, motionless interest that something dreadful had happened, but I was not prepared to hear of the cowardly murder of our President. [Caroline Cowles Richards, *Village Life in America, 1852–1872*. New York: Henry Holt and Company, 1913]

Redondo, California, 1899

minded me of a time in my own life, in the late forties, when I would ask my dad why we didn't have a television set (the first sets having been in the stores but a few months), and there was a tone in his voice—which I didn't understand then, but do now—suggesting that life was beginning to change a bit too fast.

Thursday [1857]—*I asked Grandfather why we do not have gas in the house like almost every one else and he said because it was bad for the eyes and he liked candles and sperm oil better. We have the funniest little sperm oil lamp with a shade on to read by evenings and the fire on the hearth gives Grandfather and Grandmother all the light they want, for she knits in her corner and we read aloud to them if they want us to. I think if Grandfather is proud of anything besides being a Bostonian, it is that everything in the house is forty years old. The shovel and tongs and andirons and*

fender and the haircloth sofa and the haircloth rocking chair and the flag bottomed chairs painted dark green and the two old arm-chairs which belong to them and no one else ever thinks of touching. There is a wooden partition between the dining-room and parlor and they say it can slide right up out of sight on pulleys, so that it would be all one room. We have often said that we wished we could see it go up but they say it has never been up since the day our mother was married and as she is dead I suppose it would make them feel bad, so we probably will always have it down.

And if you wonder how a girl so young possessed such a sense of history, you need only to read a few pages back to discover how a sense of history is created, where Caroline's came from, and how it happens that some among us become historians.

Saturday Night, July [1856]—*Grandfather was asking us to-night how many things we could remember, and I told him I could remember when Zachary Taylor died, and our church was draped in black, and Mr. Daggett preached a funeral sermon about him, and I could remember when Daniel Webster died, and there was service held in the church and his last words, "I still live," were put up over the pulpit. He said he could remember when George Washington died and when Benjamin Franklin died. He was seven years old then and he was seventeen when Washington died. Of course his memory goes farther back than mine, but he said I did very well, considering.* [Caroline Cowles Richards, *Village Life in America, 1852–1872.* New York: Henry Holt and Company, 1913]

Most of what we know today and just about all of the information and skills we've acquired that are essential to our survival came to us not by way of the professional historian but from our parents, our family, the children with whom we explored our world—they were our real historians, and it wasn't just the past that we learned from them: we learned the perspectives and attitudes that shaped our lives. The classroom and the book are never the principal vehicles of culture and history; for most of us it is our grandmother's lap.

Of course, every age has had its appointed historians. It is from the appointed historian that the professional of today descends. His is really a very old occupation whose lineage goes back more directly to the scribes, keepers of official records, and dynastic historians of the old civilizations.

But there is another kind of historian, most of whom, alas, remain anonymous; they are self-appointed by their sense of posterity, that same sense of mortality that makes us have our pictures taken and makes us write down recipes, that leads us to save and collect and to pass on our personal things—our artifacts—and our beliefs and values.

The historian "everyman" belongs to an old, honorable tradition whose participants extend far into the past and continue into the present day—the tellers of tales; the elders; puppeteers, dancers, and actors who initiated the young; the folksingers, clan leaders, teachers, grand-

mothers, habitués of the general store down at the fork, Sarah Endicott Ober, ten-year-old girls who keep diaries, and ninety-five-year-old Peter Duhn, who recalls a story of a long-ago childhood:

Once my father had 1,800 muskrat pelts to sell. Two men came through and wanted to buy them. Father asked 13 cents a pelt and the eldest of the two wouldn't bid more than twelve and a half.

The younger man had silver buttons down the side of his trousers and my brother and I watched him like a hawk, hoping one of the silver pieces would fall off.

Finally the younger man said, "Oh, give him the 13 cents."

The older one said, "He goes wild when he gets out into the country." But he paid 13 cents for each of the hides.

After a time the James gang robbed the bank in Wayne county of $40,000 and the Chicago, Rock Island and Pacific train near Adair. When the big city newspapers reached us, there was the story and pictures of Frank and Jesse James and their descriptions. Father took a good look and shouted, "Why those are the two men who bought my muskrat hides!" [Don Buchan, "Pioneer Tales," in *Annals of Iowa,* Fall, 1966]

*   *   *

Almost any occasion can be the starting point for a retelling of the family's history. Weddings are an occasion to recall weddings of the past and birthdays a time to recall lives long and short. Funerals and wakes are always times of historical introspection, calling once again on the magic of history to reassure and to reaffirm the continuity of the family in spite of the passing of its matriarch or patriarch. We are all historians more than we realize.

And well we Americans in particular should be, for in a very real sense we are mere children in history. Except for Native Americans among us, we're newcomers here, and though all of us remember our teachers telling us at one time or another that the United States of America is only two hundred years old and the history of the continent's settlement barely four hundred, it is sometimes difficult to grasp just what this means. It means, for one thing, that the entirety of our history as an independent nation spans at the most ten generations. This realization came to me recently when I was trading family history with a not too elderly man who remembers the opening of the Panama Canal and sailed through it many times as a young seaman. He remembers sitting with his great-grandfather one day hearing the old man relate his recollections of the death of George III. Here I was, talking with a friend not a lot older than my own father, whose great-grandfather —still alive in my friend's childhood—remembered America's last king!

Unreal? Well, look at it this way: if you are about thirty years old, then your parents, who were born about 1915, have childhood memories of the aftermath of the Great War, were children and young adults during Prohibition and the Depression, and fought in World War II.

Your grandparents, born about 1885, remember the New Year's Day that began this century, the first radios, automobiles, and aeroplanes, they may be veterans of World War I, and possibly read Jack London's *Call of the Wild* just after it appeared.

Your great-grandparents, born about 1855, remember Abraham Lincoln and the Civil War, your great-grandmother might have marched with Susan B. Anthony and might have played on her piano the latest works of Johannes Brahms to arrive in America.

Your mother and father's great-grandparents, born about 1825, remember the first wood-burning steam locomotives, the Nat Turner insurrection, and the appearance of daguerreotypes in America.

Your ancestors of six generations ago were born about 1795, when George Washington was still alive, work on the Erie Canal was just beginning, and Ludwig van Beethoven was but a concert pianist yet to write his first symphony.

Your ancestors seven generations ago, born about 1765, remember the celebrations the day the Declaration of Independence was signed, the Revolution, and the first years of the United States of America.

Think for a moment of all the memories, all the history of elderly men and women perhaps eighty years old today. Born about 1895, they were among the first to see the great inventions of our age—the exceptions being the steamship, railroad, and electricity, which preceded them—and the beginning of the widespread use of others. When they were born life in America was unimaginably different. But add to their own lives the memories of parents (born about 1870), grandparents (born about 1845), and even great-grandparents (born in the early years of the nineteenth century) and the memories of countless great-aunts and great-uncles, cousins, family friends, aunts and uncles—a family that could easily number in the hundreds—and you have some idea of the history that lies available to you if you but take advantage of it. And some idea of how much is lost at their death.

From the reminiscences again of Rae McGrady Booth:

One of my earliest memories is of my fourth birthday when my grandfather gave me enough red calico for a dress and grandmother gave me a tea set made of pewter, which I still have and not one tiny piece is missing. This was in August, 1893, the year of the "great panic" when William Jennings Bryan was making his famous speeches about "The Crown of Thorns and Cross of Gold." It was during those "panic" years that I saw my father grease his wagons with butter, which he had plenty of, rather than drive seven miles to buy axle grease. I also remember the two-bushel baskets of corn which were brought inside to be burned for fuel. The nearest market for the corn was ten miles west of the farm and the coal mines were ten miles east along the Des Moines River, so why not just burn the corn which was cheaper than coal?

We always had plenty to eat, however. We had a large strawberry patch and I can remember seeing the old extension kitchen table piled high with all the berries it would hold. It was a tiresome job for small children to sit for hours stemming strawberries, but it was worth it when we tasted the yummy shortcakes and later the strawberry jam in winter. We also had a long row of "pie plant," or rhubarb, a patch of raspberry bushes, many trees of red plums, a number of Dutchess apple trees and cherry trees. Sister Bess once picked her apron lap full of rabbit droppings under the bushes and proudly carried them to Mother thinking they were raspberries. We always had a large vegetable garden, where we found the long, slim Jersey sweet potatoes which we liked to eat with our hands, buttering each bite as we ate. We usually had mush and milk on Sat-

urday night for supper unless Dad went to the village seven miles away and brought home oysters. Then we had oyster soup with those little round crackers which the grocer dished out of an open barrel.

The historian in us is born with the realization and acceptance of our mortality. It is with this realization too that we know how much indeed we lost with the passing of our parents, grandparents, the elders of our family. Somehow, while they were alive it didn't seem important to listen to them, to record or remember what they've known, as though they would always be there just as they always were in the past.

Of course, the statistics survive, the important dates, the duties, occupations, and accomplishments, the kin and friends, all recorded matter of factly in birth and death certificates, family Bibles, and obituary notices. But what of the little things, the details that in a subtle way reach out over centuries to touch us? The fragrance of cinnamon bark evoking images of far Cathay, a little girl braiding her grandpa's white beard, the kerosene lamp's yellow light, glittering silver buttons on Jesse James's trousers, the smells of a forty-year-old house, of fresh strawberry jam and fireplaces roaring with burning pine wood, of oyster soup with little round crackers scooped up by the grocer from his big open barrel—will they survive too?

May 10th each year was the official date for starting to go barefoot and this continued until after the first frost in the fall. Although we loved to go barefoot, we also loved new shoes that squeaked. I was flabbergasted when a teacher actually suggested that I should soak my shoes in water so they would not squeak any more. I was proud of my new shoes and the squeak informed all those present that I was wearing a new pair. [Rae McGrady Booth]

Such details—and recognition of the life they evoke—will survive if you'll begin preserving them, and preserving them is now not only the easiest task of the family and community historian but in so many ways the most pleasant. In the past, historical recording was an arduous task requiring long periods of tedious note-taking, a process so cumbersome that the little

details and the spontaneity were always in danger of being lost by the frantically scribbling hand. What replaces the frantically scribbling hand today, of course, is the tape recorder, and with it the most ancient form of historical preservation has been reborn: oral history.

The oral tradition of history and literature is so much older than the written that its beginnings are obscured by time, not simply unknown but quite unknowable. Long before the written word and still today among people who do not write, the spoken word transmitted all that was to be given by one generation to the next. Even among peoples whose language has been written for centuries there are strong continuing elements of the oral tradition. Even in America, many of our ancestors who lived before this century could not read and write, and did not consciously record their own personal histories or the histories of those around them; and yet so much of that past survives, passed from elder to youngster, again, on grandmother's lap. We all have known grandfathers and aunts who could recite the name, birthplace, birth date, and countless details of every ancestor's life for generations long beyond memory, while their hands were busy embroidering, mixing batter for a generations-old family chocolate cake, or chopping firewood, without missing so much as a cousin twice removed. That's the oral tradition alive today.

The tape recorder, particularly the newer, more compact cassette recorders with built-in microphones, make oral history a simple matter of pushing a button. Well, almost. There are some rules of interviewing and recording that one should know, but these are few and easily acquired. They concern choosing your equipment, preparing for an interview, getting the interview started and keeping it going comfortably, and keeping track of all those tapes you're going to accumulate. In all, the variables are fewer and much less complicated than, say, photographic recording, making this an activity truly suited to the historian everyman, adult or child.

The suggestions that follow assume that in your quest for the past you'll first of all be recording the remembrances of family and friends, those closest to you, and the people with whom you are most comfortable. But family oral history is a habit-forming activity and often leads to regrets that you have run out of family to interview and record. The result is that you begin doing it to other people's families, which is the way community oral history surveys get started. The few basic principles that follow will hold for community as well as family history and will make recording community history as easy and as enjoyable as recording family history.

*   *   *

EQUIPMENT

Tape recorders—and wire recorders before them—were once the sophisticated gadgetry of professionals or hi-fiers with lots of money. But now even the simplest of the recorders marketed today—many under fifty dollars—are perfectly suitable for a family oral history project if not a school or community project. And children know how to use them, because before they got their own they were recording and listening to tapes in their classroom or school library media center.

Recently, I went to ride on an old restored steam railway and was pleasantly surprised to find a large number of children, none of whom had ever seen a real steam engine run before, riding the train, examining the works of the engine, and taking photographs by the hundreds. But what really excited me was that several among them had cassette recorders which they expertly dangled down over the side of the open flat cars near the wheels and pointed to just the right places from where came the old engine's great and wondrous noises. They even rode in the cabin to catch the roar of the coal fire and the talk of the engineer and fireman. No doubt those recordings will provide hours of entertainment for friends and classmates and may become the sound track for movies or slides. We need say no more on the availability and popularity of tape recording equipment.

Like most consumer goods, tape recorders come in a baffling array of models (reel-to-reel or cassette), speeds (1⅞ inches per second or ips, 3¾ ips, 7½ ips, and 15 ips), microphones (built-in, external, non-directional, omni-di-

rectional, unidirectional), tape lengths (30, 60, 90, 120 minutes), and, of course, prices. Don't worry, there's an easy way out of all this.

Let's begin with the different models: reel-to-reel or cassette. The compactness and simple controls of the cassette recorder make it the unquestionable choice of even the professional oral historian. Because of the very slow tape speed (usually 1⅞ ips), one little cassette can record up to two hours. Five of these cassettes can be stored in about the same space as one 7-inch reel of tape, and a shoebox could hold all the recordings of a large family or a small community. The cassettes also protect the tape against dust, and because only the cassette and never the tape is handled, there's little chance of the tape's breaking or jamming, even in the hands of the youngest historian. Per hour of recording time, cassettes are somewhat more expensive than reel tape but certainly not enough to offset all their other advantages. (One disadvantage of the cassette tape you should know about is that it cannot be edited. But even this problem, though a bother, can be overcome. Proper recording technique and indexing makes editing a rare need, but when it is necessary—for example, to use the tapes on a radio program, for a film sound track, or for a museum "talking exhibit"—the cassette recording can always be recorded on a reel-to-reel machine and this copy can be edited.)

Tape cassettes also come with an ingeniously simple safety device that prevents you from accidently erasing or recording over something you intend to keep. If you look at the back of the cassette (opposite the opening with the tape in it) you'll notice two little u-shaped slots. With a nailfile or small screwdriver pry out the center of the u. It will just snap out. This done, the tape may be played back but cannot accidentally be erased or re-recorded in the machine.

What about the different speeds? Tape speeds are standardized throughout the industry and the speed to choose becomes a consideration only if several recorders are being used together for a community project. In this event, be sure all the machines are of the same speed and also of the same manufacture. (Despite industry standardization, tapes recorded on one machine very often do not work as well on a machine of another manufacture, because, I think, of minute variations in motor speeds and tape-recording head alignment.) Your machine should operate on both AC (house current) and DC (batteries), and just about all of them do, though it's good to make sure. Many times you'll be out of reach of an electrical socket and will certainly need batteries. But there's no sense using expensive batteries when there is electricity around. Besides, there's more chance of batteries dying in the middle of a long tape.

Microphones present another choice, though, as with tape speed, the choice probably will be made for you. I consider a built-in, omni-directional microphone a must. Wires and little mikes strung all over the place are a hassle to set up, they intimidate the people you are interviewing (who seem to fix their eyes on the mechanical paraphernalia and, with the wires, have a harder time forgetting it's there), and in addition the wires and such invariably get moved, dropped, and tripped over, introducing a lot of distracting noises which can get bad enough to obscure what's being said. The recorder with a built-in microphone can be hung from the shoulder (even hidden under the arm), placed in the middle of the table, or just set beside the chair, and you needn't worry about another piece of equipment. The mike should be omni-directional because this allows you to record several people at once (often necessary at a family gathering around the table) without passing or pointing the microphone.

There are two other microphone features that should be considered. Automatic volume control is rapidly becoming a standard on recorders, raising the cost a little bit, but this extra device is worth the additional expense. It automatically reduces the volume of a loud sound close to the microphone but increases a sound far away, the effect being to equalize the voices of an interviewer two feet from the recorder and a couple of people six or eight feet away, all of which makes listening and transcribing much easier. The second microphone feature added to some recorders is a voice-activating device, which turns the recorder on when the speaking starts and off when there are pauses. This may save some effort, but it is in no way essential, and the device raises the price of a recorder considerably. So for my money, I'd say don't bother.

Finally, there's the matter of tape. There are several considerations here. First, tape quality. Hi fidelity—with its higher cost—is important for recording the jug bands, music, and songs that will eventually become part of many audio-history projects, but it is not necessary for the spoken word. Special tapes for recording music can be two to three times the price of tapes perfectly suitable for voice recording and, in addition, may have a frequency range beyond the capabilities of your recorder (for voice recording, 60 to 7,000 cycles per second is fine; for music, 50 to 15,000 is the minimum).

Next, tape length. Choosing the appropriate length can be a confusing business. I started using 120-minute tapes (an hour on a side) because I didn't want the person I was talking to interrupted, and so reminded of the presence of the recorder, by tape changes in the course of the conversation. For some reason tapes always end just in the middle of a childhood song newly remembered, or a lively argument between two aunts who fought in 1906 for the affections of the same boy (who is now a millionaire), or some other wonderful thing. Sometimes I'd get so enraptured with the speaker I'd forget to listen for the click at the end of the side. And you can't use warning buzzers because they're jarring too.

But a scary experience made me change my mind about long tapes. Late one night, I received a frantic call from the typist transcribing one of my prized tapes. It seems that after about an hour she glanced at the machine to discover a tangle of tape under the little plastic window and mylar beginning to ooze out of every little crevice in the machine. I rushed over with a little screwdriver and under hot, bright lamps began an operation on the cassette that for drama and tenseness rivaled any Hollywood operating room scene. If you've ever taken apart a cassette which has disgorged itself, you'll never want to do it again. (There are no little reels in there as I had imagined, only loose coils of thin, thin mylar lying on a cardboard circle!) The thin mylar used for these 120- and 180-minute tapes is even thinner than that used for the 60- and 90-minute ones, and it jammed with the constant on and off required during transcription. Although my operation was successful, I now use 60-minute tapes and figure that I can think of something to say that will get the two aunts fighting anew.

TAPE TALKS

"Interview" is a horridly formal word that can unfortunately affect the way we approach the work of oral history. No one is relaxed and has fun at an interview. But reminiscing after a pleasant dinner, indulging in a little nostalgia on the back porch swing, or just chatting about things as now, after forty years, you walk through the old neighborhood—that's very different. For the family historian, for any historian really, "tape talk" describes such reminiscing better than the word interview. If oral history is to reveal the personality and life of the subject—as only tape-recorded history can do—then recording must be enjoyable and not a chore. This doesn't mean that a tape talk can't be organized, even a little structured, it merely suggests the approach one takes toward such a project.

Tape talk recording sessions usually happen in one of two ways. There's a big event coming up—a wedding, an eightieth birthday, a golden wedding anniversary, the arrival of faraway members of a family, a cousins' party or family reunion, a retirement party, the first time grandparents or great-grandparents see a newly arrived descendant. At occasions like these you know the general direction the conversation eventually will take, and all you need do is have the recorder handy. Very little prompting is necessary; in fact you may have trouble getting the cassette in and out of the recorder fast enough.

But at other times sessions will have to be set up, planned to coincide with a brief visit by others from faraway or with your visits to elderly friends and family with less stamina than they used to have. Perhaps it means a visit to a distant relative you seldom ever see and will make a special journey to visit and record. In either case—the big event or the planned visit—these simple suggestions will help you get started and help you end up with interesting and useful family history tapes.

First of all, become well acquainted with the operation of your recorder, particularly the controls, so that you can manipulate them with ease and a minimum of distraction. If it's a new machine, practice inserting and removing the cassette and learn the limitations of your microphone.

Plan ahead for your meeting. Set aside a small shoulder bag or old briefcase and make it your oral history kit. At the minimum it should include: two extra sets of fresh batteries, the line cord for the recorder, an extension cord, a note pad or cards, pencils, lots of tape (estimate what you think you'll need and take twice that amount), and your camera.

If you're tape talking with someone you've just met or with a family member you've not seen since childhood, take the time to explain what you are doing and why. It's flattering and for the elderly reassuring that other people are still interested in them and want to preserve something of their life to pass on to younger members of the family. You might suggest that you'd be happy to send a copy of the tape to the people you are talking with or arrange for them to listen to it after it's all over.

Make your first tape talk an easy one. Start with the venerable historian of the family, who will start talking before you can get your recorder plugged in. This will not only get you over the first-try jitters, but give you lots of names and events to ask about. You might start this one by taking along a family tree and kinship chart (see Chapter Three) and using it as the focus of the talk. Filling in the blanks, trying to remember birthdays and places, limbers up minds and gets them thinking about the past. Make sure to get the correct spelling of unfamiliar names (of people or places).

Make note of follow-up suggestions. After your first talk or the first couple of talks, there will be "leads" you'll want to contact. . . .

"Talk to your Aunt Ella Steed about that, she'll surely know."

"Well, I was still in Hamburg when your granddad sailed for New York, but his old friend George Witz was waiting for him when he arrived and gave him a place to stay."

"You mention that one to Al down there at the liquor store, he's been on that same corner for thirty years."

"Oh, he's passed away. That was about a year ago, but you know, the kids from the high school talked with him not a month before he died and I think they got a recording too."

Be adaptable. Your recorder is portable, so if the day is getting too hot and it's a good time to go out in the back yard or down the street for a beer, just throw the recorder over your shoulder and go.

Say just enough to get conversation started and to keep it going in a particular direction if you wish, but let your subject do the talking. Be careful not to ask leading questions or take sides. Family matters often get complicated and tricky, so remain neutral and encourage frankness and candor.

If you're at a family gathering and someone mentions an old song they used to sing or the first rhyme they remember from their childhood, ask them to sing or recite the words. The next thing you know, there'll be old games, jokes, granddad's favorite expressions, and family sayings you may not have heard for a while.

We had sayings in our family which were based on little incidents which my mother related. Every family, I am sure, has its phrases with associations that are known to all the members and that always produce a chuckle.

In the little town where I was born, there was an individual who considered himself widely-traveled. He had been in Cairo—Illinois, not Egypt—a journey of fully 200 miles, and he had a subtle way of bringing that fact into the conversation. For example, a team of mules would be coming down the street and this latter-day Marco Polo would declare, "I've seed mules in Cairo—but I ain't never seed none like these!" And so with us it was "I've seed hot cakes—(or a picnic, or whatever)—in Cairo but I ain't never seed none like these!"

Living in the farm neighborhood where my mother grew up was a shiftless fellow who one day remarked, "My ol' woman's sick; she can't eat nothin' but 'taters, 'maters, beans and squash," which doubtless were about the only viands available at his domicile

and they came from the garden which the wife had cultivated. So when a member of our family would pile a plate high, someone would declare, "Vivian's sick—she can't eat nothin' but 'taters, 'maters—." [Boyce House, "Arkansas Boyhood, Long Ago," in *Arkansas Historical Quarterly*, Summer, 1961]

The mention of food is a sure way to get some interesting talk and some new recipes as well. Ask about memories of the family kitchen or about a person's favorite treat. For many people, like Boyce House, memories of their mother's kitchen are most dear:

My mother moved about the kitchen swiftly, poking wood in the stove, opening the oven door to inspect the progress of a roast, lifting the lids from steaming pots, and pausing, now and then, to brush a wisp of hair from her flushed forehead. She beat cake batter rhythmically—(a boy was allowed to lick the big spoon). She almost never served store bread but baked cornbread and biscuits—(using a baking powder can to cut the biscuits out). Also she made wonderful hoe cakes. She put designs on pie crusts with the tines of a fork. She made an especially fine syrup, served warm, for pancakes—and it was produced from white sugar and water. In short, she used the simplest of materials to create her culinary triumphs. Incidentally, the pancakes were a walnut tint on the outside and they were cooked all the way through. The ham-and-red-gravy she served was perfection; and there was no surpassing the sausage—with sage, of course.

When she was making apple butter or pumpkin pies or a blackberry cobbler, the kitchen had an enchanting aroma of vanilla extract, spices and other smells which gave promise of the treat that was to come.

If I have to choose any of her masterpieces for special note, the golden-fried chicken and the corn-on-the-cob would be singled out; and honorable mention would go to the vegetable soup, which was not a roll call of leftovers but was compounded of tomatoes, potatoes and macaroni, with a suggestion of onion. She was an artist in making cakes, too, with chocolate and coconut her best; well, maybe lemon, orange, banana and jelly, too. And as for pies, her mincemeat would have won at any fair; but the very best of all was her apple pie, the fruit in slices, with a latticework through which sugar and cinnamon oozed to delight the eye, the nostril and, finally, the taste.

The topics for oral history are unlimited—except perhaps by your tape budget—but here are some suggestions, any one of which might prompt a reluctant talker or become the focus of a family (or community) history project:

school days
earliest childhood memories
Lompoc in the 1920s
voyages and journeys
old country family history
a farm girl's chores
the life of a soldier
opening up a first shop or business
early automobiles, trains, and boats
first radio programs remembered
favorite actors and actresses, movies and plays from
    childhood
Saturday evening around the fire
recollections of Ellis Island
the Depression
favorite early television programs
food and cooking
clothes and fashions
toys fondly remembered
new inventions
apprenticeship and jobs
books and authors of a lifetime
ice boxes and wood stoves
phonograph records and dancing
concerts and operas

For an even livelier exchange, particularly at family gatherings or the reunions of long-lost friends, try passing around old, perhaps long-forgotten photographs, newspaper clippings, and other artifacts. If this is the first time you've met the family member you're talking to, suggest that he or she get out the family photo album, a favorite home movie, or collection of slides (tape talks can happen in the dark as well). Maybe you'll have brought along some family photographs that you've been collecting—we will talk more about this in the next chapter.

A final note on the tape talk. At the end of each talk, make sure you've got the correct names and addresses of newly located family and others with whom you might want to have a tape talk and have written down anything else that may not be clear from the tape alone. Then make sure the name of the person you've been talking with, the date, and the place are written on each cassette used in the session. You might even type or print the information ahead of the tape talk on ½-by-3-inch gummed labels and place these in the space provided on

the cassette when the talk is completed. (Some oral historians record the information at the beginning of each tape—"We are talking with Mrs.............."—but in my experience this tends to be disruptive, and with cassettes it is not necessary because unlike reels, which can get separated from their boxes, cassettes and their tape are a unit.)

ORGANIZING AND INDEXING TAPE TALKS

Your collection of tape talks might consist of just a few meetings with close family or it may begin to take on the proportions of a family or community history project. Projects like this begin to gather momentum as new events and personalities are discovered and the amateur historian discovers how pleasurable it is to spend long afternoons with family memories. "Just a few tapes for the kids" can become, many tape talks later, a life's work or a devoted hobby. But regardless of the size of your tape collection, it should be simply and conveniently organized so that rather than becoming just a jumble of tapes on a top closet shelf it can be useful in any number of ways. We seldom begin a project like this knowing exactly what it is to become. Tapes may lie unused for years to become, someday, the exciting discovery of a grandchild. Or they may be used by a local museum or historical society for a town centennial or bicentennial, or become a resource in a school library, or, very likely, be the model for a larger community oral history project. A little care now will protect a valuable historical source.

Your first and perhaps only concern at this moment will be storage. Tapes require a cool, dry, dust-free place, away from electrical motors and other magnetic fields, but the place need be nothing elaborate. A sturdy cardboard box plainly labeled ORAL HISTORY PROJECT or something like that will do well for the beginning. You'll probably want to begin numbering your cassettes and, at least in the early stages of the project, keep a sheet of paper with a list showing the number of each cassette and its subject.

At this point you've done all that is necessary for a complete, well-organized oral history project. Even with this simple shoe-box storage-

and-listing system, your collection can grow and grow and yet be manageable.

Now, one step beyond this—an index—makes your collection more accessible for research or for finding specific subjects and references quickly. A tape cassette index is no different from a book index except that instead of locating names and specific topics by page number, you refer to the place on the tape as shown by the digital counter. You can record your entries on lined notebook paper, just as with your tape list, or you might want to use a recording form like that in the illustration.

Here's how to do it. With your notebook or recording sheets ready, set the digital counter to zero (usually 000). Start the tape, and when you reach something in the conversation you feel should be indexed, stop the machine and note the number on the digital counter. Most machines have "pause" buttons that enable you to start and stop the machine with just a touch of the finger (instead of alternately pushing the "stop" and "playback" buttons). As your index begins to unfold, it might look like the following sample.

000 Preparations for leaving Budapest, 1898
036 Trip to London
048 Voyage, arrival at Ellis Island
059 Family name changed in recording papers
067 Search for a place to stay in Brooklyn
081 Meets grandma in Greek restaurant
109 Description of tenement life
128 Marriage proposal to grandma
143 Wedding
164 Looking for a job
203 Enrolling in elementary school night class

After an index has been done, there's no need to listen to a whole tape or several tapes to find a story or a specific event. You need only place the cassette in the machine, set the digital counter to zero, and run the tape through (on fast forward) until you reach the number you want. Later, through the index, you'll be able to compare different accounts of an event, compile the different recipes or old songs you've recorded, and locate the names of people with whom you would also like to have a tape talk.

And it's all right there in the oral history shoe box.

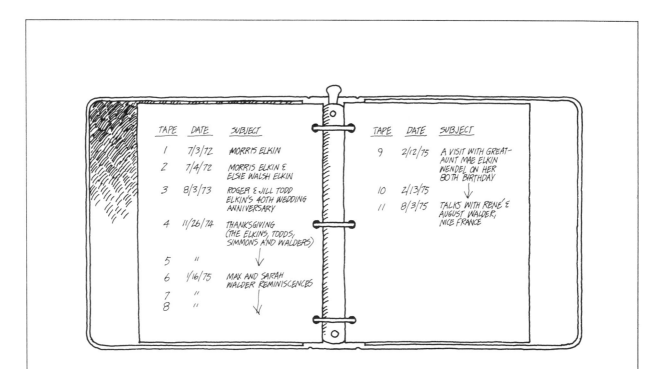

A simple oral history project tape catalog.

TAPE #6   A visit with Grandpa Morris Elkin, July 3, 1972, Lafayette, Ind.

000	Grandpa Elkin's earliest recollections of family farmstead between Fowler and West Lafayette, Ind. ca. 1890	273	Recollections of towns on his run— Frankfort, Muncie, Noblesville, Indianapolis ca. 1910
025	Description of his father Hiram and his mother Mae Spencer	330	Grandpa's boyhood fantasies of being a locomotive engineer
045	Recalls birth of brothers and sisters: Albert (1890), Beth (1891), Henry (1893) and Mae (1895). Helen Samuelson was midwife for all five children	342	Digression on the life's work of his brothers and sisters: Mae, 30 years a school teacher in South Bend, Albert the pharmacist, Beth's restaurant, and Henry's barnstorming (killed in a plane over France in 1915)
059	Childhood camping trips to Brown County and fishing with his dad and his Grandpa Spencer on the Tippecanoe and Wawasee. Reveals conspiracy among "the men" to keep his mother from finding out they'd been spelunking	360	Reminiscences on his courtship and marriage to Elsie Walsh. Details of Elsie Walsh Elkin's childhood and youth
130	Favorite caves and fishing sites	380	Story of their marriage and Grandpa having to leave the wedding party to make his run in "the worst snowstorm within memory" (1910)
145	Reminiscences on schooling and first year at Purdue ('03). Worked summers at Monon shops and found he "was more interested in railroadin' than studyin'"	400	Death and funeral of his mother Mae Spencer Elkin (1911)
200	Experiences as a brakeman, fireman, and then engineer. Remembers numbers and personalities of all his locomotives particularly his "first high six-wheeler"	410	Grandpa's thoughts on his mother, his taking more after her than his father, her favorite sayings
256	Talks about gold pocket watch engraved with a likeness of his first locomotive, a gift of his father		

A tape index showing subjects included and their position according to the digital counter.

My Furthest Back Person—The African

Alex Haley

I FIRST heard the story of our family, which had been passed down for generations, on the front porch of my grandma's house in Henning, Tennessee, about 50 miles north of Memphis. I grew up there with Grandma Cynthia Murray Palmer, and every summer she used to invite various women relatives to stay. After the supper dishes were washed and put away, they would sit in the squeaky rocking-chairs and talk about the past, as the dusk deepened into night, and the lightning bugs flicked on and off above the now shadowy honeysuckles.

Whenever they were speaking of our people, Grandma and the others spoke—always in tones of awe, I noticed—of a furtherest back person whom they called "the African." They would say that some ship brought him to some place they would pronounce as "Naplis." Somebody called "Mas' John Waller" bought that African off that ship, and took him to a plantation in "Spotsylvania County, Virginia."

When he had a daughter, Kizzy, he would tell her what things were in his native tongue. "*Ko*," he would say, pointing at a banjo, for instance. Or, pointing at a river which ran near the plantation, he would say "*Kamby Bolongo*." When other slaves would call him "Toby" he would angrily tell them that his name was "*Kin-tay*." And as he gradually learnt more English he began to tell Kizzy some things about himself—how he had been captured, for instance. He said that he had been not far away from his village, chopping some wood to make himself a drum, when four men had surprised, overwhelmed and kidnapped him.

At 16 Kizzy was sold away, on to a much smaller plantation in North Carolina. She had been bought by a "Mas' Tom Lea," and he fathered her first child, a boy, whom she named George; later she taught him all she could about his African

grandfather. In time George had seven children; one of his sons, Tom, had seven children too; and he, in turn, passed on the family story. There had developed almost a ritual in its telling. It would occur mostly during the wintertime, after the harvesting was done, and there was more free time of an evening. The family would sit around the hearth with the logs burning, and sweet potatoes would be roasting in the hot ashes, as the children listened to and absorbed the stories and the sounds. And the youngest of the seven was Cynthia, who became my maternal grandmother.

When I had heard that story over and again for around 10 years, it had become nearly as fixed in my head as it was in Grandma's, though I never then comprehended that the African they talked about was my own great-great-great-great-grandfather.

Over 30 years later I happened, one Saturday in 1965, to be walking past the National Archives in Washington, D.C. I can't be certain to this day what motivated me to walk up the building's steps, unless it was that so many times across those interim years I had thought of Grandma's stories. In the main reading room, a desk attendant asked if he could help me. I wouldn't have dreamt of telling him that I just had some curiosity in my head about some slave forebears whom I'd heard of as a boy from my grandma. What I finally did kind of bumble out to this fellow was that I was interested in the official United States Census records of Alamance County, North Carolina, for just after the Civil War.

After probably two hours of turning the microfilms through the viewing machine, I began to tire when, in utter astonishment, I saw the names of my grandma's parents. Over the next few months, whenever I could arrange it, I was back in Washington. In one source or

another during the rest of 1966 I was able to document at least the highlights of the cherished family story.

I wanted to tell Grandma, but, sadly, she had gone, in 1949. Among those who had told the story on her front porch during my boyhood, the only survivor was Cousin Georgia Anderson, in her eighties, still living in Kansas City, Kansas. So I went there to tell her what had happened. Wrinkled, bent, not well herself, Cousin Georgia was so overjoyed. When she repeated to me the old stories and sounds, they were like echoes from Grandma's front porch: "Yeah, boy, that African say his name was '*Kin-tay*'; he say the banjo was '*ko*' an' the river '*Kamby Bolongo*,' an' he was off choppin' some wood to make his drum when they grabbed 'im." The more Cousin Georgia talked of it, the more and more excited she became, until we had to stop her, calm her down. When I was leaving she said, "You go 'head boy. Your grandma, all of 'em—they up there watchin' what you do!"

In our own family's story were those strange, unknown sounds. Obviously they were bits of whatever was our original African Kin-tay's native tribal language. What specific tribal tongue? Could I maybe decipher that? Was there any way?

In New York I began making visits to the United Nations Headquarters lobby. I would stop any Africans I could, asking if my bits of phonetic sounds held any meaning for them. Across the next couple of weeks, I must have stopped a couple of dozen Africans, each and every one of whom quickly looked at me, listened, and took off— understandably dubious about some Tennesseean's imitating some "African" sounds.

Then I met Dr. Jan Vansina, a Belgian scholar who had spent his early career living in West African villages, studying and tape-recording the oral histories narrated by certain very old men. I told him our family's story. He questioned me intensely and finally said, "These sounds your family has kept are very probably of the tongue called 'Mandinka'."

"*Bolong*," he said, was clearly Mandinka for "river." And preceded by the sound "*Kamby*," very likely that meant "Gambia River." "*Kin-tay*," a very old clan that had originated in Old Mali.

I had never been to Africa or been much concerned about it till then, but I knew I must get to the Gambia River. I needed a Gambian to go with me on my search; I finally found a student named Ebou Manga; and I flew with him to Bathurst, the Gambian capital. The round trip tickets took most of my savings.

Ebou and his father assembled several Gambian officials. They listened intently as I told them every detail of Grandma's stories, "Why, yes, of course," they said, " 'Kamby Bolongo' is Gambia river!" They added, "But a greater clue is in your forefather's saying that his name was 'Kinte'." Then they told me something I would never have fantasised—that in places in the back country lived very old men, commonly called *griots*, who could tell centuries of the histories of certain very old clans—"such as the Kintes." On a map, the men pointed out to me some clan-founded villages, Kinte-Kundah, and Kinte-Kundah Janne-Ya, for instance. And these Gambians said they would do what they could to help me find a *griot* who knew about the Kintes.

To reach him, I discovered, required what seemed to me a modified safari: renting a launch to get upriver, two land vehicles to carry supplies by a more roundabout land route, and employing finally 14 people, including three interpreters and four musicians, since a *griot* would not speak the revered clan histories without background music.

After about two hours we put in at James Island, for me to see the ruins of James Fort, once a British military post. Here two centuries of slave ships had loaded thousands of cargoes of Gambian tribespeople. The crumbling stones, the deeply-oxidised swivel cannon, even some remnant links of chain seemed all but impossible to believe. Then we continued upriver to the left-bank village of Albreda, and there put ashore to continue on foot to Juffure, which was the village of the *griot*.

Finally, Juffure's playing children, sighting us, flashed an alert. The 70-odd people came rushing from their circular, thatch-roofed, mud-walled huts, with goats bounding up and about, and parrots squawking from up in the palms. I sensed him in advance, somehow, the small man amid them, wearing a pillbox cap and an off-white robe—the *griot*. Then the interpreters went to him, as the villagers thronged around me.

Rustling whispers went through the crowd, and a man brought me a low stool. Now the whispering hushed—the musicians had softly begun playing *kora* and *balafon* and a canvas sling lawn seat was taken by the *griot*. He was Kebba Kanga Fofana, aged 73 "rains" (one rainy season each year). Seeming to gather himself into a physical rigidity, he began speaking the Kinte clan's ancestral oral history. Across the next hours it came rolling from his mouth, the interpreters translating for me . . . the seventeenth- and eighteenth-century Kinte lineage details—predominantly what men took what wives, the children whom they "begot" in the order of their births; those children's mates and children. . . .

The Kinte clan he said, began in Old Mali; the men generally were blacksmiths, and the women were potters and weavers. One large branch of the clan moved to Mauretania, from where one son of the clan, Kairaba Kunta Kinte, a Muslim Marabout holy man, entered the Gambia. He lived first in the village of Pakali N'Ding; he moved next to Jiffarong village; "—and then he came here, into our own village of Juffure." His youngest son was Omoro, who in turn had four sons. Then, said the *griot*, "About the time the king's soldiers came, the eldest of those four sons, Kunta, when he had about 16 rains, went away from his village, to chop wood to make a drum, and he was never seen again."

What ship brought Kinte to Grandma's " 'Naplis" (obviously Annapolis, in Maryland)? The old *griot's* time reference to "king's soldiers" sent me flying to London. Feverish searching at last identified, in Parliament records, 'Colonel O'Hare's Forces,' dispatched in mid-1767 to protect the then British-held James Fort whose ruins I'd visited. So Kunta Kinte was down in some ship probably sailing later that summer from the Gambia River to Annapolis.

In eighteenth-century Royal Navy records I finally tracked ships reporting themselves in and out to the Commandant of the Gambia River's James Fort. And then early one afternoon I found that the Lord Ligonier, commanded by a Captain Thomas Davies, had sailed on the Sabbath of 5 July 1767. Her cargo: 3,265 elephants' teeth, 3,700 pounds of beeswax, 800 pounds of cotton, 32 ounces of Gambian gold, and 140 slaves; her destination: "Annapolis."

That night I recrossed the Atlantic. In the Library of Congress the Lord Ligonier's arrival was one brief line in "Shipping in The Port of Annapolis—1748-1775," I located the author, Vaughan W. Brown, in his Baltimore brokerage office. He drove to Historic Annapolis, the city's historical society, and found me further documentation of her arrival on 29 September 1767. (Exactly two centuries later on 29 September 1967, in Annapolis, again I knew tears.) More help came in the Maryland Hall of Records. Archivist Phebe Jacobsen found the Lord Ligonier's arriving customs declaration listing, "98 Negroes"—so in her 86-day crossing, 42 Gambians had died, one among the survivors being 16-year-old Kunta Kinte. Then the microfilmed *Maryland Gazette* of 1 October 1767 contained an announcement to prospective buyers from the ship's agents, Daniel of St. Thos. Jenifer and John Ridout (the Governor's secretary): "from the River GAMBIA, in AFRICA . . . a cargo of choice, healthy SLAVES . . ."

CHAPTER 2

Magic Boxes

Recording family lore has been chosen as the starting point in this historical odyssey because it is easily begun and as easily done, and because the tales and yarns and anecdotes living on only in some memory are the most fragile parts of our past. But we'll likely not be content for long with this eavesdropping. Beckoned by the fascination of the stories, our impulse will probably be to see our past, to look into the faces of our ancestors for reflections of our own. And it will be a kind of magic that will let us do this. Those who would scoff at the primitive's fear of cameras—the fear that to let one's image be carried away on a piece of paper is to let something of one's essence or soul be carried away—usually do so forgetting their own weakness for a charming photograph. Perhaps the magic of the camera lies in the photograph's trueness to reality. Painters control every aspect of their medium and have the power to change, to interpret, even to falsify if it is their patron's whim. The photographer too can interpret but to a more limited extent, principally through the conscious or unconscious selection of a point of view. The image on canvas forms slowly over days and months, but the film's image is formed in the click of a second, capturing unerringly a moment's reality, a graceless moment, a wince, a winsome glance, an outburst of hilarity. But in such moments, even in the smallest photographs, there are whole worlds of substance and impression. One figure projects a sense of life as burden, another projects a challenge or maybe

a boast, in a third the posture and mien express a subtle optimism or the weight of some secret oppression. And behind the figures always a background which, though sometimes nothing more than a white expanse, nevertheless provides meaning in the isolated, detached vignette.

George Eastman introduced his simple box camera in 1888 and barely a year later, when the ad on page 33 appeared, photography and Kodak—a word coined by Eastman to be a short, distinctive, and easily remembered name for his product—had become very much a part of everyday American life. Indeed, so successful was Eastman in his choice of a name that soon after its appearance, Kodak became synonymous with camera, as it remains today in the memories of older generations of Americans. George Eastman's inventive genius created the concept of the Kodak, but it was his keen insight into the American character that made the Kodak a marketing success. He had sensed in many of us the historian's impulse—that compulsion to record, to preserve for some reason never quite clear in our minds. Photography was then over half a century old but it had been, in practice at least, the realm of the adventurous, the devotee, the professional; now there would be amateur photographers who, in Eastman's words, "desire personal pictures or memoranda of their everyday life, objects, places or people that interest them in travel &c."

Kodak No. 1 showing factory-loaded 100-exposure roll

There had been great cameras before the Kodak and, by the turn of the century, a number of great photographers, among them Daguerre, Talbot, the painter Edgar Degas, the Americans Mathew Brady and Adam Clark Vroman, and countless others who are less known or remain anonymous. Even small towns all over the country had their photographer's studio on Main Street. A search of War Department records from the Civil War has revealed the names of some three hundred photographers issued battlefield passes by the Army of the Potomac. But the great photographs of the 1800s were created almost in spite of the cameras, which were ponderous wooden instruments requiring heavy tripods, quantities of glass plates, and bottles of chemicals to coat and sensitize them, all of which demanded prodigious physical feats of any photographer who would take a camera out of the studio, much less onto the battlefield. Still, the visages of generations of American ancestors were recorded by these varnished wood cameras with polished brass lens barrels and cloth bellows— if not with candidness, certainly with every bit of the sensitivity and technical perfection of which cameras are capable today.

With the Kodak, what had been hard, heavy work became no work at all. Eastman had already found an alternative to the fragile and cumbersome glass plates. His use of paper coated with a gelatin emulsion was the key to making simple photography possible. In another year, 1889, he found an even better alternative: nitrocellulose, the first clear plastic which made it possible for amateurs to process their own film. Before that amateurs had had to depend on Eastman for processing. Great-grandmother and grandfather took their first pictures of your mom and dad with a little black box which measured $3\frac{1}{4}$ by $3\frac{3}{4}$ by $6\frac{1}{2}$ inches—the Kodak No. 1—with a fixed-focus f9 lens and a one-speed shutter set at 1/25 of a second. Inside, there was already a roll of film sufficient for a hundred round pictures (the full image projected by the lens). For the camera, film, *and* the developing and printing of that first roll they paid twenty-five dollars. (They got a leather carrying case and shoulder strap too.) After the roll had been exposed, the unopened camera was mailed to Eastman's plant in Rochester, New York, along with ten dollars, which paid for reloading the camera and the eventual processing of the new film.

Soon the camera returned with its fresh load of film and a hundred little round sepia-colored photographs in their gilt-edged mounts. "You press the button, we do the rest" made photographers of all our ancestors and began a new chapter in family history.

*   *   *

The caches of photographs that abound in American households attest to the way our parents, grandparents, and great-grandparents took to the Kodak. There no longer needed to be a birthday, anniversary, wedding, graduation, or any other special occasion for a "sitting," for now photographs could be had at any time. And it wasn't just their availability, photographs now were also different in kind. In a photographer's studio, daguerreotypes might take as long as twenty minutes to expose, requiring a rigidity and tense motionlessness all too evident on the subjects' faces. Clamp-like headrests and arm supports helped somewhat, but very young children posing on their mothers' laps always dissolved into a blur of movement. With the Kodak, which used a quickly exposed film and had a comparatively fast shutter speed, photographs became more relaxed, animated, and candid. The ease with which pictures could be taken meant cameras went everywhere—to the seashore, on holiday visits with the family, to Fourth of July picnics, on hunting and fishing outings, on Sunday walks in the park with the children, to the fair, to railroad stations, and to amusement parks. The years passed, and the family's amateur photographers recorded the building of houses and barns, the new Model T on its first outing, newborn babies, and always children, at play or grinning into the camera or sitting on the front steps of the family home.

Most of us have known, somewhere in our lives, a little drawer stuffed with deckle-edged snapshots and loose strips of negatives with images just like these. In these pictures were faces we had never seen, but something about them suggested a family resemblance and we knew they were one of us. Such a drawer can become another little world for the child who happens upon it, yielding up untold secrets of the past, strange clothes, strange cars, strange

settings, all of it intriguing and compelling. But as pleased as we were to look at the pictures, few if any of us then realized what they might mean to us someday. From such a drawer can emerge a veritable history of photography—daguerreotypes, calotypes, tintypes, snapshots round and square (some of them tinted in light colors), 35mm slides, even, possibly, little spools of home movie film—and in this history our own history may be revealed to us in a way impossible with the written or spoken word.

Many of those drawers and their images are gone now, and have been for some time. From the drawer, the pictures went into boxes and from the boxes, well, who knows where. Those of us who frequent antique shops and second-hand stores know that many boxes wind up there, and often when we come upon a batch of old pictures in a worn box our pleasure and interest are mixed with a certain sadness that here are the images of someone's ancestors, a piece of someone's past, faces that once had names and brought a glimmer of recognition and remembrance to the eyes of someone of an earlier time, but doomed now to remain nameless and obscure forever.

Kodak advertisement, November 30, 1889

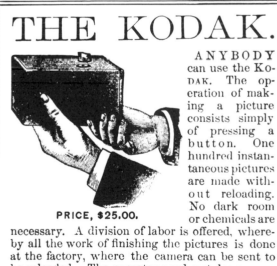

Such an experience as this started me thinking about old pictures in general and particularly the ones I remember seeing as a child. Old photographs create a kind of nostalgic warmth from within me. There was always something magical about those times when the pictures were taken out and pored over — a rare visit from faraway family or at the end of a journey which every two or three years took us to my mother's home. The albums and the loose photographs tucked away in books or in boxes (the shallow kind with a smooth white cover like the ones clothing from the store used to come in) were handled with a kind of reverence that bespoke a familiar ritual. Among the pictures were faces I had seen before on similar occasions and now these faces were old friends recalling to my mind the same stories and associations they did for my family, who originally had related them to me. When I was a child these stories and the people they described became real to me. I remember sharing with my mother a particularly poignant memory of sitting on the lap of that bearded old man looking out from a photograph when he offered me his pocketwatch to look at; I could even smell again the wool of his old suit and sense my wonderment at the Roman numerals on the face of the watch. I was perhaps five or six when I remembered all this. My mother indulged me in these memories amidst the smiles of the family there, for later when I was old enough to read the dates penciled on the back of the picture I found that the old man I had remembered so vividly, even in his manner, had died long before my time, long before my mother's.

A year or so ago I began to wonder about the old photographs in my family. Where were they? I felt uneasy because the old house with which I associated the pictures and, yes, some of the people too, were gone. I felt a kind of anxiety about the pictures, something like the feeling when you suddenly recall a childhood friend whom you haven't seen for years and years and you wonder what's become of him. I wrote my mother asking her about the pictures, and asking if, since we were so far apart now, she would help me put together all the stories that went with them. Yes, yes, they were still with her, and they would soon be in a box and on their way. I waited for that box like I used to wait for birthdays, and when it arrived I discovered that, unlike a lot of childhood joys, the ones evoked by seeing these pictures could be relived. It all seemed so miraculous. These artifacts — images on fragile pieces of paper, metal, and card — had survived, some of them for well over a century, through wars and family upheavals and through years and years in which no one cared, many of the pictures looking as though they had been picked up at the studio just last week.

What I received were prints, long ago separated from their negatives (which actually, of course, were more valuable than the prints). Many of the pictures were taken in studios no longer in existence. Several among them were daguerreotypes dating back to the very beginnings of photography, and some I could imagine my great-grandparents taking with a Kodak No. 1. In any case, there wasn't one negative in the lot and it startled me anew to think that here in the box that had come so routinely through the mail was my past. There is more to a past than "things," but somehow all the family lore, the traditional tales and anecdotes, the history and memories cannot quite do what the stories in faces do. Great-grandmother or great-great-grandfather are pleasant abstractions, but they become ours, people we know, with just one faded and yellowed snapshot of a young girl in a big, flowered hat or a grinning young man astride his mule on a dusty main street of some dusty Gold Rush town. I guess the magic of those faces is why photographs survive when sturdier things are allowed to fall by the wayside throughout the years.

*　　　*　　　*

I wanted to make sure the magic of these pictures would be kept for others, for my children, because no matter what this world may be in the future, I cannot imagine that these little images will be any less magical then. Even though their negatives were lost, they could be preserved by a very simple process of copying, of making new negatives.

But the first step in organizing family prints and negatives is to sort and store negatives and pictures so they won't get lost.

GETTING STARTED

The negatives that have survived are your first concern, and they should immediately be stored and, if necessary, cleaned. One of the simplest and least expensive ways of organizing and storing negatives is just to keep them in standard 9½-by-4-inch business envelopes, new or recycled. These envelopes will keep negatives dust free and will hold the various sizes of roll film negatives and small sheet film negatives (3 by 4 and 4 by 5) that are most likely to turn up in a family collection. The negatives should be dusted with a soft brush. If they are really dirty, they can be cleaned with a commercial cleaner or with alcohol on a wad of soft cotton. Your envelopes of negatives can themselves be easily stored in a box like the one the envelopes originally came in, usually available free from stationery stores and printers.

Developed film still in a roll (as negatives once were) should be unrolled carefully (the film might be quite brittle by now) and it should be cut into strips that fit your envelopes. Film should never be stored in a roll, for winding and unwinding it scratches the emulsion.

It's possible that your collection will include glass plates. These are precious finds indeed, probably well over a century old, and should be treated with infinite care. Each plate should be stored in a separate envelope to prevent chipping and scratching. Don't throw away a broken plate; even a badly cracked and chipped plate can produce beautiful prints with only hairline scars (plates often break at the corners, leaving most of the image area intact). More noticeable cracks can be retouched out of the print. Badly scratched negatives should be saved too. Commercial scratch removers and the old darkroom trick of rubbing a little petroleum jelly into the scratched emulsion can make imperfections invisible on the print.

There are other kinds of negative envelopes available at photography stores that can hold larger negatives (5 by 7, 8 by 10, 11 by 14) or allow you to store strips of roll film negatives in a little packet or a three-ring binder. These sleeves have the advantage of letting you look at negatives just by holding them up to the light, without having to remove them from the envelope or sleeve. They also keep each negative or strip separate, thus eliminating another possible source of scratches on the emulsion.

Family photo collections, like families themselves, can get very large, especially if you begin getting prints and negatives from other members and branches of the family. It's a good idea, then, to catalog your negatives right from the beginning. Later, when you are searching for a particular picture, you won't have to pull hundreds of negatives from their envelopes and search each frame for the missing ancestor. There are several alternative cataloging methods, but the simpler the better. If you are storing negatives in business envelopes, just print numbers corresponding to those on the margins of the negative on the outside of the envelope. Later, when you've identified the people and scenes in each frame, these identifications can be entered next to the number. Negative files that you buy usually have spaces for recording each negative, or if you decide to use the kind of file that fits into a binder, just interleave these sheafs with lined notebook paper on which you can make notes next to each negative. (If you do this, though, be sure to designate each sheet of negatives by a letter and to put that same letter on the paper for your entries so that the two don't become separated.)

The next step—if you've been able to wait this long—is to have your collection of negatives printed, or to print them yourself. One way of getting inexpensive prints is to order contact proofsheets of each envelope or roll of negatives. When you order a proofsheet made, several strips of negatives are laid directly on a piece of printing paper (usually 8 by 10 or 8½ by 11), exposed, and then developed. This is called contact printing, and if you'd like to try it in your own darkroom, or in a public darkroom, it requires no special equipment or enlarger. What you end up with is a roll or two of film printed all together on one sheet of paper. These sheets can then be filed with the negatives. The easiest way is to tape your negative envelope to the back of the proof sheet, punch holes in the proofsheet, and then store proofsheets and negatives together in a simple binder.

It's a fair assumption that at this stage you probably know very little about many of the negatives and prints in your family's collection. Negatives and prints in drawer collections are usually not too well organized, and the names of their subjects are seldom written down but exist somewhere in the collective family memory. However, now that you've begun organizing the family archives, most of your mystery pictures will sooner or later take on identities, and those that remain unknown will make for hours of talk and speculation at family gatherings.

In my own case, I began my project by making duplicates of all my proofsheets so that I could keep one set in my files. Then I made up a simple recording or catalog sheet and had copies printed to accompany each of the proofsheets on the journeys they were soon to make. On the recording sheet are spaces numbered from 1 to 36, corresponding to the frame numbers that appear at the bottom edge of the film. I filled in these spaces and then recorded the proofsheet letter on its recording sheet. Then I returned the set of proofsheets and recording sheets to my parents. Along with it went a letter explaining all this and asking for as much information about each picture as they could give me—addresses, approximate dates the pictures were taken, ages of the people in the pictures,

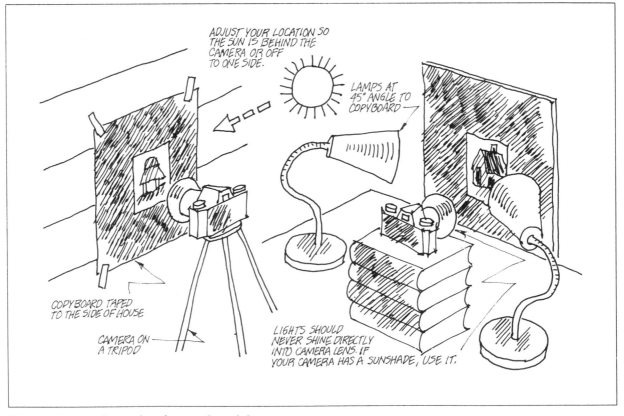

Two simple setups for copying photographs and documents indoors and outdoors.

the types of cars appearing in photos, and any other bits of family memorabilia and minutia they could think of. Pictures have a wondrous way with memories, and the notes that returned were more than I could have hoped for. Not a single picture went unrecognized, though next to some dates and locations there were question marks that my parents planned to follow up on and report on later. By now, identifying the pictures had become a family game and led to a kind of correspondence between me and several members of my family, which we all found satisfying. In this same way, you can get information on old photographs from grandparents, great-aunts and uncles, cousins, family friends, distant relatives of all kinds.

I suggested in my letters to members of the family receiving proofsheets that they keep them and make a copy of their recording sheet before returning it to me to keep with their proofsheet. (Later they may like a copy of some photograph on one of the proofsheets and will have a record of who now has the negative, or they might even think of some new information about one of the frames and will be able not only to correspond with you but to refer to the specific frame, reducing greatly any chance of error in identifying pictures by mail.) It is very likely that some of these negatives you've printed were long ago assumed to be lost, and in preserving them and printing them once again, you'll be sharing your own joy of discovery with others.

One more step you might want to take in this project, especially if your family and your collection of photographs become quite extensive, is to make an index of persons who appear in the photographs. At the front of your binder containing proofsheets and recording/catalog sheets could be a list of names, arranged alphabetically, followed by the proofsheet number and frame number of each photograph of that person.

When you stop to think that only ten proofsheets of 35mm film contain anywhere from 360 to 400 images, the chore of compiling such an index begins to seem very worthwhile, since it saves you time in the long run. Also, my experience has been that when your fame as the family's archivist begins to spread among the relations, you'll be getting requests for prints of specific pictures of Uncle Desmond or Grandma Feder, and an index makes your searching that much easier.

PRINTS ALONE

So far we've been talking about collections of negatives, but in actuality most of the photographs in your family collection will have no negatives, either because the pictures were studio portraits or because the snapshot negatives have been lost. To preserve these photographs and make it possible to print duplicates again, we'll need to have "copy negatives." Making copy negatives is nothing more complicated than taking a photograph, in this case placing your old photograph in front of a camera and making a new negative which, in turn, can be used to make more prints. Commercial photography studios will do this for you but at considerable cost, particularly when the job entails fifty or a hundred photographs or more, which is not an unusual number for a family collection. You can do it yourself with even the simplest camera, though this kind of work is best done with a 35mm single lens reflex. You might consider buying such a camera. The price of an inexpensive, single lens reflex is about equivalent to the charges for fifty or sixty copy negatives.

In a way, photographing another picture is no different from photographing anything else; the basic principles of photography still apply. Though copying is usually done indoors with artificial light, so as to allow the photographer complete control over the intensity and direction of the lighting, photographs may be copied outdoors, the process being as familiar to the amateur photographer as photographing a person or a building. If you've had even the briefest contact with cameras, you know that it's a matter of film, light, and exposure.

CAMERAS AND LENSES

The camera is, of course, your first consideration. Any camera you might have would do for copying were it not for one fact: cameras, expensive or inexpensive, come with "normal" lenses which allow you to get no closer to your subject than two to five feet. Some lenses focus as close as eighteen inches, but even this does not allow you to get close enough for copying most snapshots, daguerreotypes, tintypes, or other old photographs which are usually quite small. Therefore, the lens will have to be modified in some way to allow it to get as close as three or four inches if necessary. How you go about this depends upon your camera.

For simple cameras, those with a non-removable lens, there are available supplementary close-up lenses that clip or screw onto the front of the camera lens, permitting a closer camera-to-subject distance and increasing the size of the image on the film. The camera-to-subject distance and the area seen by the lens will vary depending on the focal length of the lens and the magnifying power of the supplementary lens, but there are lenses available that allow you to get close enough to photograph even the smallest picture in your collection. You will not be able to use your rangefinder or viewfinder for these close-ups, because your rangefinder is designed to focus only as close as the *camera* lens will focus and your viewfinder to show only what is included within the normal focusing range of the camera. You can use a small ruler or tape measure to make sure you have the correct subject-to-camera distance (information which is included in the instructions for using your close-up lens), or you can make a simple copy frame, which I'll describe below. Supplementary lenses work best at small apertures, but that's no problem because copy work should be done at the smallest aperture for maximum sharpness. The combination of a simple viewfinder camera, supplementary close-up lenses, and a home-made copy frame is the least expensive copying system available, and depending on the care with which they are used, these pieces of equipment are capable of making excellent copy negatives.

There are some disadvantages. The camera-to-subject distance is fixed and is critical, since at this very short distance the depth of field (the distance in front and in back of the object being focused on that is of acceptable sharpness) is extremely shallow, so that an error of even a quarter of an inch will result in a negative badly out of focus. The simplest cameras also provide no means of adjusting the amount of light reaching the film, so that this must be adjusted by varying the intensity and distance of the light being used to illuminate the subject. Still, when you consider that the snapshots your ancestors took came from cameras capable of producing images no better than, and in most cases considerably less sharp than, the one you're using, you can understand that there is no reason why a simple but well-designed camera can't do the job. But you will have to be very careful and learn the limitations of your equipment.

A single-lens reflex offers the most flexibility in copying. The camera-to-subject distance is not fixed and may be varied over a range of several inches. Because you are viewing through the lens that takes the picture, you can focus and center the subject in the finder accurately. And because you have more than one lens aperture and shutter speed, it's a simple matter to make the adjustments necessary for a correct exposure. Another advantage of this kind of camera is its removable lens which not only allows the use of special macrolenses (if you do enough copying to justify the expense) but allows for the use of extension rings—the least expensive way of getting your camera closer to the subject. An extension ring goes between the camera and the lens, moving the lens farther away from the film plane, in effect enlarging the image on the film.

Any number of extension rings may be placed between the lens and the camera, each extension increasing the size of the image on the film until finally it is being magnified. (Moving the lens farther from the film plane does diminish somewhat the amount of light reaching the film and requires an increase in exposure. If your camera has a built-in light meter that reads the amount of light coming through the lens, you needn't worry about this adjustment as the meter will do it for you. If, however, you do not have through-the-lens metering, you can consult an exposure chart, which lists the increase in exposure required for each extension of the lens.) You can also purchase supplementary close-up lenses for a single-lens reflex, which are placed over the regular lens. Since these lenses are not sharp at large apertures, it is particularly important to use a longer exposure time and a smaller lens opening. It is for this reason that extension rings are to be preferred.

FILMS FOR COPYING

For the beginner the array of film types available, particularly for 35mm cameras, must seem a very good reason not to get involved in photography. But choice of film is no more complex than knowing how it will be used. If we know what it is that we want the film to be able to do, then choice becomes a simple matter. In copying photographs we'll have two concerns. First, we want a film capable of rendering all of the detail to be found in a small photograph (many of those old studio cameras had fine lenses) in an enlargement which might be many times the size of the negative—in other words, we want high resolution and maximum sharpness. Second, we want a high contrast film. Often, old photographs are flat and dull, the result of fading or just poor exposure and processing. Even prints of good quality and contrast will dull down or gray when they are copied and then printed again. It's even possible that we're copying a copy of a copy which, at each remove, has been getting grayer and grayer. Sometimes, too, we'll be copying color prints of very low contrast. But if we copy photographs with a high contrast film, not only are we more likely to keep our copy negative from graying down but also we'll find that in many instances we've actually increased the contrast of the original and, therefore, actually improved it. For example, the higher contrast film used in copying will render, if the film is exposed properly, the gray of a once-white shirt or wedding dress white again, particularly if the photograph is printed on a higher contrast printing paper. All of this points to our choice of a fine-grain, high-contrast film, and the least complicated film that meets both these criteria is Kodak Panatomic-X (ASA 32). This is what we'll use.

MAKING YOUR FIRST COPIES

The two diagrams on page 36 suggest some ways for setting up for copying outdoors or indoors. Sunlight provides just the flat, even illumination we need to make good copies, but you should take a couple of precautions. Make sure that none of the equipment (camera, tripod, copy frame) or the photographer casts a shadow on the copyboard. Then, check for reflections, on glossy prints particularly. Glare will flatten out the blacks in the picture and greatly decrease the overall contrast. If necessary, position a piece of paper or cardboard to either side of the copyboard (or at both sides) to shield it from glare or the direct sun. It is important to view the subject from the same angle as the camera to make sure there are no reflections going directly into the lens. (If you do not have through-the-lens viewing, this means moving the camera aside and holding your eyes at camera level to examine the subject for any reflections.) The photograph to be copied should be placed on a dull black background. If the print is mounted with a broad white border, then the border should be covered by cutting a hole in a piece of dull black paper, allowing just the picture to show through.

Although copying indoors requires some special lighting equipment it generally offers a more controlled situation. It is best to turn off all extra room lights; the darker the room the better. And use your sunshade. These three steps—the black background, a darkened room, and a sunshade—prevent extraneous light from bouncing off the copyboard or any shiny equipment and into the lens causing flare. For the small pictures you will be copying, up to 8 by 10, two lamps in reflectors will be sufficient (though you'll often read that four are recommended). It is important that the lighting be balanced and that both bulbs be of equal brightness. Sixty- or seventy-five-watt household bulbs are adequate and nothing is gained by increasing the intensity of the light source. Adjust the lamps so that their light strikes the subject at about 45° angles.

Looking through the viewfinder or into the copy frame, check for positioning and focus. Fill the viewfinder from edge to edge with the subject, and focus accurately. If your camera has a split-image rangefinder, use it, for focusing is extremely difficult this close to the subject. If the picture has an interesting frame, mat, or folder, take two pictures, one of the whole subject, frame and all, the other of just the photograph filling the viewfinder. Later, you may want a print of just the picture area, and using this second photograph will decrease the amount of enlargement needed to make a print of a given size and so minimize the grainy quality that enlargement creates.

If the print will not stay flat, cover it with a piece of clean glass or tape down the corners. I prefer the latter procedure, as it cuts down on troublesome reflections that always seem to come with glass.

Check for reflections and uneven texture. With both hands move the lamps until there is no hint of reflections and the blacks in the picture appear as dense as they can get. Watch out for the shadows in the valleys of paper texture; these will degrade the image, particularly the whites, and should be eliminated by proper lighting balance. Look to see if the camera is reflected in the glossy surface of the print or glass covering. This is a problem with shiny chrome camera bodies and lens mounts. If this happens, cut a hole the diameter of your lens mount in a piece of black cardboard. If you slip this over the lens and then put on your lens shade, the cardboard will stay put, shielding shiny parts from the surface of the print.

Exposure, even with a good light meter, is always something of an uncertainty in copy work. It is best to expose a test roll of film, copying one or two examples of the different kinds of photographs in your collection (glossy, matte, high contrast, low contrast, color, daguerreotypes, newspaper cuts, engravings, etc.). You can use your meter, taking a reading directly off the print, but I get better results when I take a reading from a gray card (Kodak Neutral Test Card), laying it on the photograph to be copied. This gray card represents an average of middle-gray tone. If you expose for this card, the whites in old photographs (which tend to be somewhat gray) will be slightly overexposed, print whiter, and will show more contrast. Set the meter for a small aperture, say f11 or f16. Take one picture at that indicated exposure. Then "bracket" this exposure by taking a second picture at the next lower shutter speed and a third at the next higher. If,

for example, your meter reads 1/30 at f11, then take the next picture at 1/15 and the next at 1/60. Do this with one example of each of the different kinds of pictures you'll be copying and record each exposure frame by frame. Then, have this roll developed and check it before going on.

What you're looking for is a negative that has all the detail you need and no more. The dark negatives are overexposed and will not only be hard to print but will be grainy and appear to be less sharp than the thinner, lighter negative. If you also have a proofsheet made, you can see how these different negatives translate into prints. Proofsheets are made on normal paper (grade 2 or 3) and your best negatives are the ones that print best on normal paper.

Assuming nothing changes—lighting, camera, or film—you can count on these test exposures to guide you through all your work just by matching the print you intend to copy with a similar one on the test roll. By the way, if you are shooting at speeds of 1/30, 1/15, 1/8, or less, you should get a cable release to eliminate any chance of the camera's shaking, which would undo all the care you've taken so far to get a good copy negative.

SOME SPECIAL PROBLEMS

Very old photographs are sometimes stained or faded, usually to a yellowish color. The film sees this as a tone of gray, causing the final print to appear hazy and dull. Such stains can be almost eliminated by placing colored filters over the lens. The rule of thumb for filters is to use the same color filter as the color you want to remove. To remove a yellow stain from a photograph or old newspaper, you would use a yellow filter. (Often old letters and notes were written on yellow paper with pencil or ink now faded. The yellow filter would have the same restorative effect here, increasing the contrast between the blue or black writing and the yellow background.) Similarly, a blue filter will minimize a blue ink stain.

On the other hand, if all the dark areas of the print have faded into a light yellow, then you'll want to *strengthen* this color to increase contrast and make a badly faded photograph printable.

Studio photographs, early 1900s

To intensify a color, use a filter of the complementary color. A blue filter, then, will intensify yellow and increase the contrast between the yellowed and white areas of the print. A green or blue-green filter will strengthen faded sepia-toned prints.

Daguerreotypes can present some real challenges to the amateur photographer, particularly because a daguerreotype can suddenly look like a negative when an instant ago it looked like a positive. Daguerreotypes are actually pictures on mirrors of highly polished silver. This polished-silver surface forms the dark areas of the print, with the light areas and highlights coming from the whitish mercury amalgam on the silver. The picture is positive as long as the silver reflects a dark field—your dark clothing, for example. But it seems to become a negative in bright light. The solution to this problem is the black cardboard baffle suggested earlier, which will keep camera reflections out of the shiny silver surface and provide the dark field needed to cause shadows to appear in the silver and the image to appear positive.

Daguerreotypes also may need special development to compensate for the very low contrast between the silver and mercury areas. Limited overdevelopment of a negative increases the contrast and, knowing this, the historian/photographer can do some magical things with badly faded or low contrast images. Daguerreotypes and any other pictures of very low contrast (watch out, daguerreotypes appear to show more contrast than they really have to the camera) should be copied on a separate roll. This roll should then be developed 50 percent longer than the recommended time for normal development. If, for instance, Panatomic-X is normally developed in a certain developer for six minutes, the roll with low-contrast subjects would be developed in the same developer for nine minutes.

Ambrotypes and tintypes can be copied in the same way as ordinary photographic prints, increasing their contrast, if necessary, as recommended earlier. Ambrotypes are actually a kind of glass negative, and they appear positive when backed with black paper or cloth. If the black backing is badly faded and can be removed without damaging the frame or the image, replace it with intense black paper and you'll find that the contrast increases. Since ambrotypes are negatives, they can also be printed by removing the black backing and making a contact print by laying them on printing paper.

Linework—genealogy charts, wills, birth certificates, diplomas, census entries, documents, handwritten letters, maps, engravings and woodcuts, newspaper and book pages—can also be copied like photographs, and your test exposures will show you how to expose for greatest contrast. If you find that you're going to be copying a lot of linework, whole diaries or bundles of letters, you should look into special copy films like Kodak High Contrast Copy Film 5069. This film is designed for black-and-white subjects and when exposed properly does not reproduce any gray or middle tones. Exposure of films of this type is critical and must be very accurate or the results can be disastrous. Technical leaflets on this and other kinds of film are available from the manufacturer, and there is lots of literature on their use, but if you're really a beginner with a camera and are just getting started in the darkroom, it's best to get professional advice or accumulate a little more experience.

The photographic process, of course, continues in the darkroom where little negatives become prints of any size. But this is another subject which is well explained in many books. With these instructions and a little reading on your own you'll be able to make good, printable negatives and proofsheets for your files. Once you know how to do this, you've acquired one of the most valuable skills a historian can possess, to be used in all manner of ways. Now your camera goes with you on your journeys into the past, preserving that past for all those who would seek its magic.

CHAPTER 3

Strangers No More

—◆—

If the stories handed down in your family are anything like the ones in mine, it takes several languages to tell them. My family photographs are like that too, reflecting lifeways which at first seemed so different and so distant from my own. But the more I listened to the stories and looked over nearly a hundred old photographs going back at least that many years, the more stories and images all came together in some way, and soon they could not possibly belong to anyone else but me—I had made them mine. This act of claiming is what history is all about. All such pattern-making is after the fact; we select events upon which we impose some order (chronology) and then select people to whom we assign some particular meaning (*my* ancestors). It is this looking back that gives shape and form to what we then call history. "Families" are shaped in just this way too. So it is that a child may look upon the face of her great-great-great-grandmother on a little tarnished daguerreotype, listen to the family stories, and claim this distant ancestor for her own, indeed identify with her. This child has done in her own small way what all historians do—what we all may do—created her own history. We simply look back over the years, over generations and generations of men and women who were all once strangers to one another (and, of course, to us) and who came together over all manner of uncertain, random paths so that we might claim them for our own and call them family.

From a letter by Josef Kaplan to his friends back home, in Bohemia:

On May 31 [1856] we left Hamburg [Germany] on a boat named "Emma," and on the next day we sailed from Hamburg harbor. The ship was towed by another boat through the mouth of the Elbe River to the open sea, twenty-two miles from Hamburg. There were about 300 persons on the boat in all, not counting the ship's personnel and the captain. Everyone without exception must obey him.

Our crossing was smooth, without great storms. I can compare a storm at sea to a field of rye in bloom and wind playing in it: it makes such waves, only much

BELANGRIJKE BERIGTEN

UIT

PELLA,

IN DE VEREENIGDE STATEN

VAN

NOORD-AMERIKA,

OF TWEEDE BRIEF VAN

Sjoerd Aukes Sipma;

VAN DAAR GESCHREVEN AAN DE INGEZETENEN

VAN

BORNWERD,

WAARIN VELE BIJZONDERHEDEN, BETREFFENDE DE HOLLANDSCHE
VEREENIGING IN DEN STAAT JOWA, DE LEVENSWIJZE EN DE GEWOONTEN
DER AMERIKANEN, BENEVENS VELE NUTTIGE WENKEN VOOR HEN, DIE
NAAR DE VEREENIGDE STATEN WILLEN VERHUIZEN, VOORKOMEN.

VOORZIEN MET EENIGE AANMERKINGEN DOOR

N. N.

GEDRUKT
BIJ DE WED. B. SCHAAFSMA, TE DOCKUM.
1849.

Dutch poster soliciting immigrants, 1849

larger, the trough being from ten to twenty yards lower than the crest of the wave (that's in a big storm), and the ship must sail through it, so it is now in a trough and immediately after on a crest. It's a most beautiful spectacle when one wave breaks against another and soars upward; if it strikes the ship and someone is on deck, it wets him thoroughly, as happened to me. Ocean water is bitter and salty; I washed with it several times—afterward the joints grow stiff as it penetrates the body.

Only a week later did seasickness appear on our ship. Everyone breakfasted in the morning. Then came unwelcome nausea, and everyone was as though intoxicated. However, I was well, with no ill effects, at which the rest marveled, and I even more.

On June 14 we sailed past a Scottish island . . . inhabited by poor fishermen. They approached our ship with fish, for which we gave them biscuit.

On the 23rd we finally reached the open sea, for until then we could still see shores of dry land, although they appeared like dark stripes. Here we saw huge schools of fish playing; they were porpoises. On July 5 we spied icebergs, which a storm had probably blown here from the north polar sea. They were of various sizes up to that of a hut. Fog usually spread over the surface of the sea, so foghorns had to be blown in order that our ship, if meeting another, might not collide with it. However, on our whole voyage from Hamburg to Quebec we met only three ships.

On the 11th we again saw many fish near the ship— also whales in the distance, spouting water . . . like rising columns of smoke. On July 16th we reached an island not far from Quebec, where we anchored for medical inspection. Those who were ill had to land on the island. After three days we sailed on. Finally —and you know, dear friends, the immigrant to America after endless hardship on the ocean longs exceedingly for sight of the promised land for which he has yearned for so long and thought of constantly, so to speak—finally we on board the ship heard the cry: "Land! land!" You can imagine how we felt. Even though one felt quite ill, at this he became at least half well.

On the 26th we landed in Quebec . . . a beautiful, large city. From there we sailed the St. Lawrence River by steamboat to Montreal, where we arrived on the 29th. It was a huge steamboat: 100 feet long, more than 20 wide, [and] three stories high, the third very magnificent. It carried 1,150 persons [and] sailed almost as fast as the steam engine on a railroad.

From Montreal we sailed on another, smaller steamboat to Kingston [Ontario], thence by canal to Toronto. Here we took the train to Lake Huron. I must remind you that in America railroads ride much faster than at home. Cars are longer, swinging in the middle on springs.

When we went farther we saw a virgin forest burning. They cut it down partially to dry it, then set it on fire, so the whole forest is destroyed. How it burns! How you could use that wood! In short, it's a fascinating spectacle!

After that we took a steamboat and sailed on Lake Huron—that is still in Canada [and] belongs to the British empire. We reached the first United States territory at Mackinaw [Michigan]. From there [we crossed] Lake Michigan; then we stopped in Milwaukee and continued by train to Chicago. Reaching that city, we met by chance our acquaintances, the brothers

AUTOBIOGRAPHY OF JOHN STURM

When we set out from home, we went to Mannheim in a wagon, then to Mainz and Koln on the Rhine in a steamboat and then to Antwerp, a seaport, where we lay over several days until a ship was ready.

Our baggage was supposed to be in Koln when we got there, but it was not there. My father looked around for it for several days, but he did not find it. We were told it must have been sent to Antwerp and we would find it there. But to our misfortunate and almost to our utter despair, everything was lost.

In Antwerp we waited several days until our ship was ready to go to sea. My father bought food again for use on the ship, because what we had brought from home was all lost. Before we boarded ship, my father hunted for our baggage again, but in vain.

So we had nothing but the clothes on our backs. My father had his money in a belt around his waist, in silver.

When the ship was ready to go, we had to go along.

The ship was a three-master, the "Carolina." We had many a stormy day. There were many of us on the ship. There was only one kitchen for all the people to cook in for the passengers had to cook, each family for itself. So it happened that each family had a chance to cook only once in two or three days. We had little interest in eating, anyway, as most of the people were sea-sick and had no appetite.

The ship heaved and rolled almost all the time so that we had to hold on to something. Many people never came up on deck at all during the entire journey. The trunks and boxes had to be tied fast so they wouldn't be thrown about. Some of the children were happy and gay, but most of them were not.

One day a pirate ship came toward us and everyone had to come on deck, no doubt to show how many able-bodied men we had.

The sailors had their own kitchen and their own cook. Peas cooked with bacon and beans were their main foods. We also had bacon and black bread, which we almost had to split with an ax. Here a dog would hardly

eat it. Some had white bread, which was more appetizing than the black. But in spite of all this, we survived. One child died on the ship. It was buried at sea.

When at last land was sighted, we were all happy and joyful.

Because large ships could not dock, we had to land in a smaller one. Before we could get off the ship we were all examined by a doctor. We did not stay in New York long. From there we went up the Hudson in a steamer to Albany, from there to Buffalo on a canal-boat. Along the canal we saw our first peaches.

From Buffalo we went over Lake Erie on a steamboat to Cleveland. At that time, Cleveland was about one-third the size it is now. From Cleveland, we came on the Ohio Canal to Zoar. It was the latter part of June when we arrived here. Our money was pretty well used up, too.

My father found work soon as a wagoner at the upper furnace. He made barrels, flasks and such. We got a house not far from the furnace, an old dilapidated log house near the canal. It was not long before one after the other of us became sick with ague (malaria). Often we could not even get water for one another, for we had to go quite a distance to the spring. Usually, great thirst came with the fever. At first a man named Sterl doctored us, homeopathic, but

with no success. Sterl was the store-keeper at the furnace. Then we got a doctor from Bolivar, by the name of Bennet. He didn't know a word of German and we not a word of English. He was not successful, either. My father and two brothers died in September of that first year. Then there was no one left to earn a living for the others, for we were all sick.

Then old Baumeler interested himself in us and saw to it that we were taken into Zoar. My mother was put in with Anna Wilmer, an old woman, where Jacob Sylvan now lives. My sisters were put into the Children's Home in the old meeting-house, where there were a number of other girls. Mary died the following Christmas night at the age of 14. That was in the year of 1847. Eva lived about four years longer and then she died too.

I was put into No. 17, a boys' home, and also the school house. There I lived with the other boys until I was about fourteen years old. Then I was put into No. 23. I had to help in the fields, help in the summer whenever I was able and could be of use. In the spring and fall I helped make logs, pulled the rope on the saw. [John Sturm, "Autobiography of John Sturm," in *The Zoar Story*, Hilda Dischinger Morhart. Dover, Ohio: Siebert Printing Company, 1968]

Zoar, Ohio, ca. 1900

F----r. It was a happy coincidence for a man in a foreign country and especially here. In the inns here prices are established at a fixed rate: You pay one-quarter of a dollar for each meal and each lodging.

From Chicago we rode by train to Freeport. Here we stayed fourteen days with Czech settler acquaintances and bought equipment for farming: viz., wagons, oxen, cows; 2 wagons for $160, 4 oxen for $200, 2 cows for $50 and many other things such as stoves, plows, saws, axes, hoes, etc.

The towns here are growing surprisingly, and also the railroads. The town of Freeport, for example, was founded fifteen years ago and is already large, with railroads leaving it in five directions. But there are still no railroads going northwest. As we intend to go northwest to Minnesota, we have to ride from here by wagon. There are ten families of us preparing for the trip from Freeport to Minnesota over prairies and [through] forests. With this I end my letter till we reach our destination. Then I will write again. Good-bye! [Esther Jerabek, "Letters to Bohemia," *Minnesota History*, Winter, 1972]

Josef Kaplan and Barbora Zednikova Kaplan are American ancestors. They are your ancestors and mine, they belong to anyone whose people came originally from Europe, or from anywhere else in the world for that matter, and that's most of us. Barbora's death in 1881 and Josef's in 1918 place them close to our own time, and they could be the great-grandparents, even the grandparents of many Americans alive today. At some point, perhaps eight generations ago, perhaps only two, perhaps within your own memory, you were an immigrant, and thus we all share with the Kaplans, at varying removes, the experiences of people leaving one home in search of another. For unless you are a Native American—and therefore descended from earlier immigrants, indeed the very first migrants to the New World —your ancestors came to America sometime during the last three hundred years, and more likely during the nineteenth century.

The Kaplans were not, of course, among the first. They were but two people in a multitude whose Atlantic and Pacific migrations began well over two hundred years before their own leave-taking from Bohemia in 1856, and the migrations continue to this day. The migrants count themselves among those who are, in the

---

As far back as I have been able to ascertain, my ancestors on the paternal side were slaves in Rhode Island. They belonged to a family by the name of Northup, one of whom, removing to the State of New-York, settled at Hoosic, in Rensselaer county. He brought with him Mintus Northup, my father. On the death of this gentleman, which must have occurred some fifty years ago, my father became free, having been emancipated by a direction in his will.

Henry B. Northup, Esq., of Sandy Hill, a distinguished counselor at law, and the man to whom, under Providence, I am indebted for my present liberty, and my return to the society of my wife and children, is a relative of the family in which my forefathers were thus held to service, and from which they took the name I bear. To this fact may be attributed the persevering interest he has taken in my behalf.

Sometime after my father's liberation, he removed to the town of Minerva, Essex county, N.Y., where I was born, in the month of July, 1808. How long he remained in the latter place I have not the means of definitely ascertaining. From thence he removed to Granville, Washington county, near a place known as Slyborough, where, for some years, he labored on the farm of Clark Northup, also a relative of his old master; from thence he removed to the Alden farm, at Moss Street, a short distance north of the village of Sandy Hill; and from thence to the farm now owned by Russel Pratt, situated on the road leading from Fort Edward to Argyle, where he continued to reside until his death, which took place on the 22d day of November, 1829. He left a widow and two children—myself, and Joseph, an elder brother. The latter is still living in the county of Oswego, near the city of that name; my mother died during the period of my captivity. [S. Northup, *Twelve Years a Slave.* New York: International Book Company, 1895]

Granny Judith said that in Africa they had very few pretty things, and that they had no red colors in cloth. In fact, they had no cloth at all. Some strangers with pale faces come one day and dropped a small piece of red flannel down on the ground. All the black folks grabbed for it. Then a larger piece was dropped a little further on, and on until the river was reached. Then a large piece was dropped in the river and on the other side. They was led on, each one trying to get a piece as it was dropped. Finally, when the ship was reached, they dropped large pieces on the plank and up into the ship till they got as many blacks on board as they wanted. Then the gate was chained up and they could not get back. That is the way Granny Judith say they got her to America. — RICHARD JONES [Botkin, B. A., ed. *Lay My Burden Down: A Folk History of Slavery.* Chicago: The University of Chicago Press, 1945]

words of historian Oscar Handlin, The Uprooted. Before the Kaplans had come English, Scots and Irish, French and Dutch, Germans, Frisians, Scandinavians, and Slavs. From about 1820 to 1920 over thirty-five million immigrants of varying origins came to America, some to the cities and some, like the Kaplans, to be farmers.

At the beginning of this hundred years of immigration the foreign-born population of Manhattan Island was less than 20,000, or about 11 percent of the whole population. By the 1860 census, the immigrants had risen in number to 384,000, 48 percent of the island's population! Their origins? Over 200,000 of them had come from Ireland, another 120,000 from Germany, and 27,000 from England. But New York wasn't the only city with a large immigrant population. From 1820 to 1860, Boston received Irish immigrants totaling some 72,000 in a total population of 331,000. We were becoming a nation of immigrants, and in the 1890 census, for the first time the census takers asked Americans what languages and dialects they spoke other than English. The question was asked again in 1910, at which time there were 92,228,496 Americans, of whom, as their mother tongue:

2,759,032 spoke German,
1,365,110 spoke Italian,
1,051,767 spoke Yiddish,
943,781 spoke Polish,
683,219 spoke Swedish,
528,842 spoke French,
402,587 spoke Norwegian,
258,131 spoke Spanish,
229,094 spoke Hungarian,
228,738 spoke Czech,
186,345 spoke Danish,
166,474 spoke Slovak,
140,963 spoke Lithuanian,
126,045 spoke Dutch,
123,631 spoke Slovenian, and
118,379 spoke Greek.

Hundreds of thousands of others, including recently arrived Chinese and Japanese, were not recorded in this census.

Nor were Josef and Barbora extraordinary people in any way, at least for immigrants.

They were young—in their twenties—as were over half the men and women who came to America during the last century. And they were literate. Josef's letters reflect an education that was better even than that of many American men his age. (We know he attended the elementary school at Dlouhá Třebová, Bohemia, the village of his birth, about fifty miles southwest of Prague in what is now Czechoslovakia, and also, for a time, a German school in a nearby village.) Depending on which sets of statistics you use, at least 70 percent of our immigrant ancestors from southern and eastern Europe were literate—could read and write—and among those from continental Europe and England, the literacy rate was even higher (though whether people emigrated from a city or rural community may have had more to do with their literacy than nationality or geography). Only Barbora, in one way, was a bit unusual, for in those days only about 30 percent of the immigrant passengers who made the six-week voyage by sailing ship were women.

And the reasons the Kaplans left their homeland for the uncertainty of life in a new world? Well, here too they had much in common with their fellow passengers. At various times in our history, we have provided a home for those who suffered religious persecutions, French Huguenots in the late 1600s and European Jews in the 1930s. Other immigrants came to escape the ravages of war, like the Germans of Pennsylvania who fled the Palatinate in the eighteenth century. But most of our ancestors, including the Kaplans, came to find work and a better life. In what demographers sometimes refer to as the "push" and "pull" that motivates migration, the Kaplans were, in effect, driven out by the recurring economic distresses afflicting urban and rural labor in much of Europe throughout the last century and simultaneously were drawn by the riches promised in the American dream, or in a word they would not have hesitated to use, the American Utopia. For Josef and Barbora, the immediate causes of emigration were the death of Josef's father, the dividing up of the family lands among the sons, and a fire which destroyed their farm buildings and crops. For the 220,000 Irish who arrived in 1851, the immediate causes were the

[Poems in a traditional style carved into the walls of the Angel Island detention station by Chinese immigrants arriving in the 1910s and 1920s]

*I have admired America as a place of
    opportunity and happiness.
Right away, I got some money and started
    my journey.
After months of traveling in wind and
    waves, I ended up in this prison
    suffering.
I look up across the waters and Oakland is
    only a few feet away.
Oh, to return to my motherland and be a
    farmer again!
My breast is filled with grievance that I
    can't sleep.
Therefore, I write a few lines to express
    my mind.*

*I left my village behind me and now, I
    miss the bridge and flowers of my
    hometown.
I stare at the faraway clouds and
    mountains, with eyes full of tears.
A wanderer longing for treasures and a
    happy family.
Who can know that I was imprisoned on
    this island?
Thinking of China reminds me of the
    story of Juan-Chi
China is shamed by giving away her
    rights to foreign powers.
My fellow countrymen should realize this
    crisis and strive together.
I vow to take over America to right
    earlier wrongs.*

calamity of the potato famine and the evictions of the late 1840s. For the millions of Germans who came at mid-century, it was the political problems of 1848 and the related disruption of agriculture. And, in general, there was the industrial revolution, the migration of rural populations to the cities, and the effects of mechanized farming. The promise of a better life in the country across the sea was epitomized in a book on world economic changes published in 1889: "On the wheat farms of the northwestern United States . . . with wages at $25 per month and board for permanent employees, wheat could be produced for 40 cents per bushel; while in Rhenish Prussia, with wages at $6 per month, the cost of production was reported to be 80 cents per bushel." Between 1903 and 1913 nearly ten million farmers and unskilled laborers left Europe for America.

So to America they came, our ancestors, and for as many individual reasons as we could think of. And they survived—we are the testament to that. Some, like the Kaplans, struck out for the West, those less lucky than the Kaplans perishing in the cold winters or from Indian attacks. Others, packed into the tenements of lower Manhattan or Boston, knew other miseries. They started their own labor movements, social and fraternal organizations, clan associations, and churches and voiced their hopes through periodicals in their own languages. Many of them became naturalized citizens, attended schools to learn English, and in many ways passed on their energy and determination to their first-generation American children, our great-grandparents, grandparents, mothers, and fathers. That immigrant experience made a permanent mark on them, and though we may no longer be aware of it, on us too. For some that experience is close at hand, leaving us to struggle with its meaning, while for others of us it happened so long ago that we've all but forgotten that basically all Americans, including ourselves, were once immigrants.

Statistics, the stuff of census reports and farm production surveys, are, of course, only a small part of the story, and nothing of the experience. The dates of wars, the religious persecutions, the famines, pogroms, crop failures, political upheavals tell us why the immigrants came, but say little of their feelings. Statistics must by their nature ignore the agonies of great decisions, the anguish that comes of leaving behind family and friends, probably forever, the ambiguities of leaving an old life for a new, the arrival, the experience of being a stranger in a strange land. It remains for us, the children and descendants, to complete that story, to bring it to life once more, to make it our own, as only we can do it.

*   *   *

An awareness of who we are begins with the knowledge of all we once were. To find this knowledge we need only reach back into our past, not by some mystical, esoteric means, but through really simple means we all know well —a long-delayed letter to an elderly great-aunt, an afternoon with the family, another nostalgic dusty attic visit, a few minutes in the library, and once more through the well-thumbed family Bible. To the professional it's genealogy, for us it's going home—more objectively, becoming the family historian—and it all begins with a simple lineage chart like the illustration on the next page.

Just put your name and your birth date on that single line on the left. Of course, you know all about your mother and father, so fill in the next two lines. What about the next generation, do you know the names of your grandparents? All four of them? And your great-grandparents; that shouldn't be so difficult, after all they're just your mother's and father's grandparents.

The chart itself has no magic; its charm lies in the way it helps you to visualize what the last five generations of a family, anybody's family, looks like. And with the entry of a few names and dates it becomes your family, the bearers of your father's name and your mother's maiden name for four generations (or more if you add other charts). You've probably discovered that much of the information called for you either have forgotten or, possibly, never knew. But it's not lost, just a bit misplaced. If you're like most of us on the first try, you've just discovered how much there is yet to be learned about your ancestors. Here are some

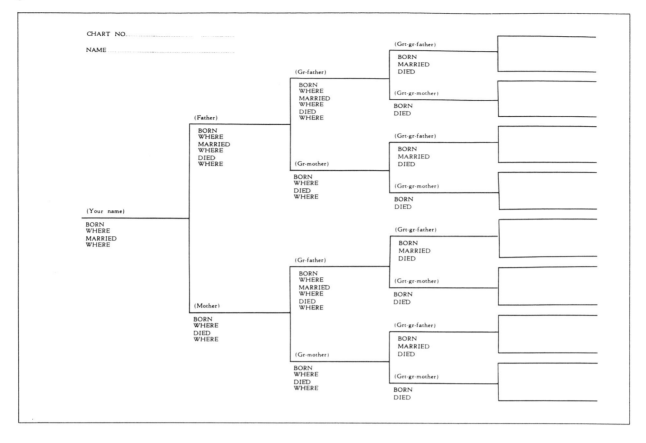

CHART NO.

NAME

(Your name)
BORN
WHERE
MARRIED
WHERE

(Father)
BORN
WHERE
MARRIED
WHERE
DIED
WHERE

(Mother)
BORN
WHERE
DIED
WHERE

(Gr-father)
BORN
WHERE
MARRIED
WHERE
DIED
WHERE

(Gr-mother)
BORN
WHERE
DIED
WHERE

(Gr-father)
BORN
WHERE
MARRIED
WHERE
DIED
WHERE

(Gr-mother)
BORN
WHERE
DIED
WHERE

(Grt-gr-father)
BORN
MARRIED
DIED

(Grt-gr-mother)
BORN
DIED

(Grt-gr-father)
BORN
MARRIED
DIED

(Grt-gr-mother)
BORN
DIED

(Grt-gr-father)
BORN
MARRIED
DIED

(Grt-gr-mother)
BORN
DIED

(Grt-gr-father)
BORN
MARRIED
DIED

(Grt-gr-mother)
BORN
DIED

suggestions, then, for completing the chart and finding some long-lost ancestors.

Begin with close family, but give priority to the oldest members, particularly elderly grandparents and great-grandparents, for they may be the last remaining link with the fifth generation and beyond. If you are seriously interested in your genealogy and if you can visit these elders to get the information, it's worth the inconvenience. Grandparents and particularly great-grandparents tire easily, and responding to even a brief letter can be exhausting for them. But visits have other advantages. You can make a tape recording of the meeting, and just talking about the past, remembering a few names and reliving old experiences, has a way of working memories loose and enables people to go back even further than they thought they could. If you can't visit with them, the chart, at least, requires less writing and explanation than a letter and helps to organize their thoughts too. In either case, make sure that you get full names for the chart, including middle names — and no nicknames. Later, when you find two

people in the family with the same name or are searching for an ancestor in some official record, the middle name will help you make certain who is who. Nicknames can be a real source of confusion because if they were used for years and years, they became the "real" names to friends and even family. You should insist on knowing if it was really Charlie instead of Charles, Andy instead of Andrew, and Liz rather than Elizabeth.

It's best to send charts to as many people as you can, even to brothers and sisters still living together. It's quite likely that a sister, for example, will know something about the family her brother doesn't, for not too long ago boys and girls, particularly in rural households, were raised separately, little girls spending most of their time with mother either in the kitchen or as she went about her work, and boys working with their fathers. Family talk was then a woman's subject to the extent that in many families part of a little girl's growing up involved being "instructed" in family history and lore as she worked along with her mother or joined her, the female cousins, and her aunts in leisure. Still, boys and their fathers probably talked about how grandpa farmed until he got his first tractor or how great-grandpa shoed horses in his blacksmith shop right there in the middle of Chicago.

So send charts to everyone you can't speak with directly. While you're waiting for the return of all these charts from around the country, perhaps even from around the world, spend time with the relatives who are close by, your mother and father, aunts and uncles, and cousins. If members of the family have just recently died or moved away, you might visit their old address and talk with next-door neighbors and friends in the neighborhood who, after years of talking over the backyard fence or perhaps playing cards together, may be every bit as close as family.

One reason for getting as many charts as possible is to resolve discrepancies, particularly with dates. These discrepancies might happen

———————◆◆◆———————

The directory makers are experiencing less difficulty every year with the names of the Russian and Polish Jews on the East Side of New York. The names with which they are burdened when they come to this country are made pronounceable by the children or the teachers when the second generation goes to school, and while in some instances the new names sound like the original, they are written differently, and in most cases, bear no resemblance to the roots from which they were taken. This is true not only of family names but of the "front" names, too. A long-bearded pushcart man was asked in court recently, "What is your name?"

"Yaikef Rabinowski," he answered.

The magistrate evidently thought that was the man's family name and asked, "What's your Christian name?"

The man became indignant at being suspected of having anything "Christian" about him, and "front name" has been the proper expression at that seat of justice ever since.

Yitzchok, the Hebrew of Jacob, has been made Hitchcock, and an old man whose neighbors know him as Cheskel has assumed the more euphonious name of Elwell. There are many similar cases of evolution, but there are more American, English, and even French names among the dwellers in the ghetto [which] are the result of accident as much as anything else. Children are sent to school, and their names are placed on the records by the teacher, who does the best he can with the unpronounceable thing. After the children have been in school a short time, they and their parents become known by the name given to them by the teacher.

An example of this kind was mentioned recently by a young woman who had been a teacher in a school where many Russian children were pupils. "A man came in one day," she said, "with two boys who could not say a word in English. Their names were impossible except for those who had acquired the East Side jargon. When the man was gone, I made one understand that his name would be John and the other that he would have to answer to the name William, and in some way or other their family name which was full of twists and turns, and ended with a 'witch,' became Holz. Within a few weeks John and William Holz made themselves understood in fair English, and within a year they were star pupils. One day the father called at the school to see me about his boys and introduced himself as Mr. Holz! He seemed to be as much at home with the name as though he had been born with it, and so there are hundreds in our district."

In many instances a sign bought at a bargain has caused men to assume a new name, and the changes are made without the least feeling in the matter. One East Side patriarch said, "We honor our fathers just as much, even if we drop their names. Nothing good ever came to us while we bore them; possibly we'll have more luck with the new names."

But there are cases where men changed their names because they wanted to obliterate their foreign origin. Thus a family came to New York with the name of Neuberger. Presently the name became Newburger; then it was changed to Newburg, and now the two remaining brothers are known, one as Mr. New and the other as Mr. Berg.

The merchant on the East Side who rejoices in the name Karzenellenbogen and his neighbor Leworosinski continue to do business despite the numerous syllables in their names, but not so Mr. Bochlowitz. His son changed his name to Buckley, and even this was too long for the second son, who cut it down a peg and made it Buck. The father and son, it is said, are in business under the firm name of Bochlowitz & Buckley, and they send checks signed that way to the young Buck, who is still at school.

"It does some people good to change their names," said an East Side observer, "and I doubt whether Mr. Gladstone would ever have been the great man he was if his ancestors had not dropped the name Freudenstein for Gladstone or whether other German names would have been as well received as their Americanized substitutes." The man could not be convinced that Gladstone was not originally Freudenstein.

One group of names on the East Side is always recognized by the knowing ones as Bohemian. To this class belong the names Yelteles, Abeles, Karpeles, Kakeles, and a number of other names ending in "les." When the owners of some of these names outgrow the East Side and move uptown they drop one of the "e's" in their name and then blossom forth as Karpels, Kakels, etc. One Bohemian said that his countrymen were proud of the "les" names, because they show that Aristotles, Sophocles, Pericles, and Hercules were all Bohemians. [*New York Tribune*, September 2, 1900]

in any number of ways, and usually do. If, for example, one of your ancestors was an orphan or bound-boy (a boy "bound out" by his father, widowed mother, or guardian as an apprentice or kind of indentured servant to a tradesman in order to be taught a trade), it's possible that he never knew, or even forgot, his real birthday. In many instances, children were orphaned on the boat bringing them to the United States, their parents dying through some mishap or illness, either aboard the boat or soon after arriving in America.

Still another problem for the family historian is the destruction of birth, baptismal, marriage, and death records in wars and natural disasters such as flood. I remember as a child being puzzled that my father didn't seem to know my grandfather's age. To a child whose every birthday was attended by a celebration and gifts, this seemed indeed strange. My father explained that my grandfather, who was something of a free spirit in his youth, had left home at an early age and apparently wandered about, though just what he did was uncertain (or at least has remained a secret to me to this day). Then, after the ravages of two European wars, there was not a trace left of his village, much less official birth certificates, and Grandpa just had no way of knowing how old he was. My grandfather had lived in Finland, one of those places in Europe where one's nationality and even one's language were changed abruptly from time to time by the fortunes of war and the inconstancies of treaties. What's more, I learned, not only didn't he know his age, he had no idea of his birth date. The day on which we celebrated his birthday was actually a date he had chosen himself (when faced with a pass-

--- ● ---

TERMS OF RELATIONSHIP

The meaning and usage of many words have changed over the years, and some, even from the first years of this century, have dropped from use entirely. This is particularly true of terms of relationship commonly used throughout early America in diaries, wills, deeds, letters, birth and death certificates, military documents, and census records. Many of these terms are still in use today but with very different meanings. Because of this, one of the most valuable research aids for the family historian is an unabridged dictionary such as *Webster's New International Dictionary of the English Language*, which still keeps track of old words and old meanings (larger libraries will have copies of this, as well as earlier editions).

Words no longer in use we have to look up. But what is confusing are words whose meanings have changed over the generations but are still used in a similar way today, leading us to think that we know what they mean when we really don't. For example, you may discover in the census records of 1850 or 1860 that someone living in your great-grandparents' household—whose name is unfamiliar to you or to anyone else in your family—was listed as an "inmate." Now, that doesn't mean that your grandparents were running

some sort of institution, as we might infer from the use of the word today. During the mid-1800s the term inmate had a very special meaning, and that person—perhaps a visitor, or some stranger given lodging for the night—just happened to be in your great-grandparents' house on the day the census was taken. Just as the meaning of that familiar word has changed in the last hundred years, so have many other familiar terms which you may encounter in your search. Here are some of the more common words which have had very different meanings during the past few centuries.

Cousin. For us the term is clear—a son or daughter of one of our aunts and uncles. But in earlier times in this country it had no such definite meaning and could refer to *any* close relative who was not a brother or sister, or son or daughter. It could be used to refer to a grandchild, niece, or nephew, and even to an uncle or aunt.

Brother. Usually means blood-brother as it does today, but could also mean brother-in-law or step-brother and may not imply any family relationship at all, as in "brother in the church." *Sister* could also be used in these ways.

Son-in-law and daughter-in-law. During the 1600s these terms were sometimes used to refer to stepchildren as well as to the husband or wife of a daughter or son.

Son and daughter. Usually have the same meaning we give them today, but were once used interchangeably with son-in-law and daughter-in-law. By the way, mothers-in-law and fathers-in-law might also have been referred to as simply mother or father.

Mrs. This term, used before a Colonial woman's name, does not necessarily mean that she was married or a widow, but was an abbreviation for *Mistriss*, a term of social distinction. I discovered this when I found Mrs. before the name of a child on a tombstone from the 1600s—she had died at the age of three! Since the term was not in general use, records and tombstones usually refer to a deceased married woman as *wife of* if her husband was still alive, and *widow* or *relict* if he preceded her in death.

Goodman and Goodwife. In Colonial days, these terms were used in place of Mister and Mistriss when referring to men and women who, though respectable, were of more ordinary social standing. A man who was not an indentured servant, and therefore entitled to vote and carry on trade, might also use the title *freeman* before his name.

port application, I suppose, or with sons asking questions like mine) and wasn't his real birthday at all. As if this weren't enough for a young lad, I then discovered that traditionally my grandfather's birthday was celebrated on the Jewish holiday of what was then called Shavous (now, it's Shabouth), which fell on the sixth day of Sivan in the Hebrew calendar (approximately June 21) and that on the "regular" calendar it might be a different date each year!

If you are ever faced with the problem of an unknown birthday, genealogists have a rule of thumb for approximating it. If you know the date of the ancestor's marriage, subtract from this date twenty-five years for a man and twenty-one years for a woman. If the ancestor was not married or the marriage date is also unknown, but the ancestor had brothers or sisters whose ages you do know, you can figure that children were born, on an average, two years apart. Using this rule of thumb, approximate the ancestor's year of birth by adding two years to the birth date of a sibling you know to be older or by subtracting two years from the birth date of a younger brother or sister.

One way of solving a date mystery is a visit to the cemetery. Making a graveside visit to the family plot, perhaps on that annual occasion which has become a tradition in some families, with your family history chart in hand, can lead to the solution of many ancestral mysteries. If grandparents and great-grandparents sometimes forget or reverse the digits of a long-ago date, cemeteries are outdoor family history files, usually with each date (although not always, even in cemeteries) literally carved in stone. Here you may discover all kinds of things for your family history—the names of ancestors who died as infants or young children, whose names have been long misplaced; or the now-forgotten first wife or second husband who brought other names into the family line. The group of markers will help you to visualize complicated step-father, step-sister, and half-brother relationships, and your great-grandparents' eighteen children all lying there right with them. (You may have had a long journey getting to this ancestral place,

so while you're about it, you might want to take your tape recorder and camera too.)

Meanwhile your charts have been out and when they return you'll be impressed with all there is to your family. (Incidentally, keep all the correspondence that comes and goes with the charts. It's important for checking other relationships later, but more important, it becomes a collection of family handwriting and personal letters.) Perhaps you've not thought about it, but of course the number of ancestors in each generation going back is twice that of the preceding generation—1, 2, 4, 8, 16, 32, on and on—so that if you could trace all of your ancestors back for ten generations (about the time New England was being settled), you'd find that you have 1,024 great-great-great-great-great-great-great-great-grandparents, or a total of 2,046 ancestors! This doesn't include collateral kinsmen—the innumerable brothers, sisters, cousins, nieces, nephews, aunts, uncles, great-aunts, and great-uncles who don't show up on the simple lineage chart, which shows only direct lines of descent. But they're part of your ancestry too, and if you are ready to assume your next responsibility as family historian, you'll need another kind of chart too.

The recording of lines of descent for collateral kinsmen is a step worthy of considerable thought. If you planned ahead for the eventuality of a chart showing family relationships when you first began your charting, the information you need can be a happy by-product of the work you do to assemble your lineage chart. Planning ahead means simply asking in your correspondence and interviews for not only the names of parents (which you need for your lineage chart) but also the names, birth dates, birthplaces, marriage dates, and dates of deaths of their children and of the brothers and sisters of your parents, grandparents, great-grandparents, and so on. This second chart provides a separate page for showing the relationships of each member of a single family—mother, father, children, and children's husbands and wives. You begin by placing the names of the father and mother at the top of the chart. Then list in the left-hand column the name of each child, moving across the chart

Generation.................... Family....................

HUSBAND'S NAME..   WIFE'S MAIDEN NAME...

Residence...   Residence..

Date of Birth...Place.................   Date of Birth..Place....................

Date of Marriage....................................Place.......................   Other marriages. Listed on a separate page.

Date of Death...Buried....................   Date of Death..

Married .... times. Listed on a separate page.   Other husbands' names ....

His father's name..   Her father's name..

Mother's maiden name..   Mother's maiden name...

CHILDREN	WHEN	BORN	WHERE	WHEN	MARRIED	WHERE	WHEN	DIED	WHERE	MARRIED TO:	CHART
1.											
2.											
3.											
4.											
5.											
6.											
7.											
8.											
9.											
10.											
11.											
12.											

References or Comments:

to fill in the birth date, birthplace, marriage information, and date of death in the column provided.

Before your project gets out of hand, you'll want some kind of system to key collateral line charts to your lineage charts. Genealogists seem to have their own way, and you might think of your own, but here's a simple system that works for even the most complicated family.

Start by numbering each of your lineage charts. Then, assign a number to each marriage in the chart. Each "family number" then goes at the top of a family chart on which is recorded all the information about the mother, father, and children in that family.

As children are born into a family, or as an elderly parent dies, or as the children themselves grow up and marry, this information is recorded in the chart. In the case of a marriage, a new family has been formed, with children likely to come, calling for a new chart with the names of the husband and wife entered at the top. All these new collateral line charts for the brothers and sisters of the family should be kept together and numbered to show their association with the parents. This can be done simply by adding a letter—a, b, c, and so on —to the lineage chart/family chart number to which the newly married children belong.

Later, you (or successive generations of the family's historians) need only add to the charts you've begun and start new ones as needed for new branches of the family. To keep your information organized and to provide assistance to future generations of family genealogists you should list on the reverse the sources of your information for the chart. This might be a reference to one of the letters that accompanied a filled-in lineage chart, a tape recorded interview, a document such as a birth certificate, or a newspaper article.

*   *   *

As you sort through your ancestors arrayed on lineage and family charts, you're going to find that no matter how careful and thorough you've been during this first step, you've lost someone. Perhaps the family line seems to end abruptly three or four generations ago. None of the replies to your queries brings to light the name or any other information about the mystery ancestor who seems just forgotten, perhaps deliberately so. For any number of reasons, many families consist of only one or two generations, all the grandparents and great-grandparents having died long ago. Moreover, if they had no brothers and sisters, or left the rest of their families behind in some faraway part of the world, their recollection of family history may indeed be very limited. Wars decimate whole generations. Childbirth and disease once brought early deaths to women. Ancestors disappear from the mind, too, as when immigrants or first-generation Americans deny and eventually obscure their origins in their own consciousness and that of their children, leading to a kind of cultural amnesia. Whatever the reasons, there are memory gaps in every family, bringing a new challenge to the family historian.

SEARCHING FAMILY RECORDS

Of course, your first step was to go back in time as far as you could in the memories of the living, and you'll try again later, of course, as new facts come to light. But now you must try other ways. This next step is digging into family records. Let's list some of the places to begin looking.

First, there's the family Bible, which sometimes contains a printed chart for entering notes on births, baptisms, marriages, and deaths. In the absence of such a chart you may find a blank page or inside cover that has been used to record family history for several generations. A long time ago, and sometimes even today, Bibles were given as wedding gifts to young couples by their parents. And if the couple didn't get one as a gift, then a very special family Bible was one of their first purchases together. Sometimes the new Bible would be dated and the family history from the Bibles of their parents copied into it. This was

probably the case if you've found entries that predate the publication of the Bible (sometimes the only clue will be the date of the editor's or translator's note). Most couples, however, recorded their marriage as the first entry and then penned in the birth dates of their children. If you know that such a Bible existed sometime in your family but no one now remembers who has it, you might look through any old wills that are still part of family records.

Letters hiding away in odd, family places (in attic-bound trunks or in the pigeon hole in your grandfather's rolltop desk) are an excellent source of family facts. They contain all kinds of information, such as names, dates of events, news of births and marriages, stories about hard work in college, and glimpses of journeys. The salutations and the complimentary closes show relationships — mothers writing to daughters and sons, husbands in faraway battlefields writing to young wives — and the contents in between the opening and the close show all manner of family lore. Addresses and postmarks on envelopes provide clues to old family residences or a honeymoon's itinerary. The words of your ancestors, written in those ornate and elegant old hands, or maybe even a foreign script, add much to a family history collection.

Diaries and journals, a rare find to be sure and every family historian's dream, nevertheless do exist. Diaries, by young women particularly, were more common in our grandmother's day than they are now and were cherished for generations. They tend now to be forgotten. Age and time have faded and perhaps broken their bindings. Or maybe they were nothing more to begin with than a little bundle of loose vellum. Such unbound diaries and journals were saved too, tucked into envelopes, and placed lovingly in the back of the old high school yearbook with a senior prom bid, or packed away with a life-long collection of theater programs, magazines from childhood, and crumbly yellow newspaper clippings.

Passports, marriage certificates, deeds, wills, and military induction and discharge papers, diplomas, awards, and hunting licenses are another solid source of family facts. Here can be found what you want to know about your grandfather's regiment at the Marne, the name of the high school in New York from which your great-grandmother and your grandmother graduated, maiden names that will help you fill in empty branches in your lineage charts, and an immigrant ancestor's port of entry.

What else? Coverlets, friendship quilts, and samplers, some with the embroidered name of the creator, others with carefully stitched family trees, not infrequently dated. On a friendship quilt stitched by your grandmother, you might find written in indelible ink or embroidery the names of her best friends. The little seamstress doing her very first sampler may work in the names and ages of her brothers and sisters in her best cross-stitching. Look carefully. A friend just discovered on a quilt she had had for some years an inscription, embroidered white-on-white and all but lost in the wrinkled cloth, which gave the maker's name, the date of her birth, and the date of the quilt's completion.

Also collections of newspaper clippings reporting graduations, births, marriages, confirmations, promotions, retirements, deaths and funerals, election to office, county fair awards, house raisings, and visiting family. Unfortunately, most such newspaper items have been clipped away from the date in the upper corner of the page, but still they contain enough of the who, what, when, why, and how to fill in all kinds of lines and spaces.

Also stories and family lore. Like this one, which might disclose the nationality and native language of your great-great-grandfather.

I remember a Dane who sold his oxen to a German. The oxen were well trained to obey voice commands, but didn't understand German. Only Danish. The German finally called on my father for help. Father spoke to the oxen in Danish and they obeyed. [Don Buchan, "Pioneer Tales," in *Annals of Iowa,* Fall, 1966]

Also engraved names, dates, and monograms on metal heirlooms such as silverware, goblets and platters, rings and jewelry, pocket watch and wristwatch cases, hairbrush and comb sets, and fountain pens. Look for both

Sampler, 1838

wedding dates and the initials of the bride and groom on wedding rings and on table settings given as wedding presents.

SEARCHING PUBLIC RECORDS

You may not have realized it, but the recording and preservation of genealogical statistics are in fact provided for in the Constitution, Article I, Section 2, though at first glance Article I, Section 2 does not seem to be about ancestral records at all:

Representatives and direct Taxes shall be apportioned among the several States which may be included within this Union according to their respective Numbers, which shall be determined by adding to the whole Number of free Persons, including those bound to Service for a Term of years, and excluding Indians not taxed, three-fifths of all other Persons. The actual Enumeration shall be made within three years after the first Meeting of the Congress of the United States, and within every subsequent Term of ten Years, in such Manner as they shall by Law direct.

The original purpose of this enumeration, or census, was not, of course, historical but political, the census being the official means of determining a state's representation in the House of Representatives.

In spite of all the problems facing the new nation, that first census was taken, though

Old Handwriting and Symbols

Reading old handwriting can be a real problem when it's in a foreign language, but it can be just as much a problem in English, especially if you're not aware of changes in handwriting and styles over the years. Many words, for instance, were abbreviated by deleting a letter or all but the first and last letters of a word; even names were shortened this way. In Colonial America this deletion was common in letters and documents and was usually indicated by a horizontal line written above or through the word. Some of your handwriting problems may require you to find some old penmanship manuals in the library (interesting browsing, actually, whether you need them or not), but here are examples of a few of the more common abbreviations and symbols.

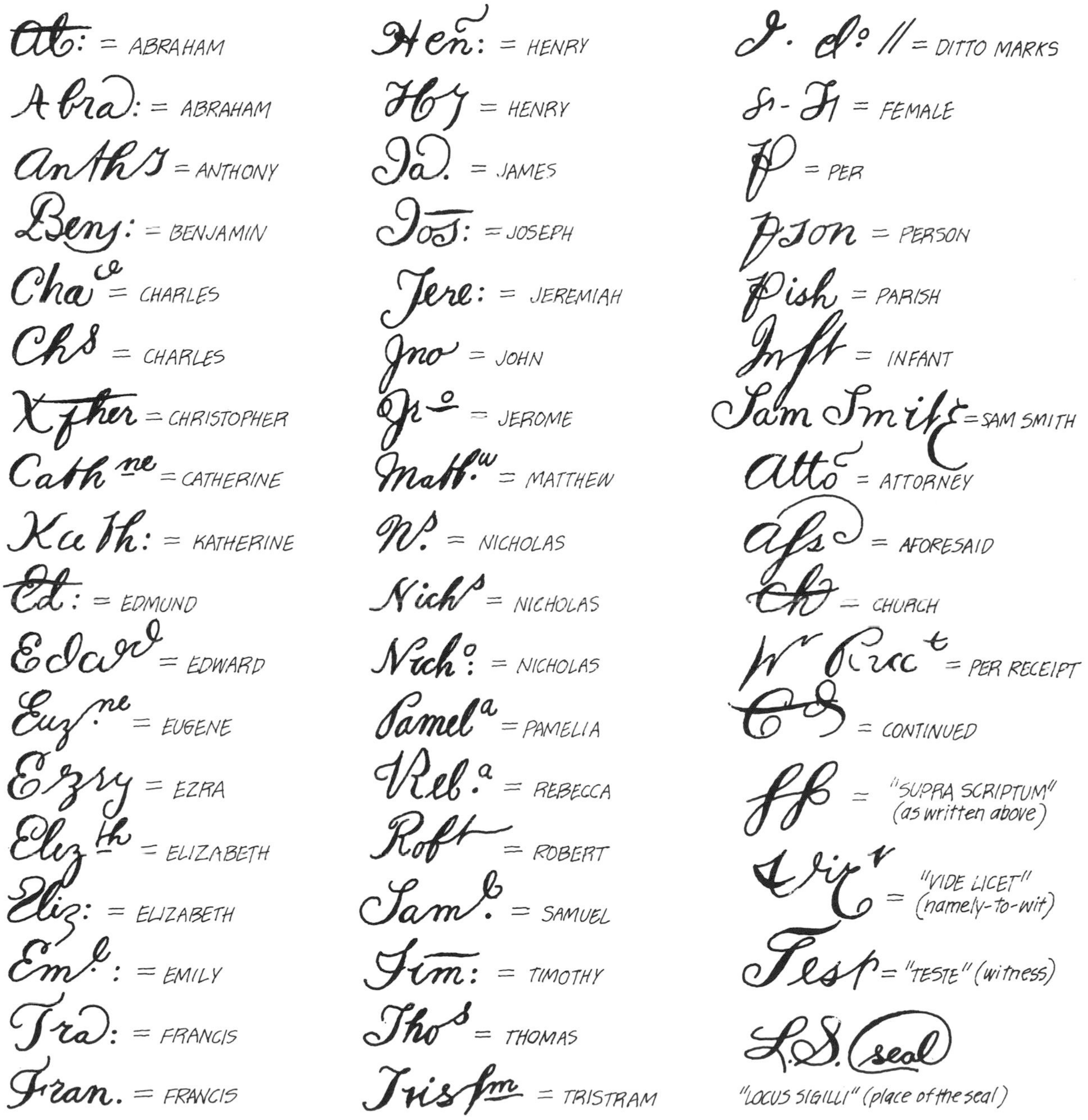

Ab: = ABRAHAM
Abra): = ABRAHAM
Anth⁵ = ANTHONY
Benj: = BENJAMIN
Cha⁵ = CHARLES
Ch⁵ = CHARLES
Xpher = CHRISTOPHER
Cath ⁿᵉ = CATHERINE
Kath: = KATHERINE
Ed: = EDMUND
Edard = EDWARD
Eug:ⁿᵉ = EUGENE
Ezry = EZRA
Eliz ᵗʰ = ELIZABETH
Eliz: = ELIZABETH
Eml: = EMILY
Fra): = FRANCIS
Fran. = FRANCIS

Hen: = HENRY
Hry = HENRY
Ja. = JAMES
Jos: = JOSEPH
Jere: = JEREMIAH
Jno = JOHN
Je:ᵒ = JEROME
Matt.ʷ = MATTHEW
N⁵ = NICHOLAS
Nich⁵ = NICHOLAS
Nich:ᵒ = NICHOLAS
Pamel ᵃ = PAMELIA
Reb.ᵃ = REBECCA
Robt = ROBERT
Saml: = SAMUEL
Tim: = TIMOTHY
Tho⁵ = THOMAS
Trisfm = TRISTRAM

I. do // = DITTO MARKS
S - H = FEMALE
P = PER
Pson = PERSON
Pish = PARISH
Inft = INFANT
Sam Smith = SAM SMITH
Atto = ATTORNEY
afs = AFORESAID
Ch = CHURCH
Wᵐ Recᵗ = PER RECEIPT
C8 = CONTINUED
ff = "SUPRA SCRIPTUM" (as written above)
Vizᵗ = "VIDE LICET" (namely-to-wit)
Test = "TESTE" (witness)
L.S. (seal) = "LOCUS SIGILLI" (place of the seal)

looking at America in 1790 one wonders how. The United States covered 867,980 square miles of territory (the United Kingdom—England, Scotland, Wales, and Northern Ireland—is only 94,212 square miles in all, about a ninth of the United States in 1790). The countryside was sparsely populated with small family farms miles apart and small towns separated by several days' travel on horseback. Maps were few and often inaccurate. In addition, marshals were feared as instruments of federal control and were received with suspicion and hostility. Each marshal devised not only his own procedures but his own recording forms as well. The marshals were paid one dollar per one hundred and fifty inhabitants of country districts and, with the exception of those in Massachusetts, were required to supply their own pen, ink, and paper besides. Written by hand on every imaginable kind of paper, punctuated with erasures, corrections, ink blots, copying errors, and miscalculations, the first census of Connecticut, Delaware, Georgia, Kentucky, Maine, Maryland, Massachusetts, New Hampshire, New Jersey, New York, North Carolina, Pennsylvania, Rhode Island, South Carolina, Tennessee, Vermont, and Virginia arrived at President Washington's desk in every manner and form, including account books, ledgers, and a volume covered with orchid-colored wallpaper decorated with ribbons and twigs. Some of these records have turned to dust with age (fortunately they've been copied), others—Delaware's, Georgia's, Kentucky's, New Jersey's, Tennessee's, and Virginia's—were later destroyed when the Capitol was burned by the British in the War of 1812. In any case, when all the records were in and the enumeration completed, the first census recorded 3,893,635 Americans.

Since that time there has been a census every ten years (some states conducting their own more frequently) and for essentially the same purpose—enumeration. But the census was to evolve into something more than just a simple head count. Even before the second census in 1800, Thomas Jefferson had petitioned Congress to expand the census to provide "a more detailed view of the inhabitants." Jefferson, always the historian, foresaw the interests of future generations of Americans who would find it "highly gratifying to observe the progress of the population."

Soon there were more practical reasons for an expanded census. The President and Congress needed information about America's diverse and scattered population to help them make decisions about postal roads, home industries, and protective tariffs. By the third census in 1810, renewed troubles with Great Britain raised once again the spectre of war and made a national stock-taking imperative. How many ships were there and how many seamen to man them? Were there smiths and millers and rope-makers enough to sustain the Republic through another war? How many men were available for the militia? Later were added questions about occupations and trades, national origins, education, land ownership, and literacy.

And what does all this mean to the amateur historian? Well, for one thing the census remains a record of our ancestors, fulfilling Thomas Jefferson's vision of a kind of pool of national history. Native Americans, immigrants, freemen and slaves, they're all there,

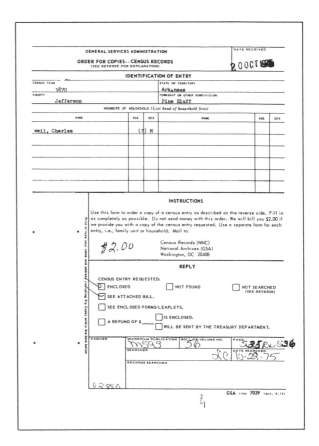

each successive census recording their birth, childhood, marriage, the birth of their own children, their movements about the country and the wars they served in. From the census you might learn, for example, your great-grandmother's native language, her age and birthplace, her occupation, or (if you are of African descent) the name of the master from whom she took her own name. You might discover that your great-great-great-grandfather, back in 1820, gave the census taker a spelling of the family name that differs in some way from the spelling you and your parents use. Checking subsequent census records might show that it was just a recording error, or then again, it could reveal the period of the family's history when the name was changed, and tell you which of your ancestors did it. For the family historian, then, that simple head count which started back in 1790 has over the years become an amazing historical treasure. But what's even more astonishing is the ease with which much of your family's history can be obtained from original census records.

How do you go about getting census information? Well it's so simple that searching census records for information about your ancestors is the ideal first step for the hesitant neophyte historian (and a rewarding elementary and high school history project, too), in spite of the fact that you'll be corresponding with not one but two government agencies. Federal census records are stored at two different locations administered by two government agencies. The original Federal census returns for 1790 and up through 1870, microfilm copies of the 1880 census, and a small fragment of the original 1890 census (most of which was destroyed by a fire in 1921) reside at the National Archives, Washington, D.C. Original records of the 1900 census and all those since are administered by the Bureau of the Census and are stored in Pittsburg, Kansas.

Many people visit the National Archives and do their own research, but most of us cannot, and because of this there is available a simple and inexpensive service for searching census returns by mail. First you'll need several copies of GSA Form 7029 (you'll need one form for each census or entry), which can be obtained

free from Census Records (NNC), National Archives (GSA), Washington, D.C. 20408. All you do is fill out and return your form(s). You need not send any money. If the researchers are unable to find the entry you're seeking, the application form is returned with an explanation and there is no charge. If the research is successful, you will receive a full-size photocopy of the page containing your entry and a bill for $2.00.

Access to census records from 1900 on is a bit more complicated and somewhat more expensive but by no means discouragingly so. This more recent census information is considered confidential and is subject to certain restrictions. Information about a child can be requested only by a parent or guardian. The request for information about a living adult must be initiated and signed by that person. To obtain information about a deceased person you must be a blood relative, surviving husband or wife, or court-appointed executor to his or her estate. In addition, your request must be accompanied by a copy of the death certificate. Let's say you know your grandparents had immigrated to the United States sometime between 1900 and 1910 but aren't sure of the year. You'll find the year of immigration, place of birth, and other information, too, in the 1910 census. Now, if they are still alive, then they must make the search request; if deceased, then you have a right to the information. More details and Application for Search of Census Records forms (BC-600) are available from the Personal Census Service Branch, Bureau of the Census, Pittsburg, Kansas 66762.

While you are awaiting your forms, you'll probably need to do some preliminary detective work. The first thing you'll have to decide is which census you want searched. (Only one census will be searched with each Form 7029; you can specify two census years on the Form BC-600.) The Form 7029 requires only the name of the head of household and the state or territory, county, township, or other geographical subdivision where the person lived. When dealing with census records from 1900 on, the address (number and street) is requested, though the search will be carried out if you cannot supply this information.

My own ancestor search began with my maternal great-grandparents, with whom, sometime in the 1860s, our family's historical consciousness began. These are the earliest ancestors I "know"; I have photographs and other artifacts from their life. It seemed to me that if I could get some information about them then I might be able to reach back at least one more generation. So here I began. There is a story in our family that my great-grand-father emigrated from Germany in the late 1850s or early 1860s to avoid becoming cannon fodder in the Kaiser's armies, only to be caught up in the Civil War once he arrived in America, probably at a port in Virginia. He ended up in Pine Bluff, Arkansas, and if the family story was accurate I figured his name should appear on the 1870 census for that district. All I knew for certain was his name.

After about three weeks I received a thick envelope in the mail containing copies of pages 20 and 21 of "Schedule 1—Inhabitants in Pine Bluff." My great-grandfather's house-hold took three lines, two at the bottom of one page and one at the top of the next. I was im-mediately struck by the simple fact that I was reading the ornately handwritten report of a man who had met my great-grandfather Charles and my great-grandmother Sarah on what must have been a very hot fifth day of August, 1870.

Assistant Marshal Sam S. Grey had appar-ently visited 205 families before arriving at my great-grandparents' door. Charles Weil was then thirty-one years old, his wife, Sarah, seventeen. His occupation was listed as "mer-chant" and Sarah's, like all the other wives on the page, simply as "housekeeper." Charles was born in Germany (Baden-Baden, I think) in 1839. Sarah was born in Mississippi. Their first child, Mabel (Aunt "May" to older mem-bers of the family, now gone but remembered by my mother) was then only five months old, or 5/12 as it appeared neatly penned into the little square. Looking for a moment over the other entries I could see that many of their neighbors were immigrants too: Joe Pender-gast and Roy McMann from Ireland, a sixty-three-year-old man from England whose name I can't read, and several German families in-

———◆◆◆———

"LICENSED TO GO BEYOND THE SEAS"

At some point in this retrospective journey you may find yourself in a port somewhere—perhaps on the very pier where your ancestors first set foot in America—looking out on the ocean which bridged the Old World and the New. That ocean, though, need be no more a barrier to you than it was for them; there are ways of reaching back to the time, even to the day, when your ancestors embarked on their voyage from a port in Europe or Asia and arrived in America. One way is through passenger arrival lists stored at the National Archives.

How would you find out if your grandfather or great-great-grand-mother is on an immigration list in Pascagoula, Mississippi, or French-man's Bay, Maine? Well, first you'll need some information, and it may already be there in your family his-tory. At the very least you should know the port and the year they ar-rived. Knowing the month will make things even easier, as would knowing the name of the ship. Read over diaries, letters back to families, and transcripts of your tape talks for clues. You might even find among bundles of yellowed letters naturali-zation papers or passports. Look for dates on the backs of photos taken soon after arrival or just before de-parture from the old country.

Then, look at the section on pas-senger arrival lists in the *Guide to Genealogical Records in the National Archives* (see page 65). Stored in the National Archives are lists—originals, copies, and abstracts—of immigrants arriving at ports on the Atlantic Ocean, the Gulf of Mexico, and a few inland ports. The earliest list is from 1798, but most of the information available is from about 1820 to 1945, and there are some gaps in these. (Immigration laws of the 1800s did not require ar-rival records for persons entering the United States by land from Canada or Mexico.) Sadly, the San Fran-cisco passenger lists were destroyed by fires in 1851 and 1940, though some lists may still be available from lines serving ports on the west coast. But still there are many lists available from ports in Connecticut, Delaware, Florida, Georgia, Louisiana, Maine, Maryland, Massachusetts, Missis-sippi, New Hampshire, New Jersey, New York, North Carolina, Ohio, Pennsylvania, Rhode Island, South Carolina, Texas, and Virginia.

While research work on passenger arrival lists must be done at the Na-tional Archives where there is a small staff to help you search, there are other lists as close as your city or county library or the library of a nearby university. These are lists published here and in Europe, usu-ally by genealogical and state his-torical societies, which not only show names, but also a considerable amount of biographical data includ-ing status, condition of servitude, native country, and occupation.

Here in these lists you may find someone who brought your name to America two, even three centuries ago—someone who was, in the words of immigration officials in London, "Licensed to Go Beyond the Seas."

Page No. 20

☞ Inquiries numbered 7, 16, and 17 are not to be asked in respect to infants. Inquiries numbered 11, 12, 15, 16, 17, 19, and 20 are to be answered (if at all) merely by an affirmative mark, as /

SCHEDULE 1.—Inhabitants in *Pine Bluff* , in the County of *Jefferson* , State of *Arkansas* , enumerated by me on the *8th* day of *August*, 1870,

Post Office: *Pine Bluff Ark*   *Alex S. Greig*, Ass't Marshal.

1	2	3 The name of every person whose place of abode on the first day of June, 1870, was in this family.	4	5	6	7 Profession, Occupation, or Trade of each person, male or female.	8	9	10 Place of Birth	11	12	13	14	15	16	17	18	19	20	
1		Blackfield Kate	9	f	w				Ark						/					1
2		— George	6	m	w				Ark											2
3		— Ford	1	f	w				Ark											3
4	191 192	Bridges Wm. H.	45	m	w	Clerk in store			N. C.	=								/		4
5		— Ella	30	f	w	Housekeeping			Va					/						5
6		— Charles	2	m	w				Ark											6
7	191 193	Franklin Edd	28	m	m	Laborer			Tenn									/		7
8		— Susan	20	f	m	Laundress			Penn							/				8
9	193	—																		9
10	192 194	Hitt Frank	29	m	w	Sadler			Miss									/		10
11		— Mary E	21	f	w	Housekeeper			Tenn											11
12		— Peter P	1	m	w				Ark											12
13	193 195	Harvey E. V.	57	m	w	Sadler			Va									/		13
14		— Wm	16	m	w				Ark											14
15		— Emily	14	f	w				Ark											15
16	201 196	Thomas Wyatt	33	m	w	Editor & Publisher	500	200	Va											16
17		Matthews Jos	15	m	w	Printer			Miss											17
18		Outham James	20	m	w	Printer			Ark											18
19	201 197	Bradford Wash	33	m	m	Taylor			Penn							/		/		19
20		— Susan A	24	f	m	Housekeeper			Penn							/				20
21	202 198	Hurlsburgh William	42	m	w	Mercht		300	Germany	/	/							/		21
22		— Sophia	41	f	w	Housekeeper			Germany	/	/									22
23		— Charles	13	m	w				Mo	/	/			/	/					23
24		— Hannah	11	f	w				Mo	/	/			/	/					24
25		— David	7	m	w				Ark	/	/									25
26		— Leo	3	m	w				Ark	/	/									26
27		— Carrie	1	f	w				Ark	/	/									27
28	203 199	Bloom Jacob	37	m	w	Retired Mercht	300	250	Germany	/	/								1	28
29		— Rachel	19	f	w	Housekeeping			Mo	/	/									29
30		— Bennett	1	m	w				Ark	/										30
31		— Julia	21	f	w	Housekeeping			Germany	/	/									31
32	204 200	Smith B. F.	44	m	w	Com Mercht	2000	100	N. C.		/							/		32
33		— Eliza	35	f	w	Housekeeper			Ark											33
34		— Beulah	8	f	w				Ark						/					34
35		— Thomas	5	m	w				Ark											35
36		— Antoine	5	m	w				Ark											36
37		Carson Eliza	18	f	w				Ark											37
38		— Lucien	15	m	w	Clerk in store			Ark											38
39	205 201	Weil Charles	31	m	w	Retired Mercht		500	Germany	/	/								/	39
40		— Sarah	17	f	w	Housekeeping	200		Miss	/	/									40

No. of dwellings, 11   No. of white females, 14   No. of males, foreign born, 3
    families, 10   colored males, 2   females, 2
    white males, 21   females, 2   blind,
12,000 150   No. of Insane,

Page No. 21

Inquiries numbered 7, 16, and 17 are not to be asked in respect to infants. Inquiries numbered 11, 12, 15, 16, 17, 19, and 20 are to be answered (if at all) merely by an affirmative mark, as 1.

SCHEDULE 1.—Inhabitants in *City of Pine Bluff*, in the County of *Jefferson*, State of *Arkansas*, enumerated by me on the *5* day of *August*, 1870.

Post Office: *Pine Bluff*

Sam S Grey, Ass't Marshal.

536

1	2	3 The name of every person whose place of abode on the first day of June, 1870, was in this family.	4 Age	5 Sex	6 Color	7 Profession, Occupation, or Trade of each person, male or female.	8 Value of Real Estate	9 Value of Personal Estate	10 Place of Birth, naming State or Territory of U.S., or the Country, if of foreign birth.	11	12	13	14	15	16	17	18 Whether deaf and dumb, blind, insane, or idiotic.	19	20	
		Neil, Elbert	5	m	m				Ark	1	1	24								1
216	202	Rolts, Samuel	39	m	w	Merchant	3000	5000	N.Y.										1	2
		" Sara	14	f	w				Ark					1						3
		" Louisa	11	f	w				N.Y.											4
217	203	Smith, John	33	m	w	Merchant			Tenn										1	5
		Wright, R.C.	28	m	w	Clerk Store			Va					1					1	6
208	204	Seymour, Alf	35	m	w	Clerk			N.C.										1	7
		" Maggie	24	f	w	H Keeper			Tenn											8
		" Mary	1	f	w				Ark											9
209	205	Henry, Jas	31	m	w	Bar Keeper			Miss					1	1				1	10
210	206	Ray, Norman	43	m	w	Saloon Keeper	8000	1000	England	1	1								1	11
		Pedegrast, Mc	42	m	w	Merchant			Ireland	1	1								1	12
21	207	Faw, N.H	30	m	w	Merchant			Tenn										1	13
		" Mary	50	f	w	H Keeper			Tenn											14
		" John	10	m	w				Tenn											15
212	208	Murphy, J.P	21	m	w	Bar Keeper	1000	500	Tenn										1	16
		" Betty	17	f	w	H Keeper			Tenn											17
		Delaney, James	45	m	w	Bar Keeper		400	Ireland	1	1									18
		Jones, James	17	m	m	Servant			Ark						1	1				19
214	211	Ginsberg, John	33	m	w	Merchant		100	Ark										1	20
		" Anna	27	f	w	Keep House			Ark											21
215																				22
216	212	Rosenberg, Sol	32	m	w	Merchant	8000	6000	Germany	1	1								1	23
		" Lucy	24	f	w	Keep House			U.S.	1	1									24
		" Alf	3	m	w				Ark	1										25
		" Flora	2	f	w				Ark	1										26
		" Franklin	63	f	w				England	1	1									27
211	213	Risher, Sol	24	m	w	Merchant		2000	Germany	1	1								1	28
		" Anna	20	f	w				Ky	1	1									29
218	214	Rosenberg, Abr	44	m	w	Merchant		2000	Germany	1	1								30
		" Caroline	35	f	w	Keep House			Germany	1	1									31
		" Rena	1	f	w				Ark	1	1									32
		Vineshine, M	16	m	w				Germany	1	1									33
219	215	Kaermstin, J	24	m	w	Book Keeper			Tenn		1	1							1	34
		Mitra, Wirke	20	m	w	Clerk Store			Tenn	1	1									35
220	216	Jones, John	30	m	w	Porter		100	Ark						1	1				36
		" Anna	40	f	b	House Keeper			Tenn						1	1				37
		" Albert	21	m	w	School Teacher			Tenn									b		38
		Wells, Henry	12	m	b				Tenn							1				39
221	217																			40

No. of dwellings 16 No. of white females 13 No. of white foreign born 9
" families 17 " colored males 6 " females
" white males 23 " females " blind

22,000 17,100

No. of insane

cluding William and Sophi Wurtzburger, Jacob and Rachle Bloom, Sol and Lucy Rozenburg, and Sol Miller. Next to all the names were listed the many occupations and trades of this small segment of Pine Bluff's population: a saddler, a taylor, a couple of printers, a school teacher, two saloon keepers, a porter, several merchants, and a bookkeeper. The value of Charles Weil's real estate and personal property are written in, and though I have no way of knowing whether he might have been considered well off in his day, the only man doing much better (or admitting to it) and apparently one of the richest men in town was the saloon keeper. Over to the right of the form were the many boxes to be checked by Assistant Marshal Grey. Both Charles and Sarah indicated that their mother and father were foreign born. Charles had become a naturalized citizen and both he and his wife had answered yes to the marshal's question about whether they could read and write.

I'm now awaiting the next chapters to arrive with the 1880 and 1890 census entries. With these will come the names of the children born in the next decade, great-grandfather Charles's answer to the Civil War questions (soldier, sailor, marine? Union or Confederate?), and, oh yes, how Roy McMann is prospering with his saloon.

——◆——

THE NATIONAL ARCHIVES

The beginning genealogist soon discovers that there is a problem of too much information, scattered throughout too many sources. This seems particularly true of information available from various agencies of the U.S. Government, but there is one little inexpensive book that serves as a where-to-find-it and how-to-get-it guide to just about all the important collections of genealogical data compiled over the years by numerous Federal offices.

Guide to Genealogical Records in the National Archives by Meredith B. Colkett, Jr., and Frank E. Bridgers (National Archives Publication No. 64–8) should be one of the first books on your family history bookshelf. It can be ordered by mail from the Superintendent of Documents, U.S. Government Printing Office, Washington, D.C. 20402. The *Guide* contains descriptions of all sorts of records: census schedules from 1790 through 1890, with suggestions on how to research them; passenger arrival lists; United States military records; United States naval and marine records; records of veterans' benefits; records concerning the Confederate states; land-entry records; miscellaneous genealogical records such as passport applications and naturalizations; as well as documents concerning Indian removal and claims. As the introduction to the *Guide* points out, the archival holdings amount to over nine hundred thousand cubic feet of files dating back to the Continental Congresses. This book lets you know what is there and helps you find what you are looking for.

——◆——

A03093857

Newly inducted military personnel often hear it said that you remember your service number for the rest of your life. It is written on countless forms, looked for among others on promotion lists, duty rosters, and military orders, and is even stenciled on equipment and clothing. This may also have been the case for some of your ancestors, perhaps as far back as the American Revolution in 1775. That's the earliest date on military records stored in the National Archives and the beginning of a long military history that holds intriguing information for the family historian.

Suppose your great-great-great-great-grandfather did fight in the Revolutionary War. Well, that might be a bit difficult to know for sure since many military records were destroyed in 1814 when government buildings in Washington were ransacked and burned by the British Army. But it's worth a try. In early Army, Navy, Marine, and Coast Guard files you might find any number of details of a distant ancestor's military career, including age at enlistment, occupation at enlistment, rank, regiment and company or vessels to which assigned, rank or rating, home state at enlistment, date separated from service, even a physical description. In addition, there's information on pensions and bounty land warrants granting public lands to veterans of the Revolutionary War, the War of 1812, Indian wars, and the war with Mexico, which just might explain the origins of a family homestead. There are records of benefits granted to widows and dependents of an ancestor who died in a war, too. Photocopies of many records can be obtained by mail. To find out all about this service, write to the National Archives and Record Service requesting a free copy of *Military Service Records in the National Archives of the United States.*

CHAPTER 4

Resting Places

—•◦◉◦•—

THE HILL

Where are Elmer, Herman, Bert, Tom and Charley,
The weak of will, the strong of arm, the clown,
*   the boozer, the fighter?*
All, all, are sleeping on the hill.

One passed in a fever,
One was burned in a mine,
One was killed in a brawl,
One died in a jail,
One fell from a bridge toiling for children and wife—
All, all are sleeping, sleeping, sleeping on the hill.

Where are Ella, Kate, Mag, Lizzie and Edith,
The tender heart, the simple soul, the loud, the proud,
*   the happy one?—*
All, all, are sleeping on the hill.

One died in shameful child-birth,
One of a thwarted love,
One at the hands of a brute in a brothel,
One of a broken pride, in the search for heart's desire,
One after life in far-away London and Paris
Was brought to her little space by Ella and Kate
*   and Mag—*
All, all are sleeping, sleeping, sleeping on the hill.

Where are Uncle Isaac and Aunt Emily,
And old Towny Kincaid and Sevigne Houghton,
And Major Walker who had talked
With venerable men of the revolution?—
All, all, are sleeping on the hill.

They brought them dead sons from the war,
And daughters whom life had crushed,
And their children fatherless, crying—
All, all are sleeping, sleeping, sleeping on the hill.

Where is Old Fiddler Jones
Who played with life all his ninety years,
Braving the sleet with bared breast,
Drinking, rioting, thinking neither of wife nor kin,
Nor gold, nor love, nor heaven?
Lo! he babbles of the fish-frys of long ago,
Of the horse-races of long ago at Clary's Grove,
Of what Abe Lincoln said
One time at Springfield.

[Edgar Lee Masters, *Spoon River Anthology*]

Cemeteries are, for many of us, uncomfortable, even dreaded places. And we really don't know why. Perhaps we nervously try to explain away our discomfort by alluding to the specters we once imagined to be there, fragments, no doubt, of gothic tales from our childhood. But there's more to it than that, of course, and it seems to me it has to do with death. Amidst the stones of a quiet little country burying ground or in the sprawling cemetery of the city, we confront thoughts that we don't otherwise normally encounter. In these places, we are reminded, more than anywhere else, of the transitory nature of human existence and of our own death.

But, then, that is what cemeteries are for—at least that is what they were for our ancestors. Beginning with the Puritans of the seventeenth century (and continuing right up to the early decades of this century), burying grounds more or less deliberately served our ancestors as constant reminders that there can be no life without death, that the passing of time and our own mortality are powerful influences in our lives. Thus the village cemetery, its graves clustered about the meetinghouse, or church, or crowning a little hill not far from the center of town, was a part of day-to-day life, never out of sight, never far from mind.

On the stones in the village cemeteries were lessons to be learned; the memento mori not only marked the place wherein lay the remains of the dead, but also proclaimed the freeing of the soul and, in addition, instructed the living. For some, the central lesson offered by the stones was to be found in the inscriptions; for others, the children and (in our earliest days) the adults who could not read, the lesson was in the graven images—grinning skeletons, for instance, atop empty hourglasses, clutching the scythe of time. The lesson was clear:

> AS YOU ARE NOW,
> SO ONCE WAS I:
> AS I AM NOW,
> SO YOU MUST BE.
> SO PREPARE FOR DEATH
> AND FOLLOW ME.

The graveyard lesson was not an obscure one. If the poetry of the early stones strikes us as melodramatic or overdone, then we need to look once again at our earliest history, back to the time of Indian hostility, severe winters, epidemics, and dwindling food supplies. Deaths occurred in such numbers that these pious Christians had to leave their dead in unmarked mass graves. These were the years called by historians the "starving time." In his report on Jamestown, Park Service archaeologist John L. Cotter tells us that "between December 1606 (when the first vessels of the Virginia Company left England) and February 1625, 7,289 immigrants came to Virginia. During this period 6,040 died. . . . Allowing for a proportion of these settlers to have been buried on plantations and settlements on the mainland, it is evident that more persons were buried on Jamestown Island during the first few years than lived there at any one time thereafter."

Still, the Puritan graveyards did not remain unchanging reminders of mortality. True, the messages and images, particularly in the earliest and most trying times, were anything but pleasant, reflecting not only the sternness of the Puritan faith, but the hardships, famine, epidemics, and cold that carried away the children and whole families. But the death's heads, the macabre skeletons, and the crossed bones eventually gave way to symbols of hope and the promise of Resurrection, the deceased's soul symbolically being borne heavenward by winged cherubs, wreathed in the vines and trees and fruits of prosperity. In a later stage, the stones carried caricatured, stylized portraits of the dead. The grave now was the way to a more comfortable life, to immortality free of the anguish and sorrows of death. It was not death that had occurred. Rather the deceased had, as it is told on the stone of Thomas Nichols, Wakefield, Massachusetts, "exchanged worlds in the month of April, 1765."

Times are different now, and though death means no less to us than it did to our ancestors, we've tended to insulate ourselves from the dread, the fears, even the reality of life cycles. One of the ways we express this is in our disregard for graveyards. Not only don't we seek them out as places of instruction or contemplation or as "museums" of our own past, but many of us assiduously avoid them, not realizing that the result is the loss, both personal and cultural, of one of our historical resources. Much of what America was once and aspires to be in the future is revealed on little slabs of wood and stone, some quite ornate, others quite simple, and for the experience we don't even have to know how to read!

Thousands of burying grounds lie around us, forgotten and deteriorating. Actually, none of us is more than a few minutes, a healthful walk, from a cemetery—even small sites with but a few stones, now possibly overgrown with vines, may surprise us with their beautiful sculpture and poetry. But relatively few realize it. And we'll probably never know how many others

Workers in Stone

Hereby informs his Customers and other Gentlemen and Ladies that besides carrying on the Stone Cutting business as usual he carries on the Art and Manufactory of a Sister Simolacrocum, or the making of all sorts of Images viz.: — 1st. Kings and Queens, 2nd. King George and Queen Charlotte, 3rd. King and Queen of Prussia, 4th. King and Queen of Denmark, 5th. King and Queen of Sweden, Likewise a number of busts, among which are Matthew, Prior, Homer, Milton, &c. also a number of animals such as Parrots, Cats, Dogs, Lions, Sheep with a number of others too many to enumerate. . . .

Until late in the 1800s, there were probably few full-time tombstone cutters, though larger cities had many craftsmen who did many things with their skilled hands, among these activities the carving of tombstones. Harriette Forbes notes in her collection of biographies of New England gravestone cutters (published in 1927) that it is unlikely, in the early days at least, that they were called stonecutters. Some were workers in stone to be sure, immigrants and descendants of immigrants from stone-culture countries like England, Scotland, Ireland, and Germany; but others were masons, woodcarvers, cordwainers, cabinetmakers, even printers. William Mumford of Boston, for one, was a brass and copper engraver, Joseph Lamson a mariner and bricklayer, and William Young the town surveyor of Tatnuck.

Probably because stonemaking was a sideline of other work, the ordering and selling of gravestones seems to have been a rather informal business. Amidst the tremendous number of business records from the Colonial period only a very few are available to illustrate the manner of buying and selling gravestones. Among them is this order discovered by Harriette Forbes:

Mr. Robert Mulican of Bradford Ser pray make; for me Two Gravestones; one for David Foster jeunier of Andover; who died the 22; day of Dec; in the year of our Lord 1736, in the 20th year of his age; the son of David and Lidea Foster of Andover.

And one for Lidea Foster, the daughter of David and Lidea Foster of Andover; who died in the 17th year of her age in the year of our Lord 1736 and when they are made; send me word; and I will come and pay you for them.

David Foster

And one for Isaac Foster; the son of Joshua and Mary Foster of Andover who died in the third year of his age in the year 1738. Pray send me word when it is made; and I will satisfie you for it.

Joshua Foster

Let them all be made; before you send us word the 3rd day of April 1739. [Harriette Merrifield Forbes, *Gravestones of Early New England and the Men Who Made Them 1653–1800*. Boston: Houghton Mifflin, 1927]

have already been leveled and built over, the ultimate cost of our neglect. The protection and restoration of cemeteries are beyond the scope of this book, but where such action all begins— in awareness, interest, curiosity, and concern —is very much what we are about.

*   *   *

Philadelphia, Pennsylvania, ca. 1700

Because we move around so much these days, the chances are, particularly if you're younger, that you're nowhere near your buried ancestors. There's a cemetery close to where you are living right now, but it's possible that not a single living descendant of anyone buried there is living close by. In some sites, individual stones, family plots, perhaps even entire graveyards are hidden from view by thickets of berry bushes. Such lack of care isn't entirely attributable to population patterns—elderly people moving away to the city, say, and the repopulation of rural communities by urban expatriates; it also happens that many old families have simply died out, their lines of descent ending years ago, with not a single living relative left. Regardless of the cause, many cemeteries today show all the signs of neglect: broken, all but buried tombstones; rotted wooden markers; fenceposts and trees undermined with rabbit warrens; many of the beautiful old stones gone, carried away to be used as hearthstones, doorstops, or even foundation footings for the new barn.

If you've ever wondered about where your ancestors are or how their mortal remains are faring, that wondering is a good sign. You may

be too far away or too late to be of much help to your own ancestors, but you can take care of someone else's and hope he will do the same for you.

The first step toward appreciation (and ultimately the protection) of old graveyards is to be aware that they are there, to visit them for their history or for the peacefulness, the solitude, and the imagery they offer. To find cemeteries in the city one need no more exotic a historical source than the telephone directory. Under the heading "Cemeteries and Memorial Parks" can be found the information you'll need to start, for the listings include cemeteries for every imaginable ethnic group (Serbians, Japanese, Italians, Germans), religious denomination (Roman Catholics, Greek Orthodox, Buddhist, Jewish), and fraternal organization (Odd Fellows, Elk) in America.

Still, the listings, as full as they are, are not complete. Many old burial grounds have dropped from sight. Some perhaps were never more than a few stones marking a small family graveyard, which at one time was located just outside of town, but now, absorbed by the growth of the city, is in the midst of downtown traffic. Even if you're an old hand at finding and visiting cemeteries around where you live, as well as in the cities and little towns through which you travel, there are probably many graveyards—some even quite close—unknown to you and to most of the more recent arrivals to the area. These cemeteries are likely to be some of the oldest in the vicinity. Here are some possible locations and sources of information you may not have considered:

1. Parks and grounds surrounding city, county, and state buildings, particularly around the meetinghouse, the old town hall, the county courthouse, the square or commons, and other green areas of the city.

2. University campuses, the oldest public grounds in many cities, which sometimes hide little clusters of stones, shaded by giant old trees and closed in with wrought-iron fences, plots going back to the church or land-grant origins of the school.

3. Churchyards, particularly near old Roman Catholic churches whose grounds are sometimes a forest of gravestones (usually for

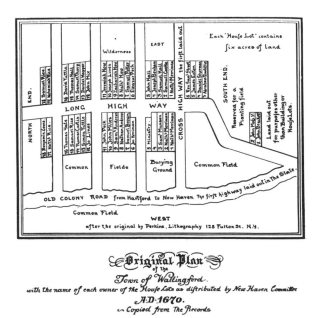

deceased clergy and children of the parish orphanage, but not infrequently for parishioners too) dating back to times when the church stood at the center of the parish.

4. Military bases and military cemeteries (United States Government National Cemeteries) which came into being during the Civil War, perhaps earlier, with row upon row of gravestones chronicling American military history.

5. Old maps of the city, available from the city clerk's office, the local history section of the library, university libraries, city planning offices, and local historical associations, which show the locations of burying grounds that are difficult to find in any other way, being tucked away in the corner of a park or hidden under a thicket on a small lot that has remained untouched for years.

6. Aerial photographs available from city offices and commercial aerial photographers.

Old cemeteries in rural areas are more of a challenge to find, but here are some hints:

1. Ask around town, particularly old-timers who know every inch of the land. They will know not only where the cemeteries are but probably the names of everyone there! This first step can save a lot of searching, and if the person you ask happens to be in a pickup truck you'll probably get a ride.

2. Examine United States Geological Survey topographic maps. They cover virtually every inch of the United States, showing churches, even pioneer burying grounds with but a few stones in them. These may be purchased cheaply enough (about a dollar) or may be found in files at the library. Surveyors, civil engineering firms, or hiker/outdoorsman friends probably have copies you could look at.

3. Talk to morticians or funeral directors and you'll probably discover that they're responsible for the care of little cemeteries and nearby pioneer burying grounds and that they arrange funerals for rural communities. If they've been there a while, they'll have burial records that will help you when a stone is missing or illegible. At the very least they'll have helpful memories. Some morticians work with county and local historical societies and museums to keep historical graves marked and recorded. Here's just such a marker placed by the funeral director in a local cemetery some forty miles from town:

WILLIAM M. MANTLE
1827–1858
1ST PERSON TO BE BURIED IN THE
VALLEY VIEW MEMORIAL PARK

4. You might also talk to the local stonecarver (listed in the yellow pages under "Monuments") who probably has some very interesting history to tell. An Italian stonecarver listed in the San Francisco telephone directory advertises that he's the "fifth generation" of stonecarvers in his family; that's a lead to about one hundred and fifty years of memories and experiences.

5. Finally, look up anyone who's spent a lot of time on the land—foresters, county maintenance crews, surveyors, public utility crews and supervisors, sheriff's deputies, and real estate agents—who may remember seeing a little group of stones (some perhaps nearly uprooted by the old tree hiding them from view).

And, by the way, when you've discovered that little graveyard, be sure to mark it on your map if it's not already there. This will help you and other local historians to find the place again.

*   *   *

Stones of Many Colors

There are vast quantities of blue or slate stone at the Pin Hill quarry in Harvard. It leases to the stone cutters in this and a neighboring town for £6.10/per annum. . . . The stones are chiefly used for grave and tomb stones and are carried to a great distance. . . . In the northeasterly part of Lancaster is the fine and valuable and perhaps inexhaustible slate pit, furnishing slates and tiles for the roofs of houses, and most excellent stones for tombs and graves. . . . No slates equal to them have been discovered on this continent. Great numbers are used in Boston every season. They are exported to Virginia, to Hartford in Connecticut. [Peter Whitney, *History of Lancaster County,* 1790]

The first stone grave markers in America were just granite boulders taken from a field to mark the newly dug grave. Earlier than that wooden planks were probably used, with inscriptions either painted on or carved into the wood, but the inscriptions, if they existed, have become weathered and mute so that we can't be sure. One of the earliest stones extant is a rough-cut boulder with the inscription "EL 1647" in Ipswich, Massachusetts. Since that time many different kinds of stone have been used either because they were easily available close by, or because they were the style, in which case they might even have been shipped from considerable distances.

Keeping in mind the fact that stones were shipped around the country and that availability obviously determined what was used — which means that a stone did not necessarily come freshly from the immediate area — you can date a gravestone roughly by the kind of stone from which it was carved, a procedure that is particularly useful when trying to date undated or badly weathered markers.

Before 1650. Unmarked rough-cut granite boulders with simple inscriptions, usually nothing more than initials. The date of death began to appear in the 1640s.

1650s. Boulders dressed or faced on one side, inscriptions set within deeply cut horizontal rules.

1660s. Slate stones, which are easier to carve than granite, began to appear in greater numbers, particularly around Boston and Charlestown. In Connecticut, especially, red and brown sandstone was used throughout this period. The use of the deeply cut horizontal guidelines went out of style in the cities, but continued in the small towns for another decade or so. From this time and continuing throughout the seventeenth and eighteenth centuries, the inscriptions were in roman lettering — which remains readable even after the stones have weathered badly.

1700s. Continued use of slate and sandstone and now greater use of cameo stones, stone naturally composed of alternate layers of different-colored material. Cutting through from one layer to the next the stonecutter could produce a stone in two colors, one for the background, the other for the design and lettering. Black designs on gray backgrounds were very common, but other combinations included red or rose on olive green, and deep orange appearing through bright cobalt blue.

Late 1700s. First use of marble for gravestones.

Late 1700s to early 1800s. Continued use of soft, dark slate throughout most of the country. Roman lettering was used almost without exception throughout the entire period.

Ca. 1800–1850. A harder, grayish blue slate came into use, but inscriptions began following the new style, which was to use italic script. This italic script, unlike the roman, weathers badly and often only the heavy, deeply carved vertical strokes remain. The delicate hairline cross strokes disappear, often leaving indistinguishable the numbers 1, 7, and 4; and 3, 8, and 9.

1840s. A harder marble came into use and the inscription style returned to roman letters, probably because the harder stone made the rounded, ornate italics more difficult to carve.

Late 1800s. Reappearance of granite stones, sometimes with raised lettering. Late in this century and in the early 1900s, sandblasting began to replace the hammer and chisel for the cutting of designs and inscriptions. More deeply incised, they lasted longer, particularly on granite. This period also marked the appearance of cast metal "stones."

Your purpose in visiting cemeteries may be nothing more than to seek the peace and quiet of these resting places. You needn't worry about being alone or conspicuous, particularly if you're visiting a larger cemetery in or near a city, for others like you will be there. Many city dwellers have discovered that cemeteries deep within the city are the habitat of birds and insects and animals who disappeared from the city scene long ago and who now nest and breed in these grassy, tree-filled spaces. Here city dwellers find fewer people (and fewer bothersome dogs) than in parks, the solitude providing them a haven from the encroaching concrete.

Many of the people you'll see are there to visit a family grave, as you might expect. But many others will be there for all manner of reasons—some just out for a walk and to relax in the sun, others to jog or to bicycle. Others might come to feed the wildlife, pick berries, collect butterflies, even to fish in the little ponds or streams there. Still others will be seen photographing unique markers, copying down epitaphs, collecting family history, or making stone rubbings. You might encounter a group of school children on a field trip visiting historic graves and having a quiet picnic. Such visitors, whether they know it or not, are actually part of a long tradition going back to the 1800s, when cemeteries, particularly in New England and in the South, were the scene of family Sunday socials in which grave visitations, reminiscences of the old-timers, and picnicking all combined to make for a pleasant and enjoyable day.

Whatever your purposes, you might want to take a few moments to become acquainted with the cemetery as a history museum. Stroll about until you find the oldest section, containing the very first graves. This might be right in the middle, the cemetery having grown outward in all directions, or perhaps in some far-off corner. Walk among the markers feeling all the different textures of slate and marble and granite, and maybe you'll discover that, without reading the inscription, you can guess the century or even the half-century in which it was carved just from its substance. If you think that a friend's ancestors are buried here, you may follow your curiosity to discover who they were. You might even come upon a stone with your own last name, leaving you to wonder if you've happened upon a long-lost ancestor. You could be treated to an unexpected history lesson were you to come upon a stone like this one in Cooke Memorial Park, Fairhaven, Massachusetts:

SACRED TO THE MEMORY OF
JOHN COOKE
WHO WAS BURIED HERE IN 1695
THE LAST SURVIVING MALE PILGRIM
OF THOSE WHO CAME OVER IN THE
MAYFLOWER
THE FIRST WHITE SETTLER OF THIS TOWN
AND THE PIONEER IN ITS RELIGIOUS
MORAL AND BUSINESS LIFE

Or this one in Round Valley, California:

HENRY L. FORD
BORN AT NORTH CONWAY, N.H. 24 AUGUST 1822
CALIFORNIA PIONEER OF 1843
LIEUTENANT OF THE BEAR PARTY
AT SONOMA 14 JUNE 1846
SUGGESTED THE GRIZZLY BEAR FOR ITS FLAG
COMMANDED DETACHMENT
AT SKIRMISH AT OLOMPALI
CAPTAIN COMMANDING COMPANY B
CALIFORNIA BATTALION 1846–1847
AGENT NOME LACKEE AND
MENDOCINO INDIAN RESERVATION 1854–1860
DIED IN THIS VALLEY 2 JULY 1860

You may even discover that a cemetery is not an unlikely place for lighter moments. Consider an epitaph such as this one in the churchyard of Saint Andrew's, Staten Island, New York:

THOSE THAT KNEW HIM BEST DEPLORED HIM MOST.

Or this simple commentary on the event of Charles DuPlessis' death in 1907, recorded on his stone at Rosehill Cemetery in Chicago:

NOW AINT
THAT TOO BAD

And there's mystery here too. Perhaps you'll come upon a stone as intriguing as this one in West Cemetery, Middlebury, Vermont, with its inscription reading:

ASHES OF AMUN-HER-KHEPESH-EF
AGED 2 YEARS
SON OF SEN WOSET 3RD
KING OF EGYPT AND HIS WIFE
HATHOR-HOTPE
1883 B.C.

It seems that the child's mummy was one of a number of archaeological finds brought from Egypt to this country during the last century which eventually became part of the collection of the Sheldon Museum in Middlebury. When the mummy began to disintegrate, the problem of its disposal was solved by a museum staff member who had the mummy cremated and the ashes buried in his own family plot and erected a stone in memory of the child's death, nearly four thousand years before.

*   *   *

On my first cemetery visit, what intrigued me most was the wide variety of names. Almost every inscription would contain a name new to me, some recalling the Bible, others the splendor of Greece or classical Rome—names deriving from the Old World and from early America. I recall during this first visit not being able to remember all the marvelous names I was discovering and, in order to keep them, began a list. Beginning that list was a fateful step, for as soon as I had come up with a pencil stub and with a scrap of paper that almost instantly became covered with names of people and faraway places, archaic spellings, and inscriptions in foreign languages, along with my clumsy sketches of the stones—I knew I was to become a constant visitor to burial grounds and a cemetery historian forevermore.

NAMES FROM THE PAST

Perhaps you've not thought much about names, about how they go in and out of style, disappearing altogether for a generation or two only to reappear again and be in vogue. A look through any telephone directory points up the sad fact that, during the past couple of generations, we've become a bit staid, a lot less creative than our ancestors about naming our children, using over and over names like Robert, Charles, Mary, Stephen, William, Carol, Linda, James, or Deborah. It's not that there's anything wrong with these names, it's just that our ancestors' names were, well let's say, a bit more colorful. Here, for example, is a sampling of names from some New England graveyards of the 1600s and 1700s. There were, of course, the usual names like Henry (5 of them), James (3), Richard (1), Frederick (1), Timothy (2), Martha (3), Mary (6), Ann (2), Elizabeth (1), and one Charles and a Ruth. But they don't add up to many among all of these:

Aaron	Jeremiah	Almira
Abel	Josiah	Amasa
Achsah	Keziah	Bethiah
Beriah	Kias	Chloe
Caleb	Luen	Clarissa
Constant	Lyman	Disire
Ebenezer	Merlin	Dorcas
Eleazer	Moses	Experience (2)
Elijah	Nehemiah (2)	Hulda(h) (3)
Elisha (3)	Omri	Jennet
Ephraim	Othniel	Margrit (2)
Enoch (3)	Penuel	Mehetable
Ezekiel	Philetus	Mercy
Ezra	Phineas	Patience
Fletcher	Polycarpus	Phebe
Fordyce	Pyam	Philomena
Gershem	Rufus	Polly (2)
Griswel	Seth	Prudence
Hazadiah	Silas	Rebekah
Hobart	Simeon (3)	Sabra
Israel	Zerubbabel	Sibbel (2)
Jared		Temperance
Jephthah		Zeruiah

What might we learn from such a listing? For one thing, the names of the kings and queens of England and other European nations were not particularly popular among Puritan Americans—the name George is absent.

Also, such English names as William, Richard, John, Ann, Elizabeth, and Katherine are there in number, to be sure, but in numbers much smaller than we would find in an English graveyard, then or now. It appears that Americans, much unlike English colonials elsewhere, were showing, albeit informally, some independence from the rigors of the motherland's traditions.

There are some other social facts we might infer from names on tombstones. It seems that sons were often named for their fathers, but daughters were seldom named for their mothers. And although gravestones sometimes referred to women as Mrs. John Brown, more often than not the wife's full name appears, and in at least several instances a wife has a stone of her own.

The names mentioned above came from graveyards of the 1600s and 1700s. What of names in the late 1800s and the early 1900s? How are they different from names of today? Are there names that are just as popular now as they were then? These and other interesting bits of name history—like local favorites, or the vogue of Juniors and IIIs, or the most popular period for your own name and for the ones you've chosen for your children—can be discovered in an hour or so at the cemetery. The names are right there with their dates; a notepad and pencil are all you need to piece together the answers.

CHANGING LIFE EXPECTANCY

You may have seen one of those charts in which changing life expectancies are plotted for the past hundreds, perhaps thousands of years, and you may have wondered how such things are known. Well, now you know, for cemeteries are a principal source of data for historical demography. Other sources are necessary too, like genealogies, family Bibles, official birth and death certificates, census data, and tax rolls, but cemeteries have certain advantages; they're outside in the fresh air, they don't move around very much (although, as we've noted, they can get lost from time to time), records on stone are more permanent than those on paper, and most of the information you'll need is in one place. Gathering information on life expectancy, then, is not particularly complicated, though to be accurate about it can be very time consuming and is best done by several researchers.

But let's assume that you want to find out what the life expectancy was in your community for men and women, say, during the last half of the nineteenth century. You'll find that some gravestone inscriptions from the early part of this period record the date of death as shown on the next page.

—◆—

FUNERALS. *The Sexton of Trinity-Church gives Notice to the Inhabitants of this Town, That he, with proper Assistance, will attend at Funerals, as there may be Occasion; and will carry the Corps to the Grave, at the Price of 24 s. He has also a handsome Pall for grown Persons at 7/6, another for Children at 4/. Attendance 5/. He may be spoken with at his Dwelling-House in Summer-Street, Boston.* [Boston News-Letter, April 9/16, 1741]

—◆—

FUNERAL PALL. *Whereas the Towns of Salem & Marblehead, and other Towns adjacent, have no Pall to accomodate a decent Funeral, without sending to Boston for one; Capt. Joseph Majory, at his House in Marblehead, has provided two handsome black Velvet Palls to Lett, suitable for such service, viz. a large one and a smaller.* [Boston Gazette, May 24/31, 1736]

Monday last were decently interred, the Remains of Mr. Ellis Callender, Son of the Late Minister of the Baptist Church. The Town had the Satisfaction of seeing in this Instance, a Funeral conducted conformable to an Agreement lately entered into by a great Number of the most respectable of its Inhabitants.— A long Train of Relations followed the Corpse (which was deposited in a Plain Coffin) without any sort of Mourning at all: Mr. Andrew Hall, the Chief Mourner, appeared in his usual Habit, with a Crape round his Arm; and his Wife, who was Sister and nearest Relative to the Deceased, with no other Token of Mourning than a black Bonnet, Gloves, Ribbons and Handkerchief. The Funeral was attended by a large Procession of Merchants and Gentlemen of Figure, as a Testimony of their approbation of this Piece of Occonomy and as a Mark of their Esteem for a

Family who have shown Virtue enough to break a Custom too long established and which has proved ruinous to many Families in this Community.

—◆—

THE GENTLEMEN AND LADIES OF THE TOWN ARE INFORMED, That Bows and Roses of Ribbands for Gentleman, and Bonnets proper for Widows and other Ladies, are made in the genteelest Manner, and sold by ANNE and ELIZABETH CUMMINGS, at the corner of Queen-Street, near the Town-House. Where also may be had: Crapes for Gentlemen's Hats or Arms, and Handkerchiefs, Ribbands & Gloves for Ladies. N.B. Bonnets for Funerals are either to be Let or Sold. [Boston Gazette, September 24, 1764]

RICHARD MORTON

DIED

MAY 1ST, 1865,

IN THE 26TH YEAR OF HIS AGE

This presents some problems if you try to work backward to find the year of birth. If Richard Morton became twenty-five sometime in April 1865, he entered his twenty-sixth year in April and was born, then, in 1840. *But*, if his birthday occurred sometime after May 1, 1864, his death then still occurred in his twenty-sixth year of life, but he was born in 1839. Unless we could find his date of birth somewhere else, we'd have to record his birth date as 1839/1840.

Another kind of inscription eliminates this problem and gives both the date of death and the age at death. For example:

THOMAS Z. BRANSFORD

DIED

MAR. 18, 1876

AGED

31 YRS., 9 MOS.

Beginning sometime during the last quarter of the nineteenth century and continuing to the present day, stones have carried inclusive dates:

ALICE

DAU. OF

H. E. & D. R. CRAMER

BORN

JULY 31, 1878

DIED

DEC. 16, 1878

Citing both dates makes things a bit easier for the historian.

Your notes for estimating life expectancy might look like the chart below.

I should say that one decision I made in compiling this list was to leave out males and females ten years of age and younger, for the reason that their deaths were probably the result of childhood diseases. (Many too died as infants.) The rationale for excluding these names is that if it's life expectancy of adults we want, then we should use in our sample only men and women who in fact have attained adulthood. But the choice is really up to you. Recording only deaths at ten years of age or less will give you another statistic, infant and juvenile mortality, which is also of interest. If

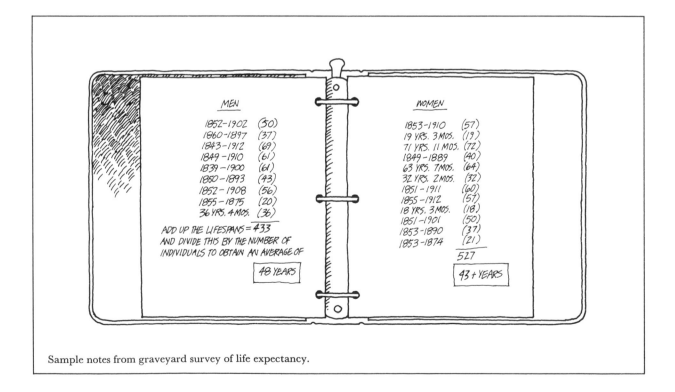

Sample notes from graveyard survey of life expectancy.

you include the deaths of children in your general list, however, your life expectancy statistics obviously will be much lower (infant mortality was very high during this period, thus adding a lot of young deaths to your sample). In either case, be consistent and let your reader know what decision you've made.

This listing was a very small sample from a small rural burying ground so I must be careful about any conclusions I attempt to draw from it. But in at least one respect, the figures are representative of larger samples from this period. Women tended to live longer than men—but *only* if they survived the dangers of childbirth. This is a very serious if. Thus, from cemeteries of this period you can expect to learn that more women than men died in their late teens and early to mid-twenties. You can expect to find this sort of inscription:

MARY WILDER
DIED
NOV. 5, 1887
AGED
19 YRS. 5 MOS.

And nearby you'll find a smaller stone with, in effect, the explanation for her death:

CHARLES WILDER
SON OF
CAPT. RICHARD & MARY WILDER
DIED
NOV. 5, 1887
AGED
1 MO.

Often, one stone served as a marker for both mother and infant.

18 YEARS A MAIDEN
1 YEAR A WIFE
1 DAY A MOTHER
THEN I LOST MY LIFE.
[epitaph for Florianna Forbes, Annapolis Royal, Nova Scotia]

I IN THE GRAVEYARD TOO MAY SEE
GRAVES SHORTER THERE THAN I
FROM DEATH'S ARREST NO AGE IS FREE
YOUNG CHILDREN TOO MAY DIE
[*New England Primer*]

AGE AT MARRIAGE

Another interesting piece of information that may be easily determined at the cemetery is changes in the marrying age of men and women over the years. (Cemeteries are particularly helpful in determining this information where church or civil marriage documents are non-existent.)

The information comes from working with a group of stones on a family plot. All you do is note the birth dates of sons and daughters and subtract these from the birth dates of mothers and fathers. You'll find two direct sources to help determine the parents' ages—and one not so direct. As in instances like the one noted earlier, where a child has died, his or her name and the parents' names and the pertinent dates are together, either on separate markers or on the same marker (you'll also begin recognizing special little stones for children, with sculptured lambs or angels). Or since parents usually precede their children in death, you'll find many stones inscribed Mother and Father close to and on the same plot with their deceased children. You will, however, have to be careful in sorting out different generations of parents and children.

If neither of these alternatives is present, you'll just have to guess which parent/children relationships are which. The result, then, will look something like this:

HANNAH GLAUER   ABEL GLAUER
OUR BELOVED MOTHER   OUR BELOVED FATHER
1845–1903   1840–1910

RICHARD GLAUER   ERIC GLAUER
1863–1928   1866–1914

WILMA GLAUER
1865–1870

Assuming that childbearing began very soon after marriage in those days, we can guess that Hannah and Abel Glauer were married at eighteen and twenty-three years of age, respectively. If we then collect this same kind of information for a sizable sample of people of, say, the early 1600s or 1700s, we can discern any differences in the marrying ages of men and women over the years, in our own town or in others whose burying grounds we might visit.

DISEASES AND DISASTERS

Wandering about the old cemetery in the little town of Palmyra, Missouri, you'd soon start to wonder why so many graves of children and adults carry dates from the early 1830s, particularly 1833 and 1834. You would soon conclude that something terrible had befallen the people of Palmyra. But the stones are mute. No doubt one of the old-timers in town could tell you the story, related to him by his parents and grandparents. Or you could turn to the town history, where indeed you would find this entry:

A tragic setback to the growth of Palmyra occurred in the spring of 1833 when an epidemic of Asiatic cholera made its appearance. It had struck St. Louis with dire results in 1832 but was not carried to Palmyra until the following year.

On June 2, a religious meeting was held at Cherry Run near the river and among those attending was William Smith of Palmyra. The next day he was stricken down and died within a few hours. The doctors in attendance pronounced his disease genuine Asiatic cholera.

The news spread rapidly but there was no panic. The people did not know their danger. The next day a Mr. Foster died and soon a Mr. Stephens died and the plague was general all over town.

In a week or more, so rapid and terrible were the deaths that panic seized the people and they began to flee to the country for safety. Many of those persons died after seeking refuge and their flight helped to spread the disease to other communities.

The population of Palmyra was believed to be about six hundred persons at the time but so many people fled or were caring for the ill that it soon began to look like a ghost town. Of the total population over one hundred, with some estimates going as high as one hundred and fifty, died. The epidemic had started to abate by the middle of June and was over by the first of July, but during the early weeks of June it raged with dreadful fury.

In a few hours after the victims had been seized they were dead and the coffin makers were working around the clock.

Wagons, driven mostly by slaves, made the rounds of the streets picking up the dead and hauling them to the burial grounds where they were interred without ceremony. Many of the dead were buried near their homes but most of them were transported to the western edge of town to a tract on the Philadelphia Road for burial. . . .

(Here we find written history which provides us a clue to the location of an old burial ground, suggesting that similar sites, now lost, exist in many towns.)

This tract is believed to lie on what is today the north side of Sloan Street in the 1100 block. Most of the graves were not marked and their exact locations are not known. [Palmyra, Missouri Sesquicentennial, 1819–1969]

Cemeteries, more than any official record or history, make us feel something of the horror that has gripped most American towns at some time in their history. Epidemics, floods, tornados, mining accidents, factory explosions, fires, and all manner of disasters, whether they claimed the lives of a dozen people or hundreds, are reflected in the recurring dates of gravestones.

BURIED IN THEIR ADOPTED LAND

Cemeteries are also an informal source of information about immigration, though the full picture comes only from a composite of several documentary sources, including passenger lists, naturalization records, and censuses. But were it not for information on gravestones, we'd probably have little if any documented evidence of when various ethnic groups first came to inland areas. Newspaper archaeology, particularly the biographical details of the obituaries, is one possible source of such information, but only if the community had a newspaper that was published continuously for many years. Even so, trying to compile data on immigration patterns by going through hundreds of crumbling, yellowed newspapers is arduous work. Graveyards, on the other hand, make our work simpler and have the added benefit of getting us out of doors on a nice day. Though there may not be as many markers as we need to draw really accurate conclusions, doing a graveyard ethnic census is simple, and it works.

Recently, while walking through a graveyard in a small northern California town, I came upon a stone with an inscription in a very unfamiliar language:

TÂSÂ HEPPÂÂ
MERIMEIS KARL WIIKGREEN
SYNTYNYD PYHÂJOEN PITAYÂÂSÂ
MELITÂ KYLÂSÂ
KUOLLU 7. PAIVÂ HEINÂKUSSA
WUONNA 1876
46 WUOTEN WÂNHÂ

Fortunately, the inscription on the lower half of the stone was in English and obviously was a translation of the lines above it:

IN MEMORY OF
CHARLES FORMAN
BORN IN FINLAND, FIRE RIVER
MELITA COUNTY
DIED JULY 7, 1876
AGED 46 YEARS

Part of my surprise was that I don't think I had ever seen written Finnish before. But the larger part of the surprise came because I just had not expected to find immigrants from Finland in California. Thinking at first that the marker might be one of those unusual stones which is one reward for spending hours in old cemeteries, I looked around and, sure enough, found several more with similar inscriptions, revealing, it seemed to me, the remnants of a small Finnish community in the area. There were six markers in all, and they represented four families (a total of eight people), all of whom—the dates indicated—arrived in the area at about the same time and died within fifteen years of one another. Since there were no later arrivals and no earlier ones either, I could only conclude that this was a family or group of friends that had come to this little settlement together, perhaps directly from the old country. The town is in fact a coastal town, and as the afternoon mist began to close in on me, I became aware of foghorns and clanging buoys. It suddenly occurred to me that, yes, this was a place which Finns would find to be much like the home they had left, just as would the sons and daughters of Nova Scotia, Denmark, Germany, Ireland, Sweden, Norway, England, Prussia, and Portugal who were also buried here.

In this same cemetery I discovered a number of families from Maine, and as I began to record the dates of their deaths, I realized that they too had apparently all arrived within a couple of decades, around the middle of the last century. Here is the community from Maine:

LUCINDA L.
WIFE OF LEANDER P. MORRILL
B. MOUNT VERNON, MAINE
1835

LEVI TAYLOR
B. MOUNT VERNON, MAINE
1838

EMMA J. TAYLOR
B. MOUNT VERNON, MAINE
1837

FREDERIC BROWN
B. OLD TOWN, MAINE
1829–1874

NANCY BROWN
B. BELFAST, MAINE
1802–1889

ALBERT BROWN
B. ARGYLE, MAINE
1849–1935

ALBERT MAXWELL
1829–1880
AND
JANE MAXWELL
1832–1898
NATIVES OF MAINE

JAMES MILLIKEN
B. SURRY, MAINE
1851–1907
AND
LIZZIE MILLIKEN
B. HOLDEN, MAINE
1857–1946

CAPT. JOHN F. TAYLOR
"DROWNED ON
SHIP COLIMA"
1854–1895
SURRY, MAINE

MARY F.
WIFE OF ABRAM EVERSON
1820–1898
NATIVE OF MAINE

LIZZIE H. HATCH
1840–1883
WINDSOR, MAINE

E. W. BLAIR
1837–1892
NATIVE OF MAINE

L. L. SAVAGE
1823–1876
BATH, MAINE

Almost the moment I had completed my recording, I suddenly became aware of a woman, friendly and curious, who was watching me. We exchanged greetings, and she told me that she was the wife of the sexton who took care of the little burial ground and was a descendant of one of the Maine people whose names I had recorded. Our talk turned to why the little group from Maine had come to this place in California. "Oh," she said, "there was the sea, and the forests, and logging just as there is now." Like the arrival of the families from Finland, it all became so clear.

A larger cemetery with more stones would, of course, allow us to make more accurate assumptions concerning immigration to the area; but it is obvious, even from this very small sample, that there were distinct periods of ethnic immigration. We could speculate further about the groups by using individual surnames as clues to the groups' ancestries. Though guesswork at best, such speculation is often the only way we have to discern the ethnic origins of the people who settled and developed our town. In any case, we're limited in our speculation to people who died here and must look elsewhere to find out about those who lived here and then moved on.

Mendocino, California, 1854

If you are going to spend much time in grave-yards, you should be prepared to be captivated. It won't be too long before you'll find a "favorite" stone or motif that so strikes your fancy, you would like to have a copy of it. Well, you can. There are two ways of reproducing and "collecting" gravestone designs: by making rubbings and photographs. Each process produces a very different kind of image with different qualities. Whichever of these qualities serves your purposes best will determine how you go about collecting your designs.

Making rubbings is enjoyable, simple, inexpensive, and requires no special equipment. The low-relief, linear quality of American gravestones provides a perfect surface for rubbing and produces dramatic, bold designs of dark and light patterns which intensify and heighten the linearity. This intensification, in fact, makes it possible to "bring up" weathered and faint inscriptions which cannot be read or even felt with the fingers. Here's the simplest way to make good rubbings:

1. Using a whiskbroom or paintbrush, remove dirt and lichen from the surface of the marker and carefully clean out the incised design and inscription. Also check to see if parts of the inscription or symbols are hidden by tall grass at the base of the stone.

2. After the stone is clean, tape a large sheet of paper to the face so that it covers the whole surface and wraps around the edges. It's important that the paper be stretched as tightly as possible and secured well with the tape, because the slightest movement will blur the design. Paper on rolls is most easily handled;

3. Then, take a large, dark wax crayon from which the wrapper has been removed and just rub its side over the surface of the paper. Work a small area at a time until the whole surface is covered. It's best to start rather lightly, adding more and more wax until you've reached a shade of darkness that you like. (Rubbing wax comes in all different colors in addition to the traditional black—red, green, blue, brown, red-orange, even gold, silver, and bronze—and in the form of either a heavy, flat wax crayon or heel balls.) The surface of the stone will come up dark, leaving the incised design and lettering in white.

Our ancestors had left a country they loved, to encounter the unknown horrors of exile in a new and distant land. . . . By such men, all the enervating emotions of grief and despondency were discountenanced. A stoical disregard of common sufferings, and of tender feelings, was a practice of religious duty. The nourishing of grief and the indulgence of excess in sensibility, were frowned at; a submission to the Divine will, and a subjection of all their passions to a rigid discipline, was constantly inculcated. Parents were called upon to yield their children, wives their husbands, and children their parents, without a murmur. All the dearest relations were habituated to attend the obsequies of their deceased relatives, and follow them to the grave. Thence arose the practice, that even the nearest relations, in the deepest moments of affliction, followed their friends to their last home. It was expected that a mother should see her beloved child, or the dear partner of her life, deposited in the grave, with pious resignation, and witness that agonizing ceremony, while listening with indescribable horror to the sound of the earth falling on the coffin of the most beloved object of her heart.

This fashion continued when the original purpose, or motive, had ceased, and when the sternness and austerity of their manners and habits no longer existed, so as to afford them any particular gratification in the practice of it. In the course of time, too, as their numbers increased, and a diversity of interests prevailed, the unity of their social state was broken up, and the sort of sympathy, which had existed in a small community, diminished. The forms, however, continued, and the processions lengthened, till at last they were composed of very incongruous materials; of a few wretched sufferers, who followed the hearse with eyes blinded with weeping, and faltering steps, and with a long train of others, who were performing with indifference or unwillingness an irksome duty. This mode of funerals continued till its inconveniences reached their height. A few years since, the procession was made as long as possible; the relatives, male and female, all walked; the acquaintances of both sexes followed, and a train of carriages, generally empty, brought up the rear; the bells were all tolling, and not, as now, at intervals, but without ceasing; so that the original purpose of this ceremony of tolling the bells, which was to keep the devil from coming within the sound of them, to annoy the dead, was very effectually answered. It was considered a mark of sympathy, and called for by decorum, to walk, however bad the weather or the walking might be. [William Tudor, *Letters on the Eastern States*. Boston: Wells and Lilly, 1821]

As I said, this is the simplest form of rubbing, and the way you'll probably want to start, but there are other kinds of rubbings too. For example, you can use the wet technique of the imported Japanese Sumi-rubbing kits—also called *Bokataku*—now available in larger art supply stores. With this technique one uses special papers and in place of wax a special paste ink applied with tamping pads. The papers come in a variety of colors, making possible a number of color combinations.

Photography is a very different way of recording stones, requiring consideration of variables like light intensity and direction, composition, and film characteristics. The delicate, low-relief sculpture of early American stones (perhaps no more than a fraction of an inch in depth) which makes for such striking rubbings makes photographic recording difficult and at times impossible. Yet photographs, unlike rubbings, are the only way to record the subtle play of light on the incised form and to capture the variety of textures of sandstone, granite, and marble. Rubbing produces an image faithful to the original in form, but one very unlike the actual gravestone in substance and spirit. For this we need a camera.

Photographing gravestones is like any other kind of photography, and the same rules of good exposure and composition apply. Light

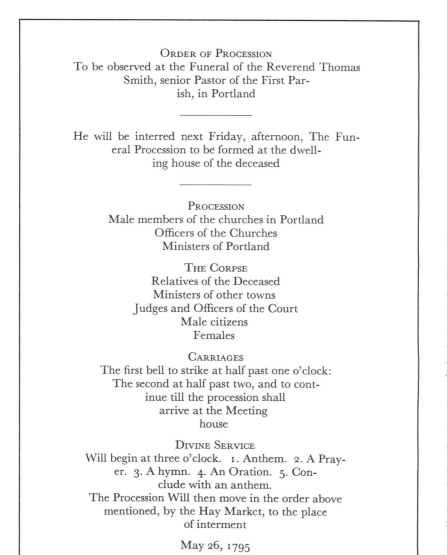

ORDER OF PROCESSION
To be observed at the Funeral of the Reverend Thomas Smith, senior Pastor of the First Parish, in Portland

He will be interred next Friday, afternoon, The Funeral Procession to be formed at the dwelling house of the deceased

PROCESSION
Male members of the churches in Portland
Officers of the Churches
Ministers of Portland

THE CORPSE
Relatives of the Deceased
Ministers of other towns
Judges and Officers of the Court
Male citizens
Females

CARRIAGES
The first bell to strike at half past one o'clock:
The second at half past two, and to continue till the procession shall
arrive at the Meeting
house

DIVINE SERVICE
Will begin at three o'clock. 1. Anthem. 2. A Prayer. 3. A hymn. 4. An Oration. 5. Conclude with an anthem.
The Procession Will then move in the order above mentioned, by the Hay Market, to the place of interment

May 26, 1795

People in those days [1880s] went all out in their demonstration of grief and my aunt and her children were no exception. Mrs. Overmyer was my father's sister.

Funerals then were spectacular and the Overmyer funeral was such a one. The hearse was, of course, black with black plumes on all four corners, and it was drawn by two black horses. There were no funeral parlors and the body was laid out in the parlor of the home until burial. The frequent trips to view the remains and the flow of unchecked tears brought everyone to a state of collapse.

Funerals were always held in the church and our church edifice was up a winding stairway, a difficult trip carrying a coffin, but they did it. By that time the church was full of spectators. Following the casket came the mourners, all swathed in black veils. Then the doleful music started and everyone who wasn't already crying began to weep.

The sermons were long and informative. If the deceased happened to be a prominent citizen the town band played, and after the town sprinkling cart had sprinkled down the dust, they marched with everyone who could find a way to go to the cemetery.

Generally they played General Grant's Funeral March and the strains of that sad tune wafting over the valley could wring tears from the most hardened hearts. [Ethel Docker, *The Good Old Days*, Ukiah, Calif.: Panpipes, 1968]

—its quality and direction—is the essence of a good gravestone photograph. Generally, the more oblique the angle at which the sun strikes the stone the better, for such an angle produces deep, dark shadows in the incised parts, which translate into good contrast on the film. If you have direct sun, it fills in the inscription, rendering it unreadable on the film and print; too much shadow, on the other hand, can result in patterns of dark that confuse the inscription and design. To get the proper angle, you'll probably want to make several visits, from early morning to late afternoon, to record each stone in its best light. Under certain circumstances, not at all unlikely, you may have to come back in a different season, so that the low winter sun comes in under that old willow or strikes a south-facing stone differently.

The film you use is the other important, but simple, consideration. Since you're taking photographs in bright or filtered sun, use the slowest film available, for example Kodak Panatomic X. Slow films not only produce fine-grain negatives that allow considerable enlargement, but also, for gravestone reading, have the added advantage of producing an image of high contrast, emphasizing light and shadow more than faster films and bringing up the texture of the stone.

*   *   *

In almost every culture throughout history, death has been the great inspirer of art, and it was no different in early America. Thousands of little graveyards and pioneer cemeteries dotting the American countryside contain examples of the poetry and images through which the first settlers and their descendants expressed their dread of the Black Angel, their acknowledgment of the inevitability of death, and their faith in the immortality of the soul. Born out of adversity, hardships, and, for us, unimaginable miseries, this was one of the earliest, perhaps the first, American art form.

Each of the New England stonecarvers had a style of his own with roots in the traditional themes of the Old World but articulated in a way that reflected the stonecutter's personal vision. From their work came a wondrous array of symbols and themes that gave life to what was perhaps the first American folk art.

As is usual with new styles, after the initial creative exuberance and spontaneity, the basic forms become fixed and serve as themes for variations by other craftsmen. So it was for the New England stonecarvers whose fresh motifs became the standard repertoire of designs for every generation of stonecarver thereafter,

———◆◆◆———

Many of the old-timers think that all burials should take place before noon; if a body is buried after 12 o'clock, another member of the family is likely to die soon. But this is no longer insisted upon, except among some very old-fashioned families. In pioneer times the funeral lasted most of the day, with hill-folk milling around the buryin' ground for three or four hours after the corpse was buried and the grave filled up. There was preachin' and prayin' and singin' all day long, with time out at noon to eat the "basket dinner" which each family brought with them in the wagon.

On no account must the mourners leave the cemetery until the last clod of earth is thrown into the grave — to do so evidences a lack of respect for the dead and is likely to bring death and destruction upon the family circle. Every one of the grave-diggers must wait, because a man who digs a grave and does not stay to see it filled and covered is marked for an early death. Many hillfolk believe that deaths always come in threes, and it may be that two more members of the group will be "called home" within a few weeks, anyhow.

There is usually a lot of gabbling and hollering at an Ozark burial. In 1944, when Rose O'Neill was buried in the family graveyard near Day, Missouri, there was no preaching, no prayer, no religious ceremony at all. We just carried the coffin out of the house, lowered it into the grave and shoveled in the dirt, without saying a word. Some of the neighbors were horrified — it was the first non-Christian burial they had ever seen. But they all did what they could to show their respect for the dead woman, even though she *was* an unbeliever. Every man of them stood stock-still until the last shovelful of earth was thrown into the grave.

Some hillfolk become quite noisy at funerals. I have seen the immediate relatives of the deceased fling themselves on the corpse with loud yells, roll groaning and kicking on the floor, and even try to leap after the coffin when it is lowered into the grave. On the other hand, I remember one man who served his children with popcorn balls at their mother's funeral, and they all sat there eating the stuff within arm's length of the woman's body. A certain amount of noise is not regarded as bad taste at a buryin', but the old-timers do not favor long periods of mourning. Some say that protracted grieving, at least in public, is likely to interfere with the dead man's repose in the other world. "The dead caint sleep," an old woman told me, "when their kinfolks hollers too loud." [Vance Randolph, *Ozark Magic and Folklore*. New York: Dover, 1964]

throughout the country, right up to the present. The importance of this fact for local historians today is that if we know something of the symbolism behind the New England stonecarver's imagery, we can then appreciate the spirit as well as the substance of stones carved any time since then.

Many of the symbols, particularly the religious symbols, used by the earliest New England stonecarvers are hundreds, some of them thousands of years old, but the style, techniques, and application of these ancient symbols on American gravestones are uniquely American. (You might ask: Can we be sure that Americans in fact made these stones? We know from bills of lading that gravestones were not shipped from England to the colonies, and passenger lists fail to reveal any large-scale immigration of stonecarvers to New England. Also, lists compiled by Harriette Forbes, biographer of early American stonecarvers, show that most stonecarvers were born in New England. Then, too, English gravestones carved at the time the colonies were being settled show obvious stylistic differences when compared to those done here, the English stones being more ponderous and sculptured, the New England stones more calligraphic.)

HERALDRY OF DEATH

For many of us, heraldry, escutcheons, hatchments, and coats of arms are trappings recalling old England and Europe and seem to have little place in American history. But in early America, particularly during the 1600s, colonists preserved these traditions, which included the use of seals affixed to documents and legal papers and the displaying of coats of arms. There were even several famous American heraldic painters, among them John Coles, whose name appears in Boston directories of 1796 as a "Heraldry Painter."

Heraldry appeared in several forms including engravings, architectural stonework, paintings, needlework, and incised tombstones still to be seen in Boston graveyards. In America, heraldry is most often associated with death. Though a gentleman might display his coat of arms on his carriage during his lifetime, the most public display of his escutcheons occurred when he died. Artists were hired to paint a man's hatchment on his coffin and on the pall of the bier. The family coat of arms might also be displayed on the front of the house of the deceased and was known as a "funeral achievement." You'll probably see heraldic designs on your outings in New England cemeteries or you might discover a funeral achievement among your own family's things — the possession of some distant ancestor. If you do, the accompanying illustration from a manuscript on early American coats of arms might help you identify its symbolism.

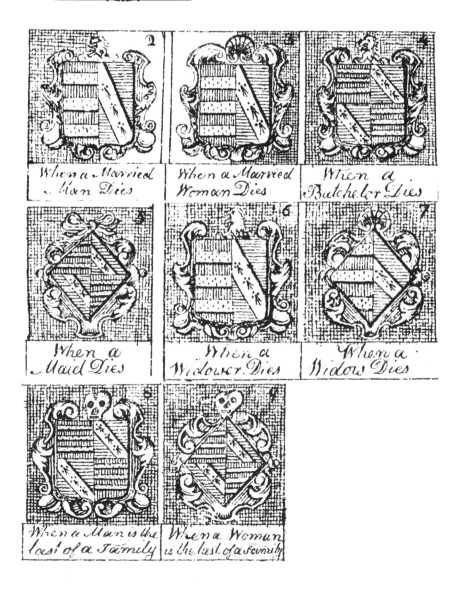

Gravestone art at first glance may seem to abound in many different images and themes. Some are borrowed from England but many come from American sources: Indian designs, furniture, engravings, woodcuts, bookplates, broadsides, and even the *New England Primer*. Yet because most of the carvers were using the same sources for their images, the number actually is not that great. Indeed, an individual stonecarver can often be identified by his few favorite symbols, which he renders in his own style over and over. What seems at first to be an overwhelming, even burdensome collection of symbols soon becomes manageable and gives way to the pleasure of wandering knowledgeably about old graveyards, photographing, making rubbings, or just looking at stones, each one a new experience that yet belongs to a clearly defined tradition.

You won't have to spend many hours looking at gravestones before becoming expert at spotting subtle differences in lettering and relief,

in little flourishes and personal ways, even at identifying an occasional set of initials that distinguishes one artist or period from another or recognizing the special symbolism of New England Puritanism. Because artistic conventions supplanted traditional themes, and because burying grounds are no longer at the center of everyday life, serving the instructional and moral function they once did in the American community, the meanings of much of this symbolism have become somewhat obscure. Even older members of a family, whose lives have spanned several generations and who now mark the passing years with births and burials, are likely to have forgotten what the symbols mean even if they once knew.

The symbolism of the New England stonecarver remains a continuous, unifying thread in the stonecarver's art from the seventeenth century to the present. And while you'll see many unusual stones, even some that are homemade, most of them reflect one or more of these traditional themes:

1. The passing of time and the shortness of life;

2. The certainty of death, a reminder of our mortality;

3. The enduring symbols of the Scriptures and Christian life;

4. Resurrection and the redemption of the soul;

5. The occupation or role of the deceased in life.

Since the recording and study of American burial grounds have only just begun, there are probably other categories that you'll discover, perhaps unique to a particular time in your community.

Remembering that all symbolism, particularly when it is centuries old, is subject to any number of interpretations and local variations, you'll still find this little guide to the symbols of the stonecutter's art helpful on your next visit to the cemetery.

Cemetery Symbology

CANDLES
(being snuffed by death's imps)

FATHER TIME
(old man with a beard)

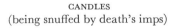

CHERUBIM
(regarded as guardians of a sacred place and as servants of God. Symbolize divine wisdom or justice)

HOURGLASS
(with the sand run out — hourglass may have wings, or may have a skeleton sitting or reclining on top of it)

*As runs the glass
Our life doth pass*
[New England Primer]

ARROWS
(in the hands of death's imps)

*Old age being come her race here ends
When God ye fatal dart he sends*
[epitaph]

CROWNS
(glory and righteousness)

Henceforth there is laid upon me a crown of righteousness, which the Lord, the righteous judge, shall give me that day: and not to me only, but unto all them also that love his appearing.
[2 Timothy 4.8]

And when the chief Shepherd shall appear, ye shall receive a crown of Glory that fadeth not away.
[1 Peter 5.4]

COCKS
(symbolize man's fall from grace and his resurrection)

The crowing cock was a monitor whereby Peter was awakened into repentance.
[Cotton Mather]

MERMAID
(half fish, half woman, a symbol of the dualism of Christ, who is half God, half man)

PEACOCKS
(eternal life)

. . . the peacock's flesh, immune from the putrification from which not even the flesh of Plato was exempt.
[Saint Augustine, *The City of God*]

SERPENT WITH HIS TAIL IN HIS MOUTH
(ancient symbol of eternity)

SHELL
(a symbol of birth and resurrection)

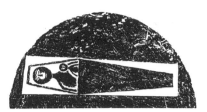

COFFINS, SKULLS, PICKAXE, AND SPADE
(tools and other objects associated with burial, reminders of our ultimate end)

DEATH'S-HEAD
(with soul effigy over mouth).

PORTALS, ARCHES, ARCHITECTURAL MOTIFS, URNS
(a symbol of the House of the Dead, death as a passageway to the unknown, a shrine or temple, a portal through which the soul passes into immortality)

Death is the portal to eternity, and carries men over to an unchangeable state.
[Samuel Willard]

SKULL RAISED ON A PILLAR
(triumph of death)

FLOWERS
(symbol of impermanence)

Death like an overflowing Stream,
Sweeps us away, our life is a dream,
An empty tale, a moving Flower,
Cut down and withered in an hour.
[epitaph]

All flesh is grass, and all the goodliness
there of is as the flower of the field.
[Isaiah 40:6]

Behold the frailty of this slender stuff Alas,
it has not long to last.
[epitaph]

BATS
(of the underworld)

BELLS
(tolling for the dead)

Oft as the Bell with solemn toll,
Speaks the departure of a soul;
Let each one ask himself am I,
Prepar'd should I be called to die?
Then when the Solemn bell I hear,
If sav'd from guilt I need not fear;
Nor would the thought distressing be,
Perhaps it next may toll for me.
[epitaph]

BIRDS
(from earliest times a symbol
of the soul)

But we are passing into an Invisible
World. *An Hades is to be looked into. But*
what then becomes of us? We then Fly
away to another world. This expression,
we fly away; it seems an Allusion to the
Condition of a Bird, which has been
hatching its full time. When the Time
for it arrives, the Shell breaks and the Bird
then does Fly Away. Our Death is the
breaking of the Shell. . . . And we have an
Immortal Spirit in us, which is, We, *and*
in this we Fly away.
[Cotton Mather, *The Soul Upon*
the Wing]

BUNCH OF GRAPES AND EAR OF CORN
(blood and body of Christ)

FRUIT
(symbolizes fecundity and
abundance)

I AM the True vine, and my father is the
husbandman. Every branch in me that
beareth not fruit he taketh away: and
every branch that beareth fruit, he purgeth
it, that it may bring forth more fruit. . . .
He that abideth in me, and I in him, the
same bringeth forth much fruit: for without
me ye can do nothing.
[John 15:1–5]

SUN, MOON, PLANETS, STARS, ORBS
(cosmological symbols with various
meanings: the saints rising, the sun as
a symbol of glorified souls, heaven as
the abode of the stars and planets)

ANCHOR
(an attribute of Saint Nicholas,
patron saint of seamen, and a
Christian symbol for hope and
steadfastness)

Which hope we have as an anchor of
the soul both sure and steadfast . . .
[Hebrews 6:19]

ANGELS
(of Heaven)

GOURDS
(deliverance from grief)

And the Lord prepared a gourd, and made
it to come up over Jonah, that it might be
a shadow over his head, to deliver him from
his grief. So Jonah was exceeding glad of
the gourd.
[Jonah 4:6110]

TREES
(weeping willow, palm tree, cedar.
The tree was not only a symbol of
paradise but it was a symbol for
human life as well. The image of the
felling of a tree [on a stone] represented the death of a person)

In the Sweet groves where pleasures dwell
And Trees of Life bear fruits of love
There Glory sits on every face
There friendship smiles in every eye.
[epitaph]

The righteous shall flourish like the palm
tree: he shall grow like a cedar in Lebanon.
[Psalm 92:12]

LAMB
(a symbol of Christ)

The next day John seeth Jesus coming
unto him, and saith, Behold the Lamb of
God . . .
[John 1:29]

LILY
(a symbol of purity, the flower
of the Virgin)

SCALES
(in general, a symbol of equality and
justice; the Archangel Michael is
often portrayed holding a pair of
scales to weigh the souls of the
departed)

TRUMPETING ANGELIC FIGURES
(accompanying the soul heavenward
and announcing the arrival of the
departed's soul in heaven)

HEART
(symbolizes the soul, the soul
triumphant over death, often with
wings or being flown to heaven by
Eros figures. A symbol of the
Trinity)

GRAPES, VINES, CHALICES
(wine, the divine fluid of
communion)

*Implant me as a branch in God's true vine
And then my grape will yield thy cup rich
 wine*
[Edward Taylor]

*Thrust in the sharp sickle and gather the
clusters of the vine of the earth; for her
grapes are fully ripe.*
[Revelations]

Here are three terms you are likely
to find on early stones — *AE*, abbreviation of *Aetatis* or years of life,
relict meaning widow, and *consort*
indicating that the husband was
alive at the time of his wife's death.

*How loved how Valued once avails thee not
To whom related or by whom begot
A heap of dust alone remains of thee
'Tis all thou art and all the Proud shall be
Survey this well, ye fair ones and believe
The Grave may terrify but can't Deceive
Yet Virtue still against decay can arm
And even lend mortality a charm*
[Sarah McKeon stone, Ipswich,
Massachusetts, 1776]

*Great God, how oft thy wraith appears
And cuts off our expected years
Thy wraith awakes our humble dread
We fear the Tyrant which strikes us dead*
[James Hickox stone, Durham,
Connecticut, 1796]

CHAPTER 5

Meetings with the Miller

All of our ancestors knew how to do something well, they had a skill they called their own, a job with which they identified and by which they were known to other members of the community. Work was then integral to one's life in a way we moderns may not be able to understand, for it requires us to imagine a life spent in the quest, development, and refinement of perhaps but one single skill. Chances are that if you have come this far in your search for your historical family, you've already discovered what many of your ancestors did for a living, finding clues, for instance, in your family name, the remembrances you've recorded, the occupations noted on census records, the photographs of ancestors at their work, even in epitaphs. You've discovered, perhaps, that your great-grandfather was a foundryman, your grandmother the town's first portrait photographer, and your great-

great-grandfather a carpenter. Is it possible, though, that knowing all this, you really don't know what they actually *did*? Did you know that carpenters once milled their own lumber to size and built houses without a single nail, that foundrymen once made their own sandmolds with wooden patterns, that your grandmother the photographer coated glass plates with emulsion she had mixed herself just before taking each picture? You see, there may be little left of the skills of fifty, one hundred, two hundred years ago in jobs with similar names today, and we must understand this fact if we are to understand our ancestors. Fortunately, many of these skills are still very much alive in the memories and hands of those who once practiced them, which we're about to discover for ourselves. And they often turn up in the places we least expect them.

Westville, Georgia, 1972

Under the spreading chestnut-tree
  The village smithy stands;
The smith, a mighty man is he,
  With large and sinewy hands;
And the muscles of his brawny arms
  Are strong as iron bands.

His hair is crisp, and black and long,
  His face is like the tan;
His brow is wet with honest sweat,
  He earns whate're he can,
And looks the whole world in the face,
  For he owes not any man.

Week in, week out, from morn til night,
  You can hear his bellows blow;
You can hear him swing his heavy sledge,
  With measured beat and slow,
Like a sexton ringing the village bell,
  When the evening sun is low.

And children coming home from school
  Look in at the open door;
They love to see the flaming forge,
  And hear the bellows roar,
And catch the burning sparks that fly
  Like chaff from the threshing-floor.
    [Henry Wadsworth Longfellow]

He was America's first all-round mechanic, and he could be found in almost every village and town, and on most large farms and plantations, from the early 1600s right up to the first decades of the present century. His many descendants—the Smiths, Schmidts, Eisenhowers, and Eisenmanns—make our telephone directories a measure of his number and importance in a burgeoning nation's economy. He was both a presage of and, later, a participant in America's industrial revolution. He did everything you needed done—smelting metals, shoeing horses, fashioning axle springs and wheel rims, fixing broken tools, and manufacturing hoes, spades, axes, pot hooks, andirons, hinges, trivets, and chisels. And so it was he became the symbol of Yankee skill and ingenuity.

What's more, he performed his wondrous skills right out in the open for all to see, often with the sky for a roof and otherwise with nothing more than a small shed to protect his hearth from the rains. Perhaps one of those children who happened by and stopped at his forge each day was later to become his apprentice and, in his turn, a village smithy. In Cambridge, Massachusetts, not far from his house,

Henry Wadsworth Longfellow passed a village smith daily and stood with him a few minutes under the horse-chestnut tree (which some years later, against the protests of the poet and his fellow villagers, was removed on the grounds that it was a hazard to drivers with heavy loads who passed beneath it!).

But if the smithy is the best known of our early anonymous craftsmen, he was really only one of many, and all were vital to the growth and development of our country. Yet in spite of our pride in American technological know-how, these early anonymous craftsmen have received little space in our history books. In fact, despite our own past, the concept of industrial archaeology and the history of industrial processes came to us from England, and then only recently.

Technology has been in one way or another central to American life since the earliest days. Manufacturing techniques came with the colonists from all over Europe, and many other techniques were developed here. Often specific skills were associated with certain ethnic groups. German communities became known for their ironwork and glassmaking, the English for their brown stoneware. At Jamestown we find a glassmaking factory begun apparently by Germans and later passing into the hands of Italian craftsmen.

And it's not as if these so-called cottage industries and their physical settings have all just vanished. True, many of the old industries are gone or their sites are now underground. But countless shops, some even filled with machinery and tools dating back well into the last century, are still around, though current knowledge of their whereabouts has often disappeared with the passing away or the migration to the cities of the old-timers. That's why exciting historical finds, though more often than not fortuitous, are still possible, and that's why, whenever we do stumble upon something, we are left wondering about what's still out there to be discovered.

*   *   *

A story of just such a fortuitous find comes from Arlington, Massachusetts. For several years concerned members of the community tried to get a conservation commission set up through the town meeting. Finally, a commission was established to assess and to preserve the town's *natural* resources, it just being assumed that the town had nothing of historical importance. "Most of the people in town were saying there's nothing here to save; it's all shot," Patricia Fitzmaurice, one of the members of that commission, remembers. "There was this brook, culverted and in many places even built over, but in other places open. And so this became the first order of business for the new town conservation commission: surveying the brook."

Just minutes from where a main street crosses over the creek, the little group of commission members, sloshing through the low waters in hip boots, came upon an old mill. What was it? No one could remember seeing it before or hearing about it. "I had never seen anything like this before, and I've been around the town more than most people," Ms. Fitzmaurice says. What had they discovered? To their surprise and delight it was the old Schwamb family mill. It had once been a gristmill, later it was a spice mill, and now, the commission discovered, it was the last remaining manufactory of oval and round wooden picture frames in America—perhaps the only one there ever was in the United States!

Elmer Schwamb, owner of the mill, had closed his business years earlier, probably because it seemed to him that there was just no way to compete with the mass producers of picture frames. Convinced that his family's century-old factory was of no value to anyone in this day and age, he had sold the mill. Before Patricia Fitzmaurice and the conservation commission could act, the new owners set about making plans for its demolition.

Ms. Fitzmaurice, the editor of the Arlington newspaper, along with a lot of newfound friends of old things in Arlington got together to raise enough money to purchase the mill and save it from decay and destruction. "The equipment was all there too," says Ms. Fitzmaurice, who became leader of the group. "We don't know of any other like it. The off-center, eccentric motion lathes are German, and no one here's seen anything like them before. They just exist here! We've gradually collected a few more of them. Each of the Schwambs had an unused one in his garage or house, not assembled but in parts, so that if this should burn and they lose everything, they wouldn't go out of business. We got one from Elmer Schwamb's attic. And we got another from the former garage of old Louis Schwamb. Somebody who had bought his house thought it was part of an old printing press and was about to throw it out.''

The latest chapter in the story of the old forgotten shingled and wood-sided building on Mill Creek ends happily. The group, with the help of Elmer Schwamb and his staff, got the factory back into operation once again.

What happened in Arlington is a good example of how most of us become historical archaeologists—by accident. But it needn't be that way (as it needn't have been that way in Arlington) if you stop to think about what's near you; for every town in America had a family industry or small shop employing two or three craftsmen—and if you're lucky, it's still there. A discovery similar to the one of the Arlington commission might be yours just around the bend in Mill Creek (for how else did the creek get its name?), or over that first rise in the rutted dirt road going out toward the hills, or in the old part of the city, down by the wharf or the railroad tracks. Here in a nearby place where you nonetheless have never been before, you, too, just might find an old mill, a pottery, a glassmaking site, a blacksmith's shop, an old garage, a forge, or maybe a historic carpenter's shop.

The men and women who worked there may be around too. The factory system of the late 1800s signaled the beginning of the end of small cottage industries like the sausage maker, the miller, and the tinsmith. Youngsters who would in earlier times have become their father's or mother's apprentices left the small towns for the glittering cities and big factories. But many of the old-timers stayed on and kept their little shops going for a long time in small towns and in the old neighborhoods of large cities, some right up to the present day. It's still not unusual to find nearby, maybe no farther away than the apartment upstairs, craftsmen who spent their youth as apprentices in these little shops and then worked all their life fashioning objects of tin, or leather, or glass, or wood. But like the Schwambs, they too will be very old, and if their story is to be told, their skills recorded and remembered, the process should begin now.

*   *   *

Interior of Schwamb Mill, 1972

How do you go about finding an old industrial site? Sometimes it's as easy as just searching your memory, thinking back over your daily movements until—there it is, the weathered old wooden building you pass on your way to work. You decide that tomorrow you'll pay a bit more attention to that part of your trip, maybe even stop and get out of the car to look at it. Sure enough, your intuition was right. There, three or four stories above the ground where you can't possibly see it from a car or bus window, is the faded but legible sign proclaiming the Acme Brick Ovens, or Dietrichs —Harness Makers to the Nation, or Rosenweig's Wholesale Dry Goods.

Coming upon something like this might even set you to thinking about all you've missed driving about town, and maybe you'll start walking to work—with your camera. Some old plants have been square in the middle of town (or the middle of a city block for that matter) all this time, so familiar as to be obscure. Perhaps you've even become aware of such a building through a friend who's come to visit for the first time and asks you about that old building she saw on the way into town. What old building? You pass through there every week or so and can't remember anything like what she's describing. Well, the next time you go to town you look for it. And as if it had been built yesterday (but there, carved above the door, is a reminder that it was actually built eighty years ago!), you are for the first time aware of Krakow's Pickles, Est. 1888, crocks, wooden barrels, and all, amidst tired but sturdy brick Victorian splendor. If this happens, don't feel bad about not having seen the building all this time. Friends of mine lived in an apartment for five or six years before deciding to investigate the odd little building *in their backyard*. They discovered that it was an old, old bakery —perhaps the first in the city—complete with ovens and all the necessary utensils.

But of course it's not always so easy to find an old factory. Sometimes you have to do some searching, and here you become a detective-historian. For example, you might spend a pleasant afternoon or two reaching back into

---

SPRING MILL

At the foot of a beautiful wooded slope about six miles northwest of Batesville on State Highway 69, known to the natives roundabout as Cushman Road, stands the near century old water grist mill known commonly as Spring Mill.

The building of Spring Mill was a huge task. Everything was built by hand labor. The whole framework of the building is made of wood, hewed, morticed, carved, dovetailed, and pegged in the most practical way with wooden pegs. The mill's grinding stones, were made from rock quarried in France near the Spanish border, and hence are known as "French Buhrs." These stones were transported to this country as ship's ballast and later distributed by dealers in the East, finding their way down the Ohio and Mississippi Rivers on flat boats. Then up the White by riverboat and by wagon to their destination—in this case, Spring Mill.

The turbine in Spring Mill is a Leffel forty horsepower, driven by water that is directed from the mill-

pond or reservoir to a "Forbay" underneath the mill. Made of cast iron, the turbine is known as a "patent wheel."

Power is transmitted from the turbine to the buhrstones by the means of a cogwheel made of wooden cogs pegged in a circular frame to correspond or enmesh with a metal gear wheel.

Persimmon being the usual wood for making such gears, it is presumed that these gears are made of persimmon wood.

The present Spring Mill was built in 1867 for Anthony N. Simmons.... Simmons, who also owned a water mill on Polk Bayou known as Simmons Mill, sold, September 30, 1871, the Spring Mill to James Miller and Thomas B. Roddy, whose sales slogan was:

Miller and Roddy
Grinds for Everybody.

In the distant past, the miller's fee was 8 pounds of corn for every 56 pounds ground, but during the long period of the Lytle ownership of Spring Mill the toll custom has un-

dergone a change. Now instead of the old toll-in-kind the fee is a cent and half per pound of grain.

Spring Mill is now (1960) the only water-powered grist mill still in operation in Arkansas. The mill pond or reservoir of Spring Mill is stocked with Rainbow Trout. [The present owner] Mrs. J. A. Lytle, Jr., ... mother, housewife, miller, country store keeper, and historian, ... operates a thriving mercantile store in the front room of the old Spring Mill building. The mercantile business is done in addition to the milling business. [E. A. Holcombe, "Spring Mill," in *Arkansas Historical Quarterly*, Spring, 1960]

the memory of an old-timer of the neighborhood who recalls finally that behind the new high school auditorium is the site of Waller Bros., the town's first garage, where Charlie and Ed Waller had a White automobile agency. As if the two of you are of a mind, you're soon heading toward the site of that dim memory, pushing in through the overgrown weeds and bushes that obscure the lot. And suddenly, standing in yesteryear, there's the old gas pump with its pump handle, looking for all the world like an abandoned barber's pole, and on the glass storage cylinder can still be read the numbers and markings showing how many gallons have been dispensed. The mechanic's pit, rusty spoked wheels, four-cylinder engine block, worn and threadbare thirty-two-by-three-and-a-half-inch tires, and the yellowed, brittle calendar pages in the shop tell you that you've stumbled on one of the first chapters in American automotive history.

When this happens, you've become an industrial archaeologist, and there's no turning back. What do you do now? With training or supervision we might, like any other archaeologist, become involved in excavating, collecting, recording, and preserving artifacts and structures at the site. But our basic responsibility is recording, and in industrial archaeology this means two things in particular. First we want to record the site—whether a mining building, a mill with its stilled waterwheel, a shoe factory, or a pottery kiln—by the best means available to us, including photography, drawing, and collecting any old pictures or even plans and blueprints we've come across. Then we want to record as fully as possible the details and circumstances of the work that went on there, to bring the hum of work back to the now silent shop—how the ore was extracted and refined, or how a gristmill works, or how shoes and boots were made, or the critical steps in firing up the kiln. At best, this means talking to someone, and here we'll use other tools like a tape recorder, fast note taking, or, least desirable but sometimes necessary, our memories. If there's just no one left to interview, we have other alternatives, like newspaper archaeology. But people are the best sources of information —perhaps the original owner, someone who once worked there, or the child or grandchild of the owner who remembers growing up there.

*   *   *

Zoar, Ohio, 1936

A few months ago I discovered a friendly old building at Main and Greeley Streets and wandered around it several times in an attempt to find out what it was. I couldn't reach its boarded-up windows, and the only writing on the building was the dates "1888–1914" in

wooden letters high above my head. Later, a friend told me that it had been a flour mill. It hasn't operated as a flour mill nor has Main Street been the main thoroughfare for years now. It's a stately old building with wood siding, reflecting even now, decrepit as it is, something of the original style and the care that went into its construction. I was to discover that inside, unknown to most people who pass by every day, is a complete flour mill looking as if the workers had just shut down for the day and gone home at five o'clock; but it has not been in use for nearly forty years! The mute, dusty machines carry printed on their wooden and metal surfaces a history and geography of milling technology dating all the way back to America's industrial revolution:

California Automatic Feeder
Patented Sept. 8th–Oct. 27th 1885
7 x 18
J. Wagner & Co.
S.F., Cal.

Barnard and Leas Mfg. Co.
Moline, Ill.
The Daisy
Pat. 1883

George T. Smith
Middlings Purifier
Jackson, Mich., No. 1–11700

Nordyke & Marmon Co.
Indianapolis, Ind.
Square Sifter

58443
Eureka Perfected
Milling Separator
The S. Howes Co.
Eureka Works
Silver Creek, N.Y. USA
Sole Manuf'r's.

The story of this mill I learned from the now aged son of the man who began it. In 1888 a local rancher, John S. Rohrbough, stood at the corner of Main and Greeley studying what was then just a little shed (housing a blacksmith's shop) and envisioned one of the only flour mills north of San Francisco. The mill he built lasted until 1937. John S. died two years later, in 1939, but his son, John D. Rohrbough, who rode horseback from grammar school to work in the mill on fall afternoons after the harvest, has vivid memories of the mill's history and the clatter of the old steam engine and the polished wooden machinery.

We met one afternoon at the mill, I with my tape recorder and John with his memories, and it was obvious that he enjoyed any excuse to talk about the past. I dragged two bags of grain into a square of light that came down into the mill's darkness from a cobwebbed window high above, and we made ourselves comfortable. Switching on my tape recorder, I began by asking John how it was that his father had become a miller in, of all places, this isolated valley.

These sketches suggesting a conjectural reconstruction of the old mill ca. 1888 and subsequent additions ca. 1914 were based on John Rohrbough's tape recorded recollections.

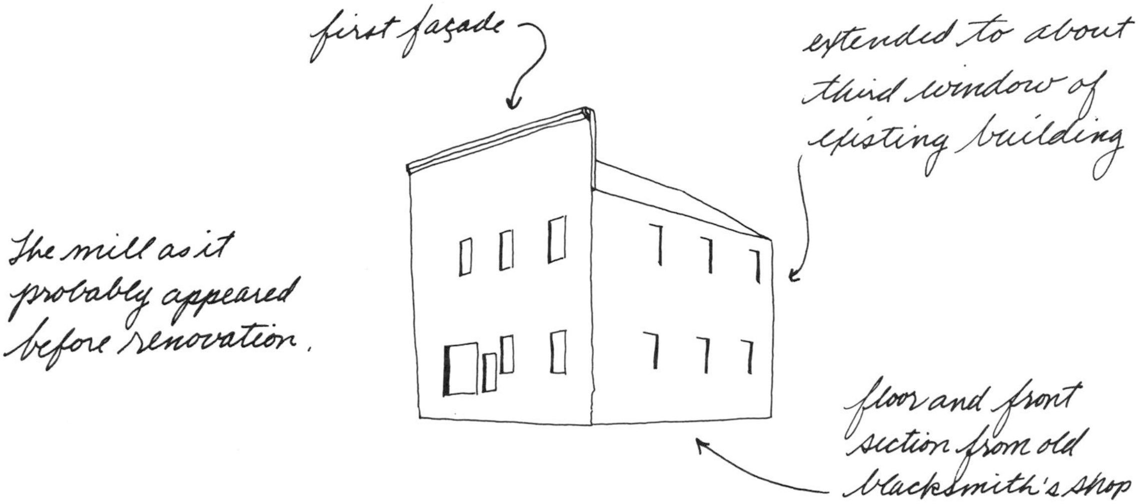

first façade

extended to about third window of existing building

The mill as it probably appeared before renovation.

floor and front section from old blacksmith's shop

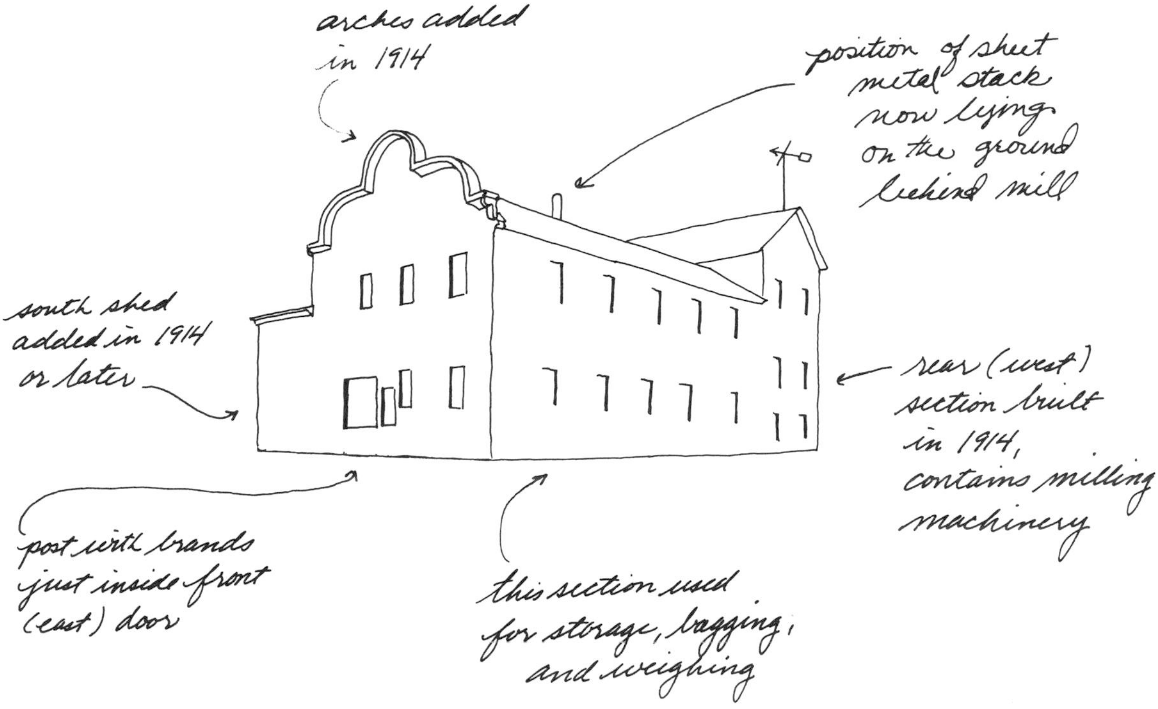

arches added in 1914

position of sheet metal stack now lying on the ground behind mill

south shed added in 1914 or later

rear (west) section built in 1914, contains milling machinery

post with brands just inside front (east) door

this section used for storage, bagging, and weighing

My father [John S. Rohrbough] came to the valley in seventy-six, from West Virginia, and went to work for his uncle George E. White who owned a ranch out here. When my father began raising wheat there weren't any mills nearby. Oh, there were some old stone mills up on the creek up there, but most of the people in the valley were pounding up their grain with rocks like the Indians did in the early days, or maybe they had little hand grinders.

All our wheat was raised right here in the valley; it was unthinkable in those days to ship commodities in. In the early eighties the closest railhead was Cloverdale—that's a hundred miles!—and everything had to be hauled in from there by mule train. Later the railroad came to Ukiah [about seventy miles away], and then on to Willits [forty miles]. I think it reached Dos Rios about nineteen twelve or thirteen. But before this, building materials—not wood, of course—but plaster, fixtures, hardware, and all the machinery, came all the way from Cloverdale.

There was a blacksmith shop here before my father became interested in this spot, probably built in the early eighties, maybe even the late seventies. . . . See here? These marks in the floor here, that's where the hot irons burned holes in the wood, and if you look at that post over there you'll see brands on it. They'd make branding irons and try them out over there.

When we started making flour here it was done with a steam engine powered by a wood-burning boiler, the very same one that's in there now. It was set the other way then, and it had a l-o-n-g belt that ran clear under the floor to about where those piles of wheat are there.

The miller would bank the fire under the boiler at night with a lot of coals and shut it up, and then he'd come about five o'clock in the morning and it wouldn't be long before we had steam. It would burn about a cord or two of wood a day; it'd take forty or fifty cord for the three months or so of operation. That's the

problem, you know, is getting wood. We'd have to cut it down at the ranch and haul it over here.

I told John how much I liked the building, with its graceful cornice and all, and wondered out loud how much he could remember of its metamorphosis.

This old building began getting pretty dilapidated, and along around nineteen fourteen my father decided he'd either have to rebuild it and put some modern machinery in it, or abandon it. So he hired this milling engineer, Spaulding [designer of the original mill] and a bunch of carpenters from the Bay Area who were good at mill work and put up this new [west] section. There was a man named Long from San Francisco who was the head carpenter and directed the building. We didn't have an architect or anything, it was just built up like a barn, and the newer part was patterned after a factory building in San Francisco. It's built with heavy timbers and bolted iron joints.

Out front there they decided to experiment a little and put those arches on that star, which they had all painted with gold paint and the words "Round Valley Flour Mills, J. S. Rohrbough Proprietor, 1888–1914." You can still read some of it. [But only through John's memory; there isn't a trace of it left below the dates and the star.]

Lord, they poured a lot of cement. I was just a kid then, and I helped pour the cement down here. This old engine foundation, boy that's deep. But this part, out here where the flour sacks were stored, we just poured some piers under here; and they've sunk a little and the floor's a little swayed now 'cause we piled up so much grain—we used to pile it in sacks clear up to those braces up there! You know, some years we'd have a

ing the name "Wagner Roller Mill," and began explaining the work of making flour.

We used a lot of machinery from the old mill and added some new things. All of it came disassembled by railroad to Dos Rios, and then here by mule train.

These old rollers, they're the same rollers. We re-babbitted the old bearings, sent the rollers [to San Francisco] to be corrugated and ground, aligned them all up, and put all new belts on them.

bumper crop and we'd just fill this thing clear full.

There was a millwright here in the valley who built all those spouts, those redwood spouts — a fellow named George Berkshire. He was a crackerjack at that, and then he ran the mill for two or three years after it was completed. . . .

Here's a picture of the flour mill when it was in good shape, right after we rebuilt it. There's two big wagon loads of wheat out in front, and that's my father in our 1910 Chandler. I'm in the picture too, but you can't really see me that well.

Flour was about a dollar and a half for a fifty-pound sack in the thirties. Wheat at three cents a pound during World War I was considered a high price; used to get a cent and a half for it! Back in the twenties, during the Depression, it went up to a dollar eighty or a dollar ninety. There were six children in our family, and oh boy, we used a lot, 'cause mother made light bread and biscuits every morning. We had a cookhouse too, and ten or fifteen men to feed. I imagine that in the course of a year we'd use two or three tons down at the ranch.

John's the kind of active man who doesn't sit still for long, so when he stood up and began walking around the mill I put my recorder over my shoulder and just followed along. It was with a touch of fondness and pride that he brushed the dust off a wooden machine, reveal-

This was a forty-barrel mill — that's 160 fifty-pound sacks a day. We started at six in the morning here. The miller blew the whistle at six o'clock, and we

ran to six at night. And we didn't shut down at noon either. We'd run about thirty to forty-five days in the fall. I remember [soon after the mill was rebuilt] I had a job before and after school sweeping up and cleaning up the mill. I was in grammar school over here then, and I thought it was big business to get in here and work and get flour all over me.

We carried grain by wheelbarrow and dumped it into these elevators here—those elevators came out of the old mill. There are belts in them with cups attached that run clear to the top—which takes it upstairs. Elevators carry things up, but things move up and down through the redwood spouts. Well, the grains go up to the separators. . . .

That separator there has a big fan in it that runs about four hundred forty revolutions a minute, and you have the grain coming in over these sieves. You can regulate the suction of the fan by opening or closing the shutters, so you could put a strong lift on it and lift the heavier grains, or a lighter lift just to lift the light stuff. For oats you'd use a lot lighter lift than you would for wheat; wheat is pretty heavy.

So you lift the shrunken kernels, and the chaff, and the dust, and everything like that, and blow it over here [into the loft of the mill]. So, up here was the light stuff, the chaff and pieces of straw. I'd put a rag on my face to keep from chokin' to death, and get up there in that itchy sun-of-a-gun oat dust, and by golly, we'd sack that up and we'd throw it out the window to the truck and haul it out. A hog wouldn't look at it; he wouldn't touch it! But a sheep would eat some of it, that old dusty stuff.

Still, there wasn't a lot of dust in the operation out in the mill. There were fans that sucked the dust off

those rollers and blew it into the machines upstairs with those stockings on them. The air went through the stockings and the dust was trapped inside. Then there were those damned things that pounded on each one as it came around and settled the dust down into the conveyor.

Anyway, from the separator, the grain went into the sifter there. It's a really good sifter, built by Nordyke and Marmon—who built the Marmon automobiles in the old days—and that thing was really a great advance. They're using them yet today, the same damned thing! The main thing about the sifter is all that silk in there. Inside the sifter there are trays stacked up with different gauges of silk, different size mesh, the bigger gauge on top, down to the smaller ones on the bottom.

That darn sifter, when it's running, it swings on a four-inch circle just like you'd shake a sieve, you know. It ran a hundred and eighty revolutions a minute, that thing, and it shook like everything. But it had a big counterweight on it so it didn't shake the building.

That's the heart of the mill, really, that darn sifter; 'cause that determines how things get separated and get to where they belong.

Of course, another big thing is getting the wheat right under the rollers and getting the rollers set to break it just about right so the sifter will handle it. You see, each time it went through the rollers, it went to a section of sifters, then it would be divided in the sifters. Some flour would come out right away. And then hulls and the bran would come off the top screens, and the finer stuff would go down to the finer screens. Some of it would come out mill run, and some would come clear through as flour.

Bran was the coarse stuff. Mill run was next to the flour, or the inner, finer part of the hull of the wheat. And then the flour itself. Of course, a lot of people now feel it's better to have that stuff left in the flour.

A MEETING WITH JOHN STEVENS

"I suppose that I am one of the very few persons living who can say that they have seen and known the entire Stevens family, from its founder, John Stevens, who was born in 1749, before the Revolution, as well as his children, grandchildren, and great-grandchildren, who have gathered around the ancestral home on the other side of the Hudson River. When I was about six years of age I was taken by my father to Hoboken to be introduced to John Stevens, because I had a few days before seen from the Jay Street Wharf a magnificent steamer, with four ponderous smokestacks, passing rapidly up the Hudson River, and had asked whose steamer it was, and where it was going.

"My father told me that there were two of these boats, the finest in the world, and that they had been built by the Stevens family of Hoboken. I said: 'Do you know the Stevens family?' To which he replied: 'Yes. I will take you to Hoboken and present you to the greatest engineer of his time.'

"And so some time between 1828 and 1830, I was taken to Hoboken and introduced to John Stevens, who was then eighty-three years of age, but in possession of all his faculties, and manifesting the greatest possible interest in this visit from an old friend

and a young boy. Familiarly he called my father 'John,' for both bore the same name, and my father said: 'This is my son. I want him to see and know you.' And then they began to talk of old times, and particularly of this remarkable story, which was so often repeated to me by my father, or else I should not remember it so well.

"My father was the draftsman and pattern-maker who had come out from England, with a party of machinists [all brought by Stevens], to erect the first stationary double-acting condensing engine which was put at work in America. It was built by Boulton & Watt at the Soho Works, near Birmingham in England, and was brought out and erected at Centre Square, in Philadelphia, to supply that city with water before the Fairmount Works, on the Schuylkill River, were erected. Thus John Stevens had built for himself the first Watt engine ever constructed in America. His corps of workers, whose chief was an engineer named Smalman, included Rhode, an ironfounder, the predecessor and instructor of James P. Allaire, who founded the Allaire Works in New York. These men, with my father as draftsman and pattern-maker, erected a new Soho Works at Belleville, near Newark, New Jersey. There John Stevens built the first low-pressure engine ever constructed in America.

"Of course, this interview with John Stevens made a profound impression upon my mind, and on my way home my father said: 'Yes, that engine was put in a boat in which I traversed the route from Belleville to New York and back again, John Stevens being the owner, builder, and captain of the boat, and Mr. Smalman, Mr. Rhode, and myself being the passengers; and we came to New York in that boat nine years before Fulton put the *Clermont* on the Hudson.'

"Portions of the engine thus constructed were for a time preserved in the Stevens Institute, and must be there still, unless transferred to the National Museum at Washington. But the boat in which the engine was placed must not be confounded with the one whose model I see here upon the table, built later, in 1804, with a double screw, and which preceded Fulton's boat by four or five years. I only remember the Belleville boat had a stern wheel, and my father said that Mr. Stevens, during the trip, remarked that wheels should have been placed at the side, and not at the stern." [Abram S. Hewitt, ironmaster, Democratic Representative to Congress, and reform mayor of New York City, 1886]

And that spiral machine sitting over there is pretty ingenious, working on a gravity feed. I got it mainly to separate the vetch [hard seeds about the size of a small pea] from the wheat because you couldn't do it with the screens in the sifter. See, it starts rollin' down, and the ones that roll fastest go to the outside spiral and out that spout, and the ones that roll slowest stay on the inside spiral and they go out a different spout. That damned vetch would roll like shot and end up outside. You can still see some of the vetch laying around—those little black seeds there.

And finally, there's this flour packer here, "The Daisy." It's one of the oldest pieces of equipment in the mill. The finished product was bagged right here.

Let's step back for a minute to see what we've learned. John in these reminiscences has told us a lot about how a flour mill was run "in the early days." But he's given us a great deal more too. He's told us something about the way people used to earn a living, doing work that may not be done anymore—people like the "millers" and "millwrights" and those who manufactured, repaired, and maintained this milling equipment. And, of course, we've learned a lot about building old buildings. There's also a bit of railroad history in John's story—the extension of the rail lines northward from San Francisco, to Ukiah, to Willits, to Dos Rios, and on up to Eureka and north. We get glimpses of the town the way it used to be before newer buildings and vacant lots appeared. Across from the mill, John remembers Perry's Saloon (which burned down in 1904) and a jewelry store where a restaurant and laundromat are now. Where the post office stands today, there was once a hotel, and across the street from that, the oldest house in town, built sometime in the 1860s and still standing (until recently, it was the office of the *Round Valley News*). Still another theme running through his narrative is the history of flour making in rural America, from grinding with stones, to gristmills, and finally the roller mill, powered by steam engine. Flour has changed, American tastes have changed, and a whole way of life is gone.

The first miller here was a man named Schrader, an old German, with a handlebar mustache and all. Then there was George Berkshire who, as I mentioned, directed the building and then ran the mill. And then . . . let's see . . . there was a miller named Pickering. He was from Modesto, and ran the mill during the late twenties and thirties. Pickering made really good flour, and in the late twenties he put a bleacher in to bleach the flour whiter. We never did bleach flour before, you know, but it did seem to improve the color of it. I think we put the bleacher in around nineteen twenty-seven and used it until the last year we made flour, which was nineteen thirty-seven.

By that time the roads got better, the trucks began runnin' in and out of the valley all the time, and they started hauling bread and big-mill flour in here. That was better for baking white bread because it was made from hard wheat and had more gluten, more protein. This soft wheat of ours is fine for pastries, and biscuits, and stuff. We did get some Australian White and Kansas Turkey Red seed wheat—they're hard wheats—and planted them here for a while, but due to the short season and mild winters they soon became soft wheats. We couldn't keep them like they were.

But still, we sold flour to beat thunder up until the thirties, when they began hauling so much bread in.

Before that there was a bakery over here near where the hardware store is now, and he used a lot of our flour to make rolls and French bread.

So we stopped making flour in thirty-seven. I hated to give it up, but there was just no business as far as selling flour any more, because freight had gotten down to where it could be shipped in, in great quantities. Of course, most people thought that anything made in a big mill is better than something made in a little mill. A lot of it was better, of course, made with hard wheat and gluten, but a lot of it wasn't any better at all. For biscuits, or hotcakes, or rolls, we made really good flour.

*   *   *

That was forty years ago now, certainly enough time gone by to dampen the wishful thoughts of even the most ardent historian that mills like the Rohrboughs' might someday be restored to working operations. After all, John Rohrbough's experiences and childhood memories go back nearly a century—back over many decades of changing American tastes and industrial practices. So when I suggested that he and his sons might someday be milling flour in that very same mill again and he chuckled skeptically, I nodded in sad agreement.

Still it was a vision that I strongly wanted to see become a reality. There was some comfort to be taken in the fact that the mill itself was still there, though that's another accident of history, the result (and evidence) of a small town remaining just a small town. Faring better than most old industrial sites, the mill in fact

had recently been purchased with some vague historical purposes in mind, perhaps to become a museum or a community meetinghouse.

Yet . . . yet . . . who could have anticipated the combination of domestic and international events—worldwide wheat shortages, inflation, energy crises, and the inevitable change in American tastes and lifestyles—that led to this report in the August 8, 1975, issue of the *Round Valley News*:

GRAIN MILL SET IN MOTION AGAIN

A tractor, instead of the traditional steam boiler, fired up the operation of the old Rohrbough grain mill on Monday noon, July 28.

After harvesting his soft white winter wheat with the help of Richard Wilson's combine, Jim Anderson looked to Mr. John D. Rohrbough's know-how to operate the old Eureka Mill Separator to filter the wheat seed from the chaff.

With help from Bud Huse, Kurt Haveman, Jim Fisher and David Boatwright, the wheat was brought to the mill and unloaded by wheelbarrow. The wheat was put in a bin from which it was blown into a wooden chute and carried by cups on a conveyor belt to the third level of the building.

The separator, which is on the second level, then received the wheat and passed it through vibrating perforated trays. The trays separated the wheat seed and filtered out the chaff.

Following separation, the chaff was blown out into a room on the third level and the cleaned wheat was returned to the first level, ready to be bagged up.

THROUGH THE MILL

Zippy led me at a run up three flights of iron-plated stairs, through a tin-covered door, and into a spinning room. When we arrived, not a wheel was stirring. I almost slipped on the greasy floor. Up and down the length of the room the ring spinning frames were standing like orderly companies of soldiers forever on dress parade. Above, the ceiling was a tangled mass of belts, electric wires, pipes, beams, and shafting. The room was oppressively heated, and was flavored with a sort of canker breath.

As I stood there, interested in my new surroundings, the wheels began

to move, almost silently, save for a slight, raspy creaking in some of the pulleys. The belts began to tremble and lap, the room was filled with a low, bee-like hum. A minute later, the wheels were whirling with such speed that the belts clacked as they turned. The hum was climbing up the scale slowly, insistently, and one could not avoid feeling sure that it would reach the topmost note soon. Then the girl spinners jumped up from the floor where they had been sitting, and went to their frames. Some pulled the levers, and tried their machines. Everybody seemed to be shouting and having a last word

of gossip. The second hand stood near the overseer's desk with his fingers stuck in his mouth. He whistled, and that was the signal for all the girls to start their frames. At last the pulleys had attained that top note in their humming, like a top, and with it were mixed screams, whistles, loud commands, the rattle of doffer's trucks, poundings, the clanking of steel on steel, and the regular day's work was begun. [A. Priddy, *Through the Mill*. Boston: The Pilgrim Press, 1911]

The Bellows' Roar

The archaeology of smiths' shops is relatively simple and straightforward. The structure in which a smith worked, his tools, and his products were rugged and durable. One of the things that historians have learned from the materials and tools found at the site of early forges is that blacksmiths often had working with them indentured servants who were trained as whitesmiths (workers in tinplate), cutlers, locksmiths, brass founders, and even armorers, the latter of whom made and repaired gunlocks, drilled musket and rifle barrels, fashioned sword hilts (the blades were made by the cutler), and cast cannonballs and shot. The excavation of a forge provides clues to what kind of fuel was used—charcoal (leaving little ash), or wood (the usual because it was the most available), or even coal (rare because although some was mined in the colonies, most of it was shipped from England). Here's a description of a blacksmith's shop of the Colonial period:

The forge used by several operators in iron is very simple: we shall instance in that of the blacksmith, to which all the rest are reducible.

The hearth, or fire-place, is a mass of brick, about two foot six inches high: the back of the forge is built upright to the ceiling, and is enclosed over the fire-place with a hovel, which leads into a chimney, to carry away the smoak. In the back of the forge, against the fire-place, is a thick iron plate, with a taper pipe fixed therein, about five inches long, called the tewel, into which the nose or pipe of the bellows is received: the use of this plate and tewel is to preserve the pipe of the bellows, and the back of the hearth from being burnt. Right before the back at about two foot distance, is the trough, filled with water to wet the coals in, and thereby increase their force; as also to quench the iron in. Behind the back of the forge is placed the bellows, one of whose boards is fixed so, that it moves not, either upward or downward; and to the other is fitted a rope, chain, or even rod; which rising perpendicularly, is fixed to a cross piece, called the rocker, which moving on a kind of fulcrum, near the middle serves as a handle.

By drawing down this handle, the movable board of the bellows rises; and by a considerable weight a-top of its upper board sinks it down again; and by this alternate agitation performs the office of a pair of bellows. [E. Chambers, *Cyclopaedia: or an Universal Dictionary of Arts and Sciences.* London, 1728]

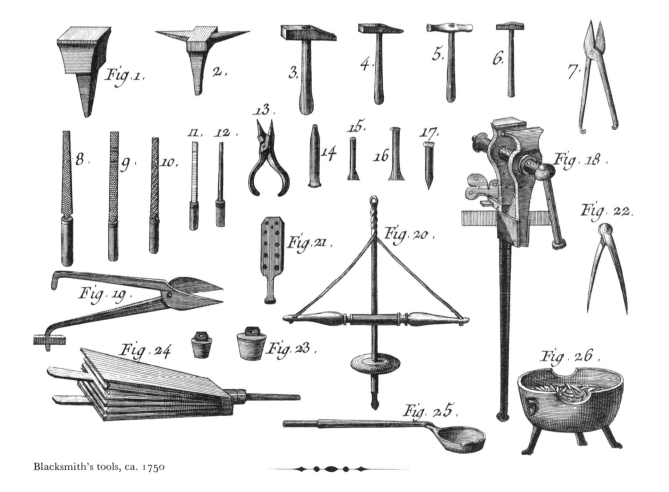

Blacksmith's tools, ca. 1750

Exterior general views and details of the Round Valley Flour Mills (March 1975)

A photographic record of the exterior of a mill or other industry should convey several aspects of the structure's life:

1. General exterior views showing each elevation (frames 1 to 3, 6 to 9, 12 and 14) place the structure in its setting and help us determine its scale. Along with John Rohrbough's commentary, these scenes also allow us to visualize the building's metamorphosis over the years.

2. Architectural details such as the eaves and supporting brackets (frames 21 to 23, and 25), massive foundation footings (frame 24), the façade (frames 4 and 31), and the weather vane (frames 27 and 29) reveal something of the architect-builder's art and sense of style.

3. Our sense of the building's function develops from details such as the loading dock and doors (frames 5, 10 to 11, and 28), the shed housing the old steam engine, furnace, and boiler (frame 33), a ventilating louvre (frame 30), and the stack (frames 35 and 36). The original position of the stack is marked by an opening in the rear (south) shed roof (frames 32 and 33).

The separation is the preliminary process in the making of flour, but it appeared to be likely that the machinery for milling flour could again do its job. The maze of chutes and machinery all seemed to be in working order and with the proper power could run.

After the wheat is examined and graded, Mr. Anderson will be selling some here in the valley through the farmers' market at the Red Circle Marketplace. This type of wheat is ideal for grinding into pastry flour.

And there are thousands of such mills and factories in America, many still capable of providing vital services to their community—and that, at the very least, should be cared for and preserved as museums of early American industry.

*   *   *

The recording of industrial sites and operations lends itself to any and all of the amateur historian's skills, not only tape recording, but sketching, note taking, photographing, and researching local histories and maps. Each is used where it is most useful, and together they constitute the historian's bag of tricks. Sketches are made to visualize old buildings before extensive modification. On notepads go the spellings of names and places mentioned on the tape, as well as manufacturers' names and patent numbers on machines hidden in corners too dark for a camera. Simple schematic drawings help us to understand a complex series of manufacturing steps and bring together operations carried out in different rooms or different buildings perhaps blocks apart. Hand-drawn maps of the surroundings make clearer

HE LIKEWISE MAKES ALL SORTS

Of all the work that has survived from the Colonial period, probably none is more familiar to us than that of the cabinetmaker. The simple, functional lines of his tables, chairs, cabinets, and clocks fashioned from native woods (oak, walnut, maple, cherry) attest to the skill and ingenuity of this worker in wood who was both craftsman and designer. And yet, it wasn't until fairly recently that very much was known about the work of the cabinetmaker—the kinds of tools and techniques he used (were they English or of his own devising?) or how he operated his shop.

Much is known about English furniture of the period simply because there was so much of it in Colonial homes and buildings and because so much of it exists today in historic houses and museums. But almost nothing of American furniture from the seventeenth century remains, and very little from the eighteenth century. Until recently, archaeologists and historians could only wonder what it might have been like to visit a cabinetmaker and watch him work. And then, in 1960, archaeologists discovered the home and shop of Williamsburg cabinetmaker Anthony Hay, and a whole new chapter could be written.

Hay's shop was erected around 1750, and he worked in it until 1767. He then leased it to another cabinetmaker, Benjamin Bucktrout, who continued to work there until about 1776. Within the shop's excavated walls and foundations, archaeologists found more than forty tools: jack plane irons, drill bits, chisels, rasps, and files. With these were found iron furniture fittings, hinges, and other hardware used to make tall-case clocks.

As if this were not enough, there was an even more important find—an unfinished, rough-hewn walnut table leg apparently intended for a straight-skirted table. Why was this single table leg so important, particularly one so rough and unfinished? Well, it was very clear that even in this state the cabinetmaker was intending to carve a ball and claw foot, a style that scholars had considered "almost unknown on Virginia furniture."

But there was to be still another surprise. A section of a boxwood oboe with two brass stops was found in the excavations. Could it be that the cabinetmaker was also an instrument maker? He certainly was. An important clue was the number of stops on the oboe. Checking into a history of musical instruments, the archaeologists discovered that in the early

eighteenth century, oboes had *three* stops, but then, by the middle of the century, they were being made with only *two* stops, which meant that the oboe in the shop must have been made in Bucktrout's time, not before. The proof that Bucktrout made the instrument was found not on the site but in the *Virginia Gazette* of January 6, 1767:

MR. ANTHONY HAY *having lately removed to the RawLeigh tavern, the subscriber has taken his shop, where the business will be carried on in all its branches.*

He hopes that those Gentlemen who were Mr. Hay's *customers will favour him with their orders, which shall be executed in the best and most expeditious manner. He likewise makes all sorts of Chinese and Gothick* PALING *for gardens and summer houses.*

N.B. SPINETS *and* HARPSICHORDS [and, one can assume, oboes] *made and repaired.*

BENJAMIN BUCKTROUT

And just where would an archaeologist begin looking for a cabinetmaker's shop? Along a creek bed. Cabinetmakers, then as now, worked with lathes; and, as with flour mills in Colonial days (and in more recent times), the power was provided by a stream.

the several generations of buildings and businesses that occupied a place in town.

A few days before calling John Rohrbough and arranging to meet with him at the mill, I looked through some local history pamphlets published by the county historical society for mention of the Rohrbough family and their life in the valley. There was enough there to get me started thinking about questions I would ask. Why was a mill started here? (Wheat is not a major crop here today.) Who had conceived this interesting building with its ornate (for a mill) cornices and wrought-iron weathervane? How much could John remember of what went on here? Had others nearby been involved with the mill, and what had been their work? Are any of the original plans and drawings extant? There were personal questions too. Since I had come to this area only recently, I wanted to know what it was that brought John Rohrbough's father here nearly a century ago.

I thought up and phrased my questions, not with the intent of getting specific bits of information, but to make this, our first meeting, comfortable and informal. At first the questions were very general, allowing John to answer as he wished and to bring in all the rich background which he so obviously enjoyed. Specific questions—dates, spellings, clarifications, names, definitions of terms—were asked when needed, gently and unobtrusively so as not to interfere. Some questions I just wrote down to be asked later. New questions came to mind as he talked, and I scribbled these on my notes too, though most of them were answered in time. At the end of nearly two hours of recording, I realized that I had asked perhaps six or eight general questions (though I had prepared about three times that) and came away with so much information that only a couple brief follow-up sessions were needed to check my notes.

The old mill worked its magic on the second-generation miller, and as we moved around the machines and climbed ladders and stairs to the mill's four levels, John's memories of half a century ago, and then some, came as though the events had happened yesterday. Here and there we stopped to read (and record) the name and patent date off a piece of machinery. (Yes, that was just about when they started making them—the very latest equipment when they were chosen for the Round Valley Mills.) And as you have read, there followed wonderfully detailed descriptions of the workings of each device and how it fit into the whole process. I had never been in a mill before, so John helped me sketch a little schematic diagram that brought together all the steps and machines in the proper order. Clustered around this went my scribbled definitions of millers' terms unfamiliar to one of another generation raised in the city: "middlings," "vetch," "separator," "hard wheat," "Kansas Turkey Red seed," "soft wheat," and pages of others.

Soon afternoon had turned into the early evening dark of the fall, and we both felt the chill of the unheated and unlighted interior (for this was the time of day the mill's work would end). Moving outside to catch the sun's last warmth and to look up at the mill's gray, weathered façade, we talked about the setting seventy years ago, about the buildings and houses gone long ago. We talked of other meetings too, but first there were the tapes to be listened to, new questions to phrase, and a couple of hours spent in the mill with my camera, where, in the silence, I might bring back all the old sounds—the steam engine, the whirring pulleys and flapping leather drive belts, the clatter of separator and sifter, and, perhaps, even the voice of the old miller himself.

Buried Boots and Brogues

Have you ever heard of *shoe* archaeology? Well, Adrienne Anderson and a group of archaeologists from the Arizona State Museum have been collecting, preserving, and classifying odd bits of shoe leather unearthed in one of Tucson's urban renewal areas. Their first problem was how to preserve the now brittle, dried pieces of leather, some over a hundred years old. Their solution was the easily available leather conditioners like neatsfoot oil, mineral oil, and a commercial preparation called Lexol. Then a visit to a shoe-shop in the city—Johnny's Shoe Shop run by John Huston—helped them learn how to identify shoe styles and details of shoe construction, and shoe manufacturers' terminology. Back in the field, they began to realize that shoe history parallels the history of invention and manufacturing in America. They found, for

example, that American mass-produced shoes fell into three categories, which represented three separate periods in time: (1) nailed, screwed, or pegged; (2) sewn; or (3) cemented. Here is the chronology they put together to help other shoe archaeologists date their finds:

1811. A machine was built to make the tiny pegs used to hold shoe parts together. Before this time the shoe-maker had to whittle each little peg.

1829. A hand-operated pegging machine was patented.

1830s. Shoemakers began to use patterns to cut out parts rather than doing each one individually.

1844. Charles Goodyear discovered how to vulcanize rubber so that by the

1850s. The first rubber inserts appeared in leather heels (though it wasn't until 1895 that the first all-rubber heel appeared).

1860. The pegging machine was replaced by a stitching machine that sewed soles to uppers and allowed the machine manufacture of shoes. This was also the first year that left and right shoes were made on different lasts. (Before this time the shape of the instep was not accounted for and shoes for left and right feet were identical.)

1875. Goodyear's welt stitcher made shoes more comfortable because now the stitches were on the outside!

1888. Standardized shoe sizes first adopted.

1926. First practical shoe cementing methods.
[See "The Archeology of Mass-Produced Footwear," in *Historical Archeology,* 1968]

CHAPTER 6

Others Too Tedious to Mention

————◦◉◦————

The tape recorder and camera have helped us to find out about some of the jobs that were once the work of America but, unfortunately, there are still others—more than we realize—that have not been performed for so many years that no one knows or remembers how to do them anymore. Many jobs from centuries past have their modern counterparts—furniture making, for one example, which used to be done almost entirely by hand but is now mostly the work of machines. Walking into a modern cabinetmaker's shop we would need only a little historical imagination and a look at the old hand tools still hanging there above the workbench or in a little-used and dusty corner of the shop to reconstruct in our minds, or do once again with our hands, a fair equivalent of the work done centuries ago. But many, many other skills are just not practiced any more because, well, there's simply no need for them. The tools for these jobs, when found, tantalize the historical imagination and often leave us wondering, "Just what was that used for?" There are tools in museums and attics so unusual or, perhaps, ingenious and specialized that no one

alive can do anything but guess at how they were used. These kinds of tools and the skilled hands that used them are no longer alive, but neither are they completely lost. We just have to look for them someplace else than the living memory—in such places as the advertising and illustrations of old newspapers, magazines, tradesmen's journals, business directories, and other treasures of the library. Of course, finding out about work of the past in books and magazines doesn't hold out the promise of meeting a new friend or watching practiced hands perform again some intriguing work, but it has its own pleasures. Besides, if among your newly discovered ancestors a japanner, feather renovator, salt caster, wharfinger, or street waterman turned up, the library may well be your only alternative.

For John Rohrbough's millers, millwrights, and teamsters, a long era was ending, and American life was changing in imperceptible but fundamental ways. Small businesses and personal skills—in fact an entire work ethic—were being supplanted by large factories producing standardized, mass-produced products, so that many workers, who had spent their lives at a job their parents and grandparents had done before them, suddenly discovered that somehow all this had changed.

But how could it be any other way? American life and work were changing because America was changing in every aspect. And so, woven into John Rohrbough's narrative are the themes of change we would expect to hear in any description of American life from, say, the 1880s to the 1930s. One of those themes is the rise and fall of the fortunes of towns, some towns growing into cities and industrial and commercial centers, others receding from the scene. Another theme, which some would suggest is the most important of all, is the changing forms of transportation.

In thousands of towns in America the story of change was repeated. The basic services of the town must grow with the times; the little gristmill, the smithy's shop, the brick factory, and the sawmill had to become big businesses to supply the needs of big populations. Products that were mass-produced and less expensive than handmade products of the small shop were, of course, more desirable. The railroad and the motor truck made them more widely available. Wheat could be transported hun-dreds of miles from the farm to the mill in the big city; then the flour could be shipped hun-dreds of miles more to a small town where, after all the transporting and changing of hands, it still could be sold at a price competitive with locally milled flour (although today's high prices make many wonder if this still can be true).

The story of this change, particularly the change in the jobs and skills that once were and are no more, has not been lost and is in fact quite easily accessible. As we've seen, part of the story lies in the reminiscences of millers and miners. But much of it is beyond the reach of memory. So, for either the casual browsers, whose curiosity sends them in search of, for example, pictures of early steam locomotives, or for the modern-day craftsperson who would like to see what the tools and products of the craft were like one hundred, two hundred, or three hundred years ago, or for the local his-torian in search of a community's beginnings, there is the library marketplace—books and newspapers and magazines, filled with all the wondrous things made by American hands, telling the story of a changed America.

*   *   *

Bernardi Hotel (provenience unknown)

Let's go back for a moment to the days before the industrial revolution in America, when work had another meaning. If we go back far enough, to the 1700s and early 1800s, in rural and small-town America, we would find an economy very different from the standardizing, mass-oriented economy of today. There was little that a family purchased. Almost everything around you was made by hand, by your own hands—the cloth of your clothing, the tools by which you made your living, the house and most of the furnishings, the barn, your wagon and sled, even your children's toys—all came of your many skills. Some raw materials like iron, of course, would have to be purchased or bartered for, but many homesteads consisted not only of barns and agricultural buildings but also of small mills and even a forge to make and repair tools. Though there was some specialization of labor, the time was one, by and large, when everyone knew just about everything he or she needed to know to survive and to prosper. All of which was certainly a point of pride among rural Americans.

But cities—as always—were different. In the cities of early America, there already was specialization of labor—though not yet to the detriment of skill—and also, of course, there was the commerce, the buying and selling that takes place because cities function as centers of exchange. To the cities came all manner of workers from the Old World, and their multitude of skills was cataloged in the newspaper announcements of their ship's arrival.

SCOTCH SERVANTS

A number of Indentured Servants, viz. Weavers, Taylors, Coopers, men and Maid Servants, to be disposed of for a certain Time:—For terms, inquire on board the Ship Douglass, *Captain* Montgomery, *from* Ayre *in Scotland, now lying at the Long-Wharff in* Boston. [*Boston Gazette,* October 31, 1763]

IRISH SERVANTS

Arrived from Ireland per the Globe, Capt. Nicholas Oursell, *Commander, and to be disposed of by him, the following Protestant Servants—viz. Men, Anchor & Ship Smith, House Carpenters, Ship Joyners and Carver, Cooper, Shoemakers, and Pattoun Maker, Naylors, Lock-Smiths, Currier, Taylor, Book Printer, Silver-Gold Lace Weaver, Silver Smith. And Women, Milliners, Ribband & Lace Weavers, Button Maker, Earthen Ware Potter Maker, House Keepers, Washer Women and Cooks.* [*Boston News-Letter,* June 18–25, 1716]

This information, note, was in the regular newspaper announcements, not in advertisements. For although the trades and commercial activities of urban Colonial America were numerous, they were also limited in scope and generally served only their community, the city. Commercial activities seldom extended beyond the home colony's boundaries, except in the importing of goods from England. This limitation is only logical of course, for a craftsman fashioning everything by hand could supply only a small market perhaps no bigger

PEWTER. Just Imported from London and to be Sold by wholesale or retail by Gilbert Deblois, at the sign of the *Crown and Comb* near the Prison in Queen Street, Boston: . . . London pewter dishes, plates, basons, porringers, breakfast bowls, table spoons, pint and quart pots, cans, Tankards, butter cups, newest fashion tea pots, table salts, sucking bottles, plate & dish covers, cullenders, soop kettles, new fashion roased [*sic*] plates, communion beakers and flaggons, pewter measures, chamber pots, bed and close stools. [*Boston Gazette,* July 26, 1756]

SCALE MAKER. Made and sold by Jonathan Dakin, Mathematical Ballance-maker, at the sign of the Hand and Beam, below the Mill-Bridge in Middle street, Boston. All sorts of Scale Beams ready prov'd and seal'd as the Law directs: likewise Money Scales with Weights, such as Ounces, Penny Weights and Grains; where all Persons in Town or Country, may be supply'd at the lowest Rates for ready Money. [*Boston Gazette,* August 7, 1753]

CROWN SOAP. Made and Sold by *Elizabeth Franklin,* at the Post-Office, the best sort of Crown Soap; also hard soap by Wholesale or Retail, at the lowest Rate. [*Boston Gazette,* August 23, 1756]

CHANDLER. Made and Sold by Edward Langdon & Son, in Fleet Street, near the old North Meeting-House, Sperma-Ceti Candles, Bayberry Wax Candles, mould and dipp'd Tallow Candles—also refin'd Sperma-Ceti Oil, by the Barrel or smaller Quantities for Lamps. [*Boston Gazette,* May 25, 1761]

than the neighborhood. By the way, as you go through newspapers from the early 1700s you may be puzzled by what seems to be a disproportionate number of advertisements placed by silversmiths. The apparent reason was that there were few safe places for well-to-do colonists to store their wealth, which was then measured by the amount of silver one had acquired. One of the things they could do with it was to have it fashioned into tableware. Since there was a considerable amount of wealth in the colonies, there was considerable demand for silversmiths (as well as watchmakers, pewterers, and goldsmiths).

Still, as you go through these newspapers you'll notice that very little space is devoted to advertising. Why advertise if you are able to supply only a limited local market? Beyond that, even cities were small then, and the craftsmen's work would be known to city people just as it would be to the citizens in any small town. Look at the city populations in 1730: Boston, 13,000; Philadelphia, 11,500; New York, 8,600. There were still other reasons for the local orientation of the early craftsmen. Protective tariffs at Colonial boundaries, taxation, limited transportation links, conflicting laws,

and diverse coinage—in short, all those ailments enumerated in our history books combined to make each colony a separate economy and each little business very local.

But when, in 1775, the populations of Philadelphia and New York increased to four times the 1730 figures—to 40,000 and 25,000 respectively—advertisements for an immense array of products and services began to appear in city papers. Much of the early advertising was for imported goods, mostly from England, but the change in the advertisements over the century, particularly in the years before the Revolution, reflect a growing pride in American products and encouragement of home manufactures. The familiar "just imported from London" notices were more and more to be replaced with statements to the effect that products "are equal if not superior in quality to any imported from Europe" and that storekeepers showed "preference to what is American made." American pride was fed by advertisements such as this one, in the *Boston Gazette* of August 23, 1756, for American-made snuff:
. . . which will be found at least as good and much cheaper than any Foreign Snuff, and it is at the same Time a Manufacture of our own. It is therefor pre-

---

WM. DONALDSON, Coachmaker, from Philadelphia Begs leave to inform his friends and the public that he has purchased the stock in trade of James Hallett, who has resigned in his favour. . . . From the great experience he has had in the line of his profession, and as he has finished some of the most superb carriages that has been finished on this continent, he flatters himself from this strict attention to business, to be able to give those gentlemen full satisfaction, that may please to call on him with their commands, with carriages of every description. Patent Axels will be procured at gentlemen's request, the utility of those axels has been much approved of. . . . [*New-York Gazette, and General Advertiser,* March 4, 1797]

MUSTARD MAKER. John Ingram, the Original Flower of Mustard Maker, from Lisbon, now living at the House of Mrs. Townsend, near Oliver's Dock, Boston, Prepares Flower of Mustard to such Perfection, by a Method unknown to any Person but himself, that it retains its Strength, Flavour and Colour Seven Years; being mix'd with hot or cold water, in a Minute's Time it makes the strongest Mustard ever eat, not in the least Bitter, yet of a delicate and delightful Flavour, and gives a most surprising grateful Taste to Beef, Pork, Lamb, Fish, Sallad, or other Sauces. It is approved of by divers eminent Physicians as the only Remedy in the Universe in all nervous Disorders, sweetens all the Juices, and rectifies the whole Mass of Blood to Admiration. If close stopt it will keep its Strength and Virtue Seven years in any Climate. Merchants and Captains of Ships shall have good Allowance to sell again. [*Boston Gazette,* September 19, 1752]

UMBRILLOES, with Ivory or Bone Sockets and Sliders, and Mehogany Sticks, made in the neatest Manner by *Isaac Greenwood*—Ivory Turner, next Door to Dr. John Clark's at the North End of Boston. He also covers Old sticks at a reasonable Rate. [*Boston Gazette,* June 20, 1763]

WIG MAKER. Made by James Mitchell, at his Shop in King-street, next door to Richard Dana, Esq.: After the best and newest Fashion: Tye Wiggs, full bottom Wiggs, Albemarles, Scratches, cut and curl'd Wiggs; also black Bags, and Rambilees for Wiggs: And has all sorts of Pomatum. He also cuts and dresses Hair after the London, French, Spanish, or Italian Fashion. And makes all sorts of Gold, Silver, or Common wire Wiggs. The said Mitchell has lately visited and work'd at the most noted Cities in Europe. [*Boston Gazette,* December 18, 1753]

sumed that private Interest, as well as Regard for the Publick, will give it the Preference to any that is imported from Abroad.

And this one, from the *Gazette* of September 18, 1769:

It is with pleasure we inform you the Public, That a few days since was shipped from Newport, a very curious Spinnet, being the first ever made in America, the performance of the ingenious Mr. John Harris, of Boston. . . .

The boycott of English goods, which was part of the independence movement, further stimulated home manufactures.

But despite the increased shift toward self-sufficiency, the colonies were still dependent on imports, and they came more and more from continental Europe, particularly from Paris, Amsterdam, and Switzerland (again, reflected in newspaper advertisements of the period). If, after the Revolution, political independence had been won from England, it would be a long time before the country would attain economic independence from Europe. Thus, it was a matter of pride for newspapers to note that on his inauguration President Washington was dressed in a suit of homespun, "a circumstance which must be considered as not only flattering to our manufacturers in particular but interesting to our countrymen in general. His Excellency the Vice-President appears also in a suit of American manufacture and several members of both Houses are distinguished by the same token of attention to the manufacturing interest of their country."

*   *   *

Ah, the humble, modest, and respectable beginnings of American advertising. I suppose many a beleaguered magazine and newspaper reader or television viewer might wish that advertising had never begun. (If it's any comfort, Americans didn't invent advertising. Like almost everything else we've come to regard as traditionally ours, newspaper advertising has its roots in England and continental Europe.) In any case, though our feelings about advertising may well be justified, we shouldn't let them make us overlook an entertaining and very real source of information about work and life

in America. In many ways the ads in the early newspapers are more revealing of American life than the articles that accompanied them—just as ads are today. Take a look at an early newspaper or magazine, bound or on microfilm, and see for yourself.

In the beginning, particularly during the 1700s, ads were apparently written by the person placing them and were submitted to newspapers in much the same way one would write a letter to the editor. The tone of early advertising, in fact, has just that quality—an open letter to the reader.

JOHN LAWRENCE, *Drawing-Master, presents his respectful compliments to the Ladies and Gentlemen of New York, and its environs, begs leave to inform them that he purposes teaching Drawing.*

A Naturalist, lately arrived from Europe, takes this method to inform his friends and the public in general that he has brought with him, a large collection of birds, insects, butterflies, and several quadrupeds, from different parts of the world. . . .

National Smith begs leave to recommend his incomparable beautifying cakes for making shining Liquid Blacking. . . .

And often the ads shared intimate facts with the reader. One John Simnet tells us that he arrived from London in 1764 to continue his work as a watchmaker, but like many craftsmen was caught up in the turmoil of the Revolution.

[He] *was at last driven by the Tempest of the war to Albany; and from being most out of employee for eight years, has reduced his circumstances to require the revival of his old advertisement, soliciting the favours of his curious surrounding neighbors, who will ever prove his performances excellent, and his charges very easy.*

All very polite and proper indeed, but even in National Smith's ad above—recommending "his incomparable beautifying cakes"—we can see the American huckster aborning. Later American advertising will sound more familiar to us, and one almost suspects an immediate ancestor of Madison Avenue at work in the following cosmetic ad that appeared—well, why don't you guess when.

The bloom of imperial rose is the constant toilet companion of ladies of the first rank and fortune . . . giving to the cheek a rosy hue, perfectly resembling nature, from the palest to the deepest tint and giving to the whole countenance a beautiful and healthful appearance; it will not change or rub off . . . and it is so truly innocent that it may be used on the delicate texture of an infant's skin.

Maybe it isn't quite the pizzazz we're used to, but it's clearly in the same tradition. You might like to know that that lyrical bit of fluff was placed (in a magazine called the *Weekly Museum*) by a gentleman with the lotion-cool name of Courtenay. The date? September 16, 1797!

But there is a good deal more to be read from newspaper ads than the rise (or is it the fall?) of the American advertising copy writer. Patterns of immigration, for example. Judging from his name, Mr. Courtenay was probably French and, if he was, the date of his ad is significant. During the Reign of Terror that followed the French Revolution of 1789, America —as it had been so many times before and has been so often since—became a refuge to French immigrants fleeing the political, economic, and social uncertainties of their homeland. Census figures and ships' passenger lists for the period are incomplete, but from the newspaper advertisements alone we could guess that French immigration was significant. For among the names of tradesmen and artisans who advertised in the newspapers of the 1790s, particularly later in that decade, there now appeared many that were obviously French—Verger ("Artist from Paris, Intending to remain a short time in this city, offers his services to the Public"); Renault (*Citizen* Renault the ad said); St. Mémin & Valdenuit, engravers; Pascal, an upholsterer; Parise, a tinner; Vergh, another Parisian artist; Artaud, a portrait painter; Badollet, a watchmaker whose advertisement in fact appears in French; another Renault, this one a gilder; and as if to remove any doubt about his origins, the portraitist who signs his ad Charles-Balthazar-Julien Fevret de Saint-Mémin. There were other signs of French immigration too—French fashions becoming very much in vogue, Americans singing French

revolutionary songs, and even the appearance in 1795 of *The French and American Gazette*, with one half of each page printed in French and the other in English translation. The bilingual *Gazette* was published for only four years, until 1799, but long enough to leave the newspaper historian with a vivid impression of the life of French emigrés in America.

Browsers through papers of the middle to late nineteenth century will be able to detect similar patterns of immigration for Irish, Germans, Russians, Greeks, Finns, and many other groups whose newspaper ads announced their arrival to the American marketplace.

The early newspaper ads also provide hints of life changing in the cities and signs of villages and towns becoming huge population centers and acquiring the attributes of large cities all over the world, such attributes as street names and numbers. One of the joys of early advertisements, before the Revolution particularly, is the colorful directions for finding the advertiser's place of business—or the description of his building which had no number.

AT THE SIGN OF THE DIAL,
NEXT DOOR EAST OF THE COFFEE-HOUSE
WITH AN ELEGANT PROJECTING WINDOW.

AT THE SIGN OF THE BRASS-KETTLE, TEA KETTLE,
AND COFFEE-POT BETWEEN THE DWELLING HOUSE OF
CAPT. ISAAC SEARS AND BEEKMAN'S SLIP.

CABINETMAKER. AT THE SIGN OF THE
CHEST OF DRAWERS IN WILLIAM STREET.

BETWEEN THE FIRE-ENGINE HOUSE AND
THE SIGN OF THE UNICORN & MORTAR.

AT THE SIGN OF THE CROSS-DAGGERS IN SMITHS-FLY.

OPPOSITE TO FROGGS POINT AT WHITE STONE.

IN THE BROAD-WAY AT THE SIGN OF THE RIDING CHAIR.

AT HIS LODGINGS AT THE HOUSE OF MRS. GEORGE,
IN THE FIRST LANE FROM THE BOWLING-GREEN,
THAT LEADS TO THE NORTH RIVER.

NEARLY OPPOSITE MR. HULL'S TAVERN.

ON GOLD-HILL-STREET, AT THE HOUSE OF
CATHERINE HUBBS, OPPOSITE MR. SCADARET'S BEER
AND OYSTER HOUSE.

AT THE SIGN OF THE GILT DISH IN DOCK STREET.

AT HIS SHOP IN CORNHILL (NEAR THE HEART
AND CROWN) AND CROCKERY STORE IN PUDDING-LANE
(A LITTLE SOUTHWARD OF THE LOWER END OF THE
TOWN HOUSE).

Within a very few years in the late 1700s all this just passed away, and advertisements, if somewhat more brief, were now less colorful. I'm sure it was with the same shock and dismay felt by many of us at the telephone company's decision several years ago to convert exchanges like Murray Hill, Sunnyside, and Thornwall to three digits that our ancestors reacted when addresses like these appeared in ads:

NO. 20 BEEKMAN STREET

NO. 21 CROWN STREET

NO. 63 PEARL STREET

Just as there are those today who still use the old telephone exchanges, there were many then like Robert Montgomery, a clock- and watchmaker, who continued to give his address as "No. 33 Wall Street, opposite the Coffee-House Bridge."

*　　　*　　　*

What about the people at No. 20 Beekman Street or those in the shop across from the Merchants' Coffee-House—what kinds of work did they do? Well, there are few mysteries to the readers of old newspapers, for everything's right there for all to see.

The "subscriber," as was the custom for the advertiser to call himself then, tells us about his origins ("recently from Glasgow," "recently of London," "having just removed from Pamroupough"), his fortunes and misfortunes, even his training and apprenticeship. Here, for instance, is Thomas Burling, cabinetmaker and chairmaker, who refers to himself in the third-person style of the day:

He served his time with Samuel Prince, a conspicuous character in his way, and esteemed one of the first workmen in this city.

About their work, subscribers then spoke in some detail. You should realize that in the 1700s, the 1800s, and even in the early years of this century, all manner of work in small shops was open to the street. There were not yet huge factories surrounded by forbidding fences. Be-

---

BELL FOUNDER. This is to give notice to all Persons that have occasion for a Bell or Bells in Churches or Meeting-houses, that in New York they may be supplyed with New Bells, or if they have any old Bell broke they may have it new cast at a reasonable Price, and warranted good for Twelve Months, that if it Crack or Break it shall be new Cast for nothing: And all New Bells shall be made of better mettal than any other that comes out of Europe for Churches or Meeting-houses. [*Boston Newsletter*, June 10, 1717]

SADDLER'S WARES. Lately Imported from London, and to be sold by *Isaac Cazneau*, at his House in Water Street, by Wholesale or Retail; All sorts of Sadler's Ware, viz. Cannon-pad Bits, large and small, Snaffle and Trench Bits of all sorts, large and small white Setts, Girth and Straining Webb of all sorts, Lace and Fringe of all Colours, Women's Reins, all sorts of Whips and Bridles, and Tuff Nails, &c. Also choice *Bohea Tea*, All at a very reasonable Price for ready Money. [*Boston Gazette*, March 2, 1742]

HATS. Daniel Jones, at the *Hat & Helmit*, South-End, Boston, . . . makes and sells Beaver, Beaveret, and Castor-Hats: and has also a good Assortment of English Castor and Beaveret Hats, English and Felt ditto; Hat Linings and Trimmings of all sorts: Red Wool, Coney Wool, Camels Hair: Logwood by the 100 Wt. by Wholesale or Retail, cheap for Cash or Treasurer's Notes. [*Boston Gazette*, December 10, 1759]

CHARLES OLIVER BRUFF, Goldsmith and Jeweller, at the Sign of the Teapot, No. 196 Queen-street, at the corner of Golden-Hill. Those gentlemen of the navy and army and others in want of swords, may be suited with all sorts, silver mounted; cut and thrust and cutteaux de chase, mounted with beautiful green grips, or whatever other forms gentlemen may chuse; and light horse swords with death's head and cross bones, all sorts of jewellery made and mended. Has for sale ladies paste buckles, stock and knee buckles, stone broaches, seals stone rings, ear rings, an excellent skelleton watch, a variety of stone sleeve buttons; black ebony, red wood and buck handle table dessert knives; pen knives and scissars; plated shoe stock knee buckles. He has employed a cutler who makes, grinds and polishes all sorts of work in his way, and forms scabbards of vellum, parchment, and calfskin. Wants to employ jewellers, silversmiths, chape forger and filers. Has for sale, screw drivers and double worms, fit for our army's use. [*New-York Gazette: and the Weekly Mercury*, October 20, 1777]

fore you even walked into a shop you might see the engraver, the locksmith, the printer, the spectacle maker, the coppersmith, or the jeweler working at the window. Much of the heavy work, like smithing or plumbing or carpentry, was done outside. Before the use of woodcuts and, later on, engravings and photographs, we can find in the words of the craftsman's advertisement descriptions of just what he or she did. Turning the pages of the old newspaper (or going to the next microfilm frame, as the case may be), we can walk down those streets and meet:

CHARLES OLIVER BRUFF *who engraves arms, crests, cyphers, figures, and fancies . . . with the heads of Shakespear, Milton, Newton, Pope, Homer, Socrates, Hannible, Mark Anthony, Caesar, Plato, Jupiter, Apollo, Neptune, Mars, Cleopatra, Diana, Flora, Venus, Marcellany, and others too tedious to mention.*

GERARDUS DUYCKINCK *at the Sign of the Two Cupids, near the Old Slip Market . . . will teach any young Gentleman that art of Drawing, with Painting on Glass. Looking-glasses new Silvered, and the Frames plaine Japan'd or Flowered, also all Sorts of Picktures, made and sold.*

ELIZABETH EVANS . . . *makes up in the neatest manner and newest taste, all sorts of Upholstery work, such as festoon bed and window curtains, field or camp beds, Ketty fishers, wrought quilts, chair, sofa, and settee cases; also ladies boned waistcoats and stays.*

ISAAC HERON. *At the Sign of the Arch'd Dial, Has an Assortment of Watches, and the best, second, third, fourth, fifth, bad, and worse Sorts; some very neat, some very ugly, and others—so, so; most of them in plain, and a few in engrav'd, gold, silver, gilt, and shagreen'd double and single Cases; some he warrants for a long Time, some for a shorter Time, and others for no Time at all.*

GOTTLIEB WOLHHAUPTER, *living at the sign of the Musical instrument-Maker, has just imported from London, a Choice Parcel of the best English Box-wood; where he continues to make and mend, all Sorts of Musical Instruments, such as German Flutes, Hautboys, Clareonets, Flageolets, Bassoons, Fifes, and also Silver Tea-Pot Handles.*

WILLIAM MUCKELVAIN, *Baker, at the Sign of the Three Bisquets, on Pot-Baker Hill, will continue to heat his Oven at Ten o'Clock every Day during the warm Weather, for baking Dishes of Meats, Pyes, &c. N. B. He likewise continues baking of Flour into Bread for Family Use, &c.*

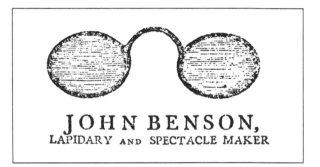

WILLIAM HINTON, *Mathematical Instrument Maker . . . Makes and sells all sorts of Mathematical Instruments, in Silver, Brass, Ivory, or Wood, viz. Hadley's Quadrants, Crostaf's Nocturnals, Gunters Scales, Cases of Instruments, Surveyors Chains, Dividers with and without Points, Protractors, paralelled Rulers, Rods for Gauging . . . and common Wood Compasses, three Foot Telescopes, Backgammon Tables, Dice and Dice Boxes; Billiard Balls and Tacks, Violin Bows and Bridges; with a Variety of other Articles too tedious to mention.*

SARAH SELLS, *Muffin-Maker, in Broad-Street . . . continues making Muffins and Crumpets hot twice every Day.*

UMBRELLAS.

PETER JAILLET,
No. 142, Queen-ſtreet,
lately arrived in this City,
Makes and mends
UMBRELLAS,
on reaſonable terms.

JOHN BALTHUS DASH, *Tinman, from Germany;* *At his house near the Oswego Market, makes the best* *of French Horns, Philadelphia Buttons and Shoe* *Buckles, and will sell them very reasonably by whole-* *sale or retail.*

If you lived in the days of these advertisements you would be acquainted with many people like the subscribers who placed them— people like Sarah Sells, muffin maker, and John Balthus Dash, tinman, for they would be your neighbors. Perhaps you've already noticed just from the few examples in this chapter that most people carried out their business in or very near their homes. There was not then the distinct separation of residential and business areas, particularly for home industries and small shops. To be sure, there were places in town where one found heavy industry—the mills lined up along both sides of the river, for instance. In cities, there were commercial areas, downtowns (though this term really didn't apply then), where row upon row of businesses lined the streets. But people lived here too and in many cities continued to live in such areas as recently as thirty or forty years ago (most of the apartments I knew, while growing up in Chicago, had small businesses on the ground floor). Indeed, this is still true of Europe today, where in London, Paris, Amsterdam, and most other cities, small businesses— stores, garages, craft shops, book stalls, shops of all kinds, even little one- and two-pump gas stations—are inconspicuously tucked in among the rows of apartments and single residences. There were also street markets all throughout American cities, not unlike the colorful little markets Americans now travel all over the world to find.

In such a community, where living and working intertwined—the children going to and from school, younger children and their mothers going about their daily activities, everyone who ventured out onto the street—all were part of everything that was happening. There was no mystery about what you bought and how it was made, for there were other items just like it, in various stages of manufacture, right there in the shop, and the shopkeeper from whom you bought it was also the craftsman who made it—unmistakably so, as you could see from the pride and satisfaction with which he handled and offered the little tin funnel or the earthenware pitcher almost warm from the kiln.

So it was, and not that long ago either. As I said, I can remember something of this in my own childhood, not forty years ago. And certainly within our parents' and grandparents' memories, most men and women boasted of their life's work, work they had done since they were children, which they had learned from their parents. It was by no means uncommon to find in a family third-, fourth-, perhaps fifth-generation carpenters, printers, millers, dressmakers, instrument makers, railroad engineers, or teachers. Today we can still see a few stores and businesses with signs proclaiming "Est. 1888" or "Serving the People of Chicago for Fifty Years," and some of these places are still in the family, though few if any among us today can duplicate George Hedderly's boast in a *New-York Daily Advertiser* ad in 1794 announcing the establishment at No. 20 Little Dock Street (in the Bowery) of his New York Bell Foundry:

G. Hedderly's ancestors, having been in the bell *foundering, and bell hanging business, for upwards* *of three centuries and he having made it his study from* *his infancy, hopes that his abilities in the art of bell* *casting and hanging will merit the attentions of the* *citizens of America.*

Ebenezer Clark, *Coach-Maker*

People identified with their work then, and their entire being—not just from eight to five—was tied up in what they did for a living. Talking with older, retired people today, we're probably surprised to discover that some of them worked twenty, thirty, forty, fifty years for one company or in one little shop! They often started as youngsters and, so to speak, became one with the place where they worked.

Another side to this, of course, is that a youngster had but little say in the choice of his or her life's work, it all being decided by mother or father. Most children, it was just assumed, would take up the work of their parents and like George Hedderly, the maker of bells, would continue with what they'd known best since infancy. (When work space and home space are one, a child comes to know the parents' work more or less automatically.) Other young people, in the 1600s and 1700s, were hired out as indentured servants, acquiring or perfecting their skills in servitude as payment either for their passage to America or for some other debt. Still others were apprenticed—which in reality, for many, was just indentured servitude under another name. Newspapers from the period are filled with ads for servants and apprentices who had disappeared.

*William Fletcher, a bought Servant,
is Run away from his Master.*

Runaway—Irish apprentice lad . . .

*Run-away . . . an apprentice lad named
George M'Clary, about nineteen years of age,
by trade a shoemaker. . . . Thirty Shillings reward.*

Still, for most youngsters then, being an apprentice, or even a "boundboy," was an opportunity to learn a trade that our children today might envy.

Part of the problem for young people today is that, although they have more freedom of choice, there is not the variety of satisfying jobs that was available in previous days: there seem to be fewer interesting things to do. The transition has been subtle, taking place gradually over the past two or three generations, and most of us probably aren't even aware of the tremendous variety of occupations that used to

be but are no more. For example: when was the last time you needed a surcingle, isinglass, teazles, oiled clothing, oakum, shoddy, guttapercha; or the services of a grainer, a wharfinger, a street waterman, a japanner, or a saw gummer? If you were living in an American city one hundred years ago, all of these goods and services and countless more would be yours to buy. Actually none of these products or occupations, or those offered in the newspaper ads that accompany this chapter, were very exotic, and most would have been known to children of the day, whose fathers and mothers might also be shipsmiths, mustard pressers, penmanship teachers, regalia manufacturers, or slaters. If you've no idea what these occupations are, that's the point. It's because they recall a time in our grandparents' and great-grandparents' day when Americans did all kinds of things and sold everything imaginable, and sometimes unimaginable.

*   *   *

In the 1800s in larger cities, there appeared, in addition to the advertisements in newspapers and magazines, business directories—thick volumes of information about the local business world. Today we'd look for the goods and services we need in the telephone book, but before telephones and telephone books existed, businesses in large cities were listed in city business directories. Many directories are still available and are just as dusty and neglected as old newspapers and local histories. They usually can be found in the local history section of the library (sometimes the chamber of commerce also has a collection of business directories).

Like newspapers, these directories contain illustrated advertisements of businesses, tradesmen, and professional services. But they contain other kinds of information too—city maps, birth and death statistics, lists of churches, city agencies, libraries, schools and universities (with enrollment figures), post offices, police and fire departments, even the salaries of civil servants, the mayor, and other political figures. So if you're interested in searching through newspapers and local histories in search of information on work in America, you should explore business directories too.

The addresses given in the directories may help you find old shops and factories and neighborhoods in larger cities now largely devoted to one kind of manufacturing or trade. Because tradesmen, manufacturers, and merchants are listed under the goods and services they provided, it is even possible, if you are sufficiently interested, for you to make a list of occupations for at least some of the years (library collections of older directories often being incomplete). Some directories also arrange entries alphabet-

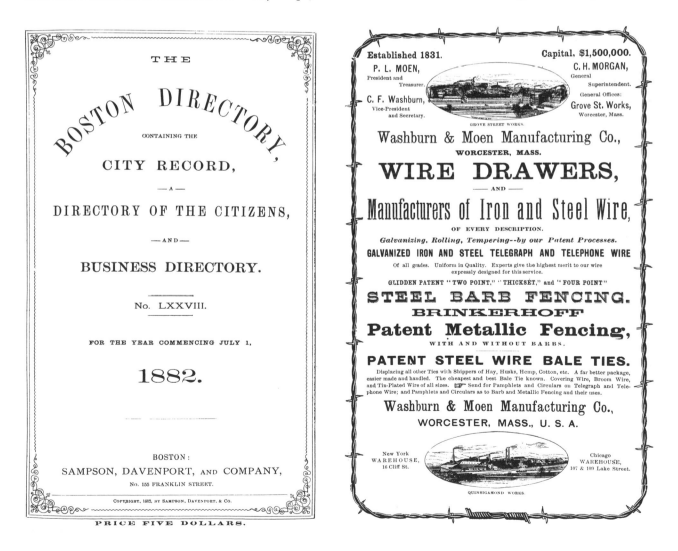

ically, by the name of the subscriber, making it possible for one to find, in cities with diverse immigrant populations, trades and occupations traditionally associated with various ethnic groups. Just as with newspaper ads, a study of directories over several years can reveal the arrival of immigrants in significant numbers and the arrival with these groups of new skills, materials, and techniques (for instance: stone cutters, mosaic and tile setters, and every kind of food from every corner of the world).

Another feature of the directories is that they are full of fine engravings of machines and other products, and in the printers' section you'll find the latest samples of printing, typography, and press design as well as some of the earliest examples of halftone and color printing. Once you turn open the cover and get your first glimpse of those beautifully detailed engravings and the circus of type fonts, it will be at least another hour before you reach the back cover —and then you'll hurry back to the shelves hoping to find a directory for the next year. That's what happened to me when I discovered the *Boston Directory* for 1882. I also became intrigued by the advertisements for goods and services (many of which sent me to the dictionary) and began to make a list of items and occupations hard to find in today's yellow pages.

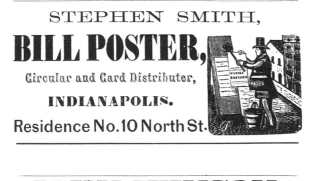

Anvils
Ballast
Bell Founders
Bellows
Bird Skins
Blacksmiths (123)
Boilermakers
Bonnet and Hat Bleachers
Boot and Shoe Buckles
Botanic Medicines
Button Hooks
Canopies for Parties & Weddings
Capstans
Carvers (ornamental)
Cast Iron Kettles
Chamois Skins
Charcoal Dealers
Chimney Sweeps
Chocolate Machinery
Clairvoyants (23)
Coffee and Spice Mills
Conductor's Ticket Punches
Conjurers
Cooperage Stock
Coopers
Copyist
Cork Cutters
Cracker Bakers
Crestings
Curriers
Demijohns, Bottles, &c.
Dentophile
Dumb Bells
Engraving Restorers
Excelsior Manufs.
Feather Renovators
Fresco Painters (9)
Galvanic Batteries
Gilders of Pictureframes
Gold Beaters
Gongs and Cymbals
Grainer
Grist Mills
Gunny Cloth and Bags
Hair Felt
Hair Mattresses
Harness Makers
Hearing Trumpets
Hoof Ointment
Hoop Skirts
Hop Presses
Horse Plumes
Horse Radish Grating Machines
Horse Shoers (70)
India Rubber and Gutta Percha
Iron Finials
Iron Fountains

Isinglass
Ivory Turners
Japanners
Juggler
Kaolin
Lamp Wicks
Lard and Tallow Presses
Leather Suspender Trimmings
Loom Straps
Maltsters
Marble Workers
Medicinal Waters
Mill Stones
Model Makers
Mourning Goods
Mustard Presses
Oakum
Oiled Clothings
Organ Stop Knob Maker
Ostrich Feathers
Penmanship
Pew Numbers
Pilot Bread
Plaster Image Makers
Pneumatic Dispatch Tubes
Railroad Lights and Lanterns
Razor Strop Makers
Regalia Manufs.
Salt Casters
Saw Gummers
Settees
Shafting Hangers and Pulleys
Ship Bread Bakers
Shipsmiths (18)
Shipwrights and Calkers
Shoddy Manufs.
Shoe Buckles
Slate Mantels
Slaters (25)
Soap Molds
Speaking Tubes
Spokes and Rims
Stove Polish
Street Watermen
Surcingles
Tachigraphy
Teazles
Tinners
Troches
Turners
Vest Makers (10)
Wax Flowers
Weather Vane Manufs.
Wharfingers
Wood Carvers
Wood Engravers
Yeast Manufs. (12)

*   *   *

Still another source of information on the work of Americans are the U.S. Government census reports. The original purpose of the census, as I've said, was to determine the number of representatives each state was to have in the House of Representatives. Yet even before the first census taken in 1790, it was suggested that the concept of the census be broadened. The result ultimately would be to increase the value of the census to American historians.

James Madison proposed that the census include additional questions to allow "the description of the several classes in which the community is divided . . . to make proper provision for the agricultural, commercial, and manufacturing interest." Madison's proposal to list all Americans under thirty separate occupations was considered impractical at the time because of the nature of American manufactures. The *Boston Gazette* of February 8, 1790,

reported the concern that Madison's plan "divided the people into classes too minute to be readily ascertained," because a number of Americans "pursued two, three, or four occupations. . . . Some followed weaving in the spring and summer, but the making of shoes was predominant in the fall and winter: under what class are these people to be thrown, especially if they joined husbandry and carpenter's work with the rest?"

The proposal was not adopted, and it was not until the census of 1820 that some data on the work of Americans were collected under the broader classifications of agriculture, commerce, and manufactures. But because the instructions to the takers of the first census were not specific, and each of the census marshals carried out his count as he saw fit, there were some surprises. Madison's suggestions were taken up by marshals in some areas of Phila-

delphia who classified heads of households according to their occupations and so recorded not only the work, but something of the seafaring flavor of the city. The picture of Philadelphia is that of a thriving port with numerous ship chandlers, rope makers, caulkers, and shipwrights. There appeared the names of a bookseller and a professor at the Academy (now the University of Pennsylvania), a mantua-maker, a soap boiler, a "Dr. of Physick," and manufacturers of everything from buckskin breeches to hair powder.

By 1810, in the light of what seemed certain war with the British, Congress's concern for American manufactures prompted a more thorough survey of American industry to reveal a nation working at home. In Hancock County, Maine, for example, marshals recorded that 66,746 yards of cotton cloth were woven on small family looms and that most villages had their own mills and blacksmith shops. Incidentally, some of the specialties we associate with various regions of the country were already beginning to appear, such as the distilling of 2,220,773 gallons of whiskey in Kentucky and the manufacture of 14,565 wooden clocks in Connecticut and 16,000,000 "American segars" in Philadelphia.

If you'd like to see for yourself how the work of America was to grow and change throughout the nineteenth century, you'll find in the censuses data on many occupations and manufactures.

1820. "*Number of persons (including slaves) engaged in agriculture, commerce, and manufactures.*"

1840. "*Number of persons in each family employed in each of seven classes of occupations.*"

1850. "*Profession, occupation, or trade for each male and female over 15.*"

1870, 1880, and 1890. "*Profession, occupation, or trade.*"

1900. "*Occupation, trade, or profession of persons 10 years old and over.*"

1910, 1920. "*Occupation, industry, and class of worker.*"

1930. "*Whether family lives on a farm.*"

1940. "*If at work, whether in private or nonemergency government work, or in public emergency work (WPA, NYA, CCC, etc.) . . . usual occupation, industry, and class of worker.*"

1950, 1960, and 1970. "*Occupation, industry, and class of worker.*"

*　　　*　　　*

The discoveries in census data and newspaper, magazine, and directory ads are unending. Here on every page are details of the jobs and technologies of long ago, of the then latest styles in costume and custom, of foods arriving for the first time in the New World (lasagna, wiener schnitzel, dolmades), of the changing modes of transportation (from wagons and sleds to canal barges and trains), and even of the then most recently enacted and amended laws (published with ads in early Colonial newspapers), all of it chronicling the work Americans have done for centuries. Future newspaper archaeologists will use our classified ads—items for sale or rent, jobs wanted, positions open, services for hire—to discover something of work in our own time. But these will record a sad event in our history—the passing of many a craftsman and artisan from the American scene.

THE CONNECTICUT PEDDLER

I'm a peddler, I'm a peddler,
I'm a peddler from Connecticut.
I'm a peddler, I'm a peddler,
So don't you want to buy.

Many things have I in store,
So many things you never saw,
So many things you never saw before.
So very many things you never saw
  before,
So listen while I name them o'er.

Here are pins, papers of needles and
  pins,

Tracts upon popular sins,
Any of which I will sell you.
And here are the seeds of asparagus,
Lettuce Beets, onions and pepper-
  grass,
From the limited society,
Seeds of all kinds and variety.

I'm a peddler, I'm a peddler,
I'm a peddler from Connecticut.
I'm a peddler, I'm a peddler,
So don't you want to buy.
[Traditional]

WANTED, BOY — High-school graduate to work in general merchandise store in small interior town and learn to be a shoemaker. One who can help milk the cow and play in the band preferred. Must be youth of clean habits; cigarette smokers, sheiks and loafers need not apply. Boy who understands Diesel gas-engine and Fordson tractor will be given preference. Users of intoxicating liquors and profane language will not be considered. Boy who gets this job must not be too proud and aristocratic to mingle with the livestock and chickens and help out in the kitchen now and then. Tenor singer who is a good strike-out baseball pitcher will find this an ideal situation. Must be early riser and not afraid of work. You will work in a very healthful climate with beautiful surroundings, fine fishing, woodlands abound in wild game and flowers. Horse to ride Sunday afternoons. Good chance to learn a trade and the principles of business and see the country. Must be a good salesman. Apply in your own handwriting, sending late photographs with three recommendations. $12 a month to start for live wire, with chance to buy interest in the business. Employer can furnish board and room at $9.50 if you will mow the lawn in your spare time. Address "Newton," care Orange Daily Leader. [Advertisement in the Orange, Texas, *Daily Leader*, 1925]

CHAPTER 7

Balsam, Bitters, and Borax

Americans like to collect things. Some would say that we're just terribly acquisitive, but it seems more likely that Americans experiencing the acceleration of life over recent years sense just how easily examples of the material culture of even a decade ago can be misplaced and destroyed. Collecting is one of the ways we have of preserving an aspect of our past that is somehow appealing and captivating but also very much exposed and endangered. Our interests are limitless. Belt buckles, barbed wire and bottles, match boxes and mill stones, toys and tools, jewelry and junk of all kind become, for one or another of us, a passion. All of which makes it harder for us to understand the worry with which professional historical archaeologists view the collecting activities of amateurs. The problem, from the professional's point of view, is that much collecting is done with total disregard for crucial—but very simple—recovery techniques and leads to the destruction of more historical data than it preserves. On the other hand, professionals are frustrated by their inability to recover much of what needs to be recovered, for they can't outdig backhoes or earthmovers. Realizing this, most professional archaeologists would agree that trained and experienced amateur historians are valuable in the field. So their quarrel with amateurs is not that the amateurs collect (for deep down inside every scholar, too, is something of a collector) but the way they collect. Can amateurs be professional in their collecting? Of course. Collecting old bottles is chosen here as an example of historical inquiry and preservation because it is a popular activity and because it requires attention to a very few simple rules of recovery and recording to be done correctly. The rules apply to other kinds of collecting as well and are the bases for more intricate and demanding work certain to face the amateur historian.

The adventurous traveler wandering through California and Nevada in the 1880s, perhaps on the way from Bullfrog, California, to Carson City, Nevada, was certain at some point in his journey to arrive at the top of a low ridge and look down on the sprawling shacks, stores, company buildings, and burying grounds of a mining town. Dozens of these boom towns dotted the vast emptiness east of the Sierra, little rough-and-tumble settlements with names like Rhyolite, Goldfield, Klondyke, Tonopah, Manhattan, Sodaville, Mammoth, and Mono Mills.

Moving down onto the main street (ankle deep in mud or dust, depending on the season), the traveler would find signs that would tell him he had arrived in, say, Bodie. Bodie, a gold mining town dating back to 1859, was in every way typical of the mid-century boom towns. Bodie just seemed to grow out of the dust and the hopes of miners who came there searching for gold—which they discovered. The discovery brought more miners, the town grew helter-skelter, and in the process death by drunken shootout or winter blizzard made unwitting permanent residents of some of the first arrivals (including W. S. Bodie himself). In these temporary towns, the gold and the miners' dreams vanished together within a few years. But Bodie in its grandest days—like many of the other towns—was a flourishing community, its population of about twelve hundred boasting twenty-eight saloons and four drugstores!

The history of Western mining towns is usually written in terms of gold, silver, borax, and bullet lead, but from the number of saloons and drugstores in Bodie, it would seem that whiskey and Hall's Pulminary Balsam might be more appropriate. And in fact, the most vivid history of everyday life in the many little towns across the country during the last decades of the nineteenth century is written in *glass*, in hundreds of thousands of bottles and jars, the durable remains of a difficult life that left little time for writing and made the acquisition and collecting of personal belongings—the artifacts for later generations of historical archaeologists—all but impossible. In the home, the boarding house, or the hotel, there were room and time for but few luxuries, and many of these luxuries were things that came in glass. This simple fact makes possible a whole field of historical archaeology (in the West particularly), and now all over America a new breed of miners, called bottle collectors, are digging into the past and writing chapters in our history not usually found in books.

It may come as a surprise, but glass objects are among the most often cited artifacts in American historical archaeology, whether the excavation is being done in Colonial Jamestown or Williamsburg on the East Coast, in pioneer settlements of the Plains, or in the missions of the Southwest and California. There are very good reasons for this. Glass is a durable substance almost unaffected by centuries of weathering and able to withstand anything except intense heat and abrasion. In addition, the gummed paper labels are a comparatively recent development. The earliest bottles had the maker's or owner's seal cast into them, and beginning in the 1860s, bottles appeared with raised or incised lettering identifying the contents and, often, extolling its virtues. Thus, with bottles, we are able to create a detailed reconstruction of life styles, even of personal tastes and fads. What's more, glass is the almost perfect substance for storing everything from food to strong acids and so had and has countless uses for everyone (and don't forget that the metal can is a very recent invention). Small wonder, then, that bottle collectors and archaeologists find bottles and jars not just occasionally but by the dozens in even the smallest domestic site.

But there is another, equally important reason for the abundance of bottles and jars: the long (though not immediately thriving) history of glassmaking in America. Glassmaking was one of the first industries to be transplanted from Europe to the New World, arriving in the wake of the Spanish conquistadores. One of the earliest known glassmaking centers was at Puebla de los Angeles in Mexico, where the site of a glass industry dating to 1535 has been discovered. The industry in the English colonies began with the establishment of the Jamestown glasshouse in 1608 by the London Company of Virginia. But this first effort was unsuccessful, and indeed the earliest bottles found in Virginia—tall, four-sided, with short necks (shipped and stored in wooden or wicker baskets called "cellars" which held about a dozen bottles)—were probably made in England. I say probably because the bottles were so thin-walled that too few survived to tell definitely whether they were made in the colonies or in England.

The details of American glassmaking become clearer as we turn to the early 1700s. One of the most important finds of mid-eighteenth century glass bottles was uncovered in the course of excavating for the foundations of a new post

Reminiscences of Glassmaking

In connection with the drawings of the ancient glass-furnaces, we deem it proper to give a drawing of glass-makers' tools in use at that period, so that the glass-makers of the present day may observe with what instruments their noble predecessors in the art performed their labor.

In many of these tools we perceive the same general characters as mark those in use now. In some, improvements have been effected; while others are quite obsolete. It is quite curious to observe the etymology of many of the technical terms of the art in use at the present day. The name of the present polished iron table, *i.e.* the MARVER, is derived from the practice of the Italians and French in using slabs of polished marble. The iron now called the *punty*, from the Italian *ponteglo*. The tool now called *percellas*, from the word *porcello*. In fact, nearly all the technical terms in the glass manufacture, appertaining to the tool or furnace, are derived from the Italian. By referring to the drawing, we see that the tool marked A is the blow-iron, that marked B the punty-iron. Their character plainly indicates

that the work made on them must have been confined to small or light articles. C, the scissors, D, the shears, correspond to those used at the present day. The tool marked E was used to finish part of their work. F and G were their large and small ladles, — the small used to take off the then called alkalic salt, showing that they were troubled with an excess of this in their time. The shovel, then called stockle, marked H, was used to

carry glass articles to the annealing oven, forks not being then in use. The crooked iron I was used to stir up the metal in the pots. The tool L was used to form or hold large articles, their punty-iron not having sufficient strength. The tool M was used to carry flat articles to the annealing ovens. The tool N was used in refining their alkalic salts, and served to take off the salt as crystallized in course of its manufacture.

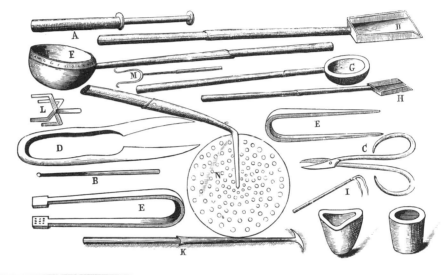

The workmen of the present day will see that, as before remarked, many tools are not altered in form, while in others there is a decided improvement, — in none more than in the tool E. Tool D is exactly like those now in use; but many new tools have been introduced since that period, rendering most of the old tools useless. Improvements in the form of glass-furnaces, construction of the glass-house, tools, &c., have been very gradual, — more so, in fact, than in almost any other art, when we consider that a period of about four hundred years has elapsed since the furnaces, tools, &c., herein referred to, were in use, and that they remained very much the same until the present century. [Deming Jarves, *Reminiscences of Glass-Making*. New York: Hurd and Houghton, 1865]

Glass peddler

office in Williamsburg in 1961. In what must have been a storage cellar used later as a refuse pit, archaeologists found over eleven hundred bottles! (If it strikes you as strange that bottles should be found in one place in such large numbers, stop for a moment to think about how we dispose of our refuse. Even before the municipal dump, there was usually a place in town, or down in the creek behind the house, or on the farmstead that for generations was used as a refuse heap—awaiting some archaeologists from the distant future.)

Despite these early beginnings, there was no large-scale glass production in America until over a half century later. In 1800 there were only nine operating glasshouses in the United States. This number increased to one hundred and eight by 1837, and another seventy-two were established between 1846 and 1860, the latter producing mostly window glass and bottles. Some of these bottles the forty-niners carried with them to mining towns like Bodie. Later the railroads carried westward tens of thousands more, filled with medicines and the miners' famed "drinkin' likker." One indicator of the growing demand for glass bottles was the appearance of glassmaking establishments in San Francisco around the mid-sixties, when mining towns were flourishing.

By the middle of the nineteenth century California had already begun to develop a food industry of considerable importance, an indus-

try eagerly looking for ways to preserve foods and get them to distant markets. And that method was already known. Earlier, experiments in France (by Nicholas Appert) had led to the discovery that if foods were cooked thoroughly and sealed properly in bottles, they could be preserved for long periods of time. This discovery, in turn, led to the beginnings of a "canning" industry, as well as to an increased demand for glass bottles and jars and, undoubtedly, to the Mason jar patent in 1858. Bottles collected in mining towns show that miners bought food packed in glass which came from California, the Eastern United States, Germany, England, and the Mediterranean! The bottles also reveal the mining camp population's gourmet tastes. Olive oil was widely used for cooking, not just one type but rather two brands from California (Sylmar's of Los Angeles and Aeolea), another with the French trademark "A.E.B.B. Depose," and yet another, the Rey Umberto brand from Italy. Among the other foods whose containers (jars and bottles) were found in the mining camps were: Hires root beer extract, coffee (Folger's and Shillings), baking powder, catsup (Curtis and Heinz), horseradish, mustard (Gulden's or

Bottles used ca. 1870

Moutarde Diaphne from France). From California came olives, Mrs. Reed's Pioneer Brand relishes, and gherkins by the Lewis Packing Co. of San Francisco. If this doesn't alter our image of the miner's palate, then consider the discovery of a not insignificant number of glass jars that once contained Lea & Perrins Worcestershire, Sauce Maggi (from Switzerland), and caviar! We can identify these bottles so confidently because they came from pre-label days and their names are part of the bottles.

In all, the durability of bottles with their incised and raised lettering, the large quantities in which bottles have been produced over the years, and the long history of glassmaking in America make bottles and glassware one of the most important and most informative historical resources. While it might seem that artifacts available in such quantities are historically less valuable than rare, occasional finds, the opposite is actually the case.

*   *   *

Since we are fortunate enough to have these glass clues in large enough numbers to allow very accurate and intimate reconstructions of life in early America, we should be careful not to lose them. Let's consider some of the critical steps for the recovery, recording, and preserving of glass artifacts.

Glass is durable but certainly not indestructible. This makes the first step—the recovery —crucial in the process of unearthing glass artifacts. Too many artifacts that have survived

Glassblowers and their tools, ca. 1860

hundreds of years in the ground are destroyed in the few minutes of excavation and recovery. Early bottles particularly may be of extremely thin-walled construction or, even if thick-walled, may be in a state of some decay. The process of recovery must proceed with care, even delicacy. Needless to say the pickaxe and shovel are not suitable tools. The best tools as yet discovered by experienced archaeologists cost nothing; you already own a matched, co-ordinated pair—your hands.

The usual sites for bottle collecting are refuse dumps, old cellars, and cess pits (it was the common practice to throw anything and every-thing, including empty bottles, down the privy). But since these areas will by now con-sist of heavily compacted soil, it may be neces-sary to prepare in advance for the recovery, perhaps even weeks in advance. If possible, the area of the site—particularly if it is a small confined area like a cess pit where the soil has become rock hard—should be soaked with water before you attempt to dig and separate bottles from the soil. The softer the soil, nat-urally, the easier it will be to recover glass artifacts and the less the danger of damage. Once the artifact has been carefully removed from the soil, the process of recovery has been completed and that of recording begins.

Recording is not just some ritual for the pro-fessional, it is an essential process. So important, in fact, that archaeologists consider the re-corded information in many ways more im-portant than the artifact. While a great deal of collecting centers on the object itself, the circumstances of discovery—the object's loca-tion and depth, the buildings and structures on or around the site, and the object's physical association with other artifacts—along with an accurate, detailed description and a drawing or photograph of the object ultimately provide more data and historical insights.

For example, let's assume that you have an attractive little crock on which are printed the words "Moutarde Diaphne, by Louet Frères, France." It's indeed a pretty object, as many French mustard jars are, but by itself is it of any interest, can it really tell us anything? Can we tell just from the jar alone, for instance, how old it is, when it arrived in this country and under what circumstances, who used it, where it was used, or anything else about it? Well, probably not. But suppose the little jar (or a picture of it) is accompanied by even the most basic information about the circumstances of its recovery. Then we are much more likely to find the answers to our questions. Here's how we might reconstruct the jar's history.

Location (city, county, state): That this mustard jar was found in the United States is interest-ing, but if it had been found, say, in Massa-chusetts or New York, then the finding of it

---

UPON THE MANUFACTURE OF GLASS. Bottles, black or green, are the most simple of all glass manufacture—the profits in making which depends upon the greatest number of work-men being employed at the smallest expense of fuel. From eight to sixteen blowers can work all at once, at one melting furnace, six feet diameter, which will take six cords of wood every twenty four hours. The best constructed green glass furnace in this country is in New Jersey—where the whole business of smelting, blow-ing, and cooling is done with one fire, by the particular construction of the furnace.

White glass may also be made in the same furnace: but it is much more curious in its composition; for to make it white, it must partake of all the colours—for this reason—in smelting the purest materials, they naturally have a greenish and pur-plish tinge; to dislodge which a black-ish fossil substance is made use of—upon this principle, that one colour in glass making will destroy another; so that at last a beautiful glass is pro-duced called white; but like the christaline humor of the eye, it par-takes of all the colours, as may be seen in the best English white glass which has a changeableness like soap bubbles; but in the best London crown glass, or mirrours, you will not perceive any of that sparkling, changeable power, because it would destort the object seen through or reflected, on account of the refracting power of such glass; therefore this glass is made of pure salts and sands only and has a native greyish colour, as may be seen by the broken pieces that, like water, they may reflect the objects truly.

Crown glass may be made here to greater profit than any other glass—on account of the plenty and cheap-ness of materials—the quantity that can be made—and the great con-sumption of it—The method of making which—form and dimen-sions of the furnace—preparation of the materials—I shall waive for par-ticular reasons. A Glass Maker. [*Gazette of the United States*, July 25, 1789]

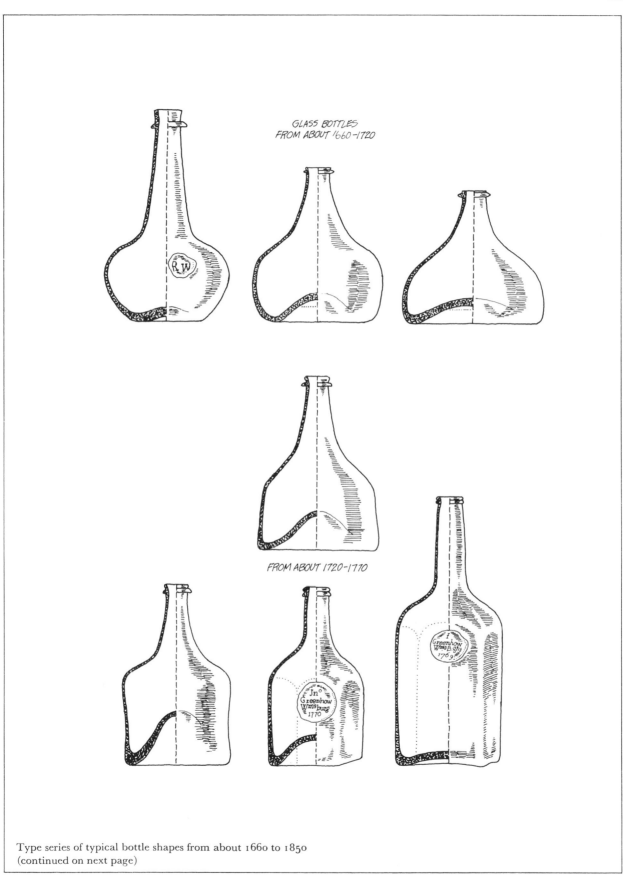

GLASS BOTTLES
FROM ABOUT 1660-1720

FROM ABOUT 1720-1770

Type series of typical bottle shapes from about 1660 to 1850
(continued on next page)

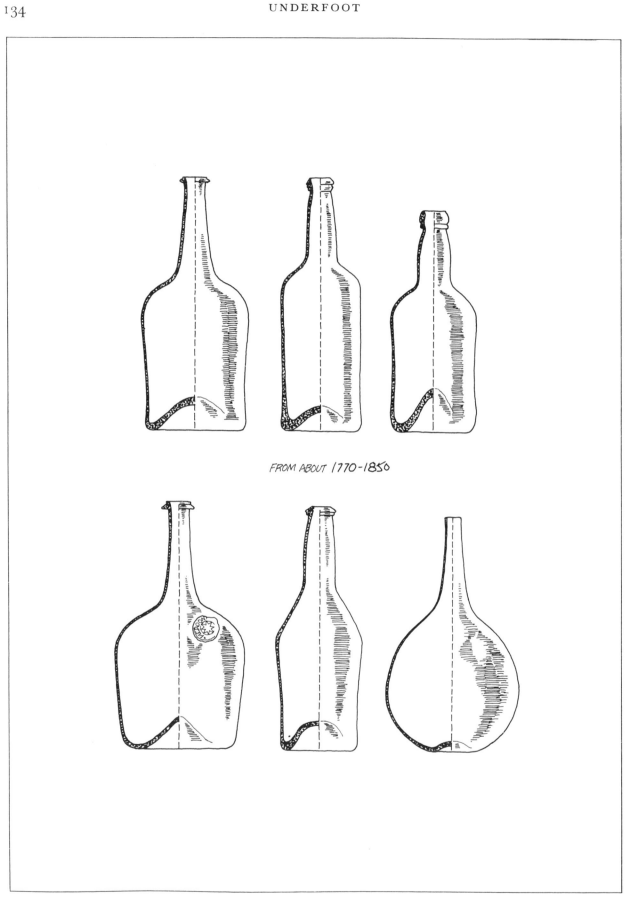

FROM ABOUT 1770-1850

would not be particularly remarkable. One would expect to find all sorts of European products in and around old Colonial ports, areas that remain large import centers even today.

But what if our jar of Moutarde Diaphne had been discovered in California? Well, that's a little different. That means the jar might have traveled across the continent by railroad or around Cape Horn (or through the Panama Canal). It suggests that a food distribution system or import/export industry was a part of our earliest commerce (but how early?). It might tell us something about the movements of French immigrants in the United States.

And if the jar had been found specifically in the city of San Francisco? Well, that wouldn't tell any more than we already might have surmised. It would be interesting for all the reasons we've just noted, but, of course, one would expect to find foreign products in large cities, and lots of foreign visitors too.

But this jar was found in Goldfield, Nevada! Moutarde Diaphne in a little mining camp—that's history.

Site: Our curiosity is really aroused now; is it possible, we're wondering, for us to learn more about how this gourmet delight ended up among whiskey-drinkin' miners? Well, where was the jar found? Was it discovered in the cellar of an old saloon? If so, we could conclude that the saloon was also an eatery and likely a good one. But all restaurants, even then, had exotic little treats, "specialties of the house" to attract customers. So a saloon location doesn't tell us much. What if the jar was found in the large house up on the hill, the one owned by the president of the Gilt Edge Mining Company? That might suggest less general use; the president of a mining company would, after all, have lots of money for luxuries. But if the jar were found among the old bottles of a miner's shack? Well, now we'd be on to something intriguing, and we might have to change our whole image of mining camp days.

We need more information to be sure, like a detailed description of the site and other things we found there. If we've found just the one bottle, can we really say anything about its place in American history? It might be just a household item brought over by a French pros-

pector—or perhaps even a souvenir from the First World War, a possibility we can't discount, you know. But suppose our mustard jar turned up among twelve others, still in the remains of their wooden shipping crate, still sealed in wax? And that along with this crate we found others filled with loose jars and bottles which once contained catsup, coffee, sauces, relishes, vegetables, and meat? Well, judging from the structure of the building where we found everything and also from some other data we'd need, you'd have probably guessed by now that our mustard jar was not an unusual item, but the sort of thing once bought at the general store. If the weathered old sign were still legible, we should note in our report that the jar came from the Goldfield Grocery.

Now, we need only note the depth of our find to complete the picture.

Depth: The relationship of depth, kind of soil, and age of the find is a technical issue best determined by archaeologists and anthropologists, but we can help by recording, if nothing more, how far down we found the bottle or jar. This will give us clues to age, and other information too. If all the mustard jars were found at only one level, the mustard may have been only a passing fad. But if they were found at different levels, we might surmise that the Louet Frères' mustard was the miners' favorite for many years. The depth at which the jar was found may also date it sufficiently for us to determine how French products got to the West, whether they traveled around the Cape, came by train from the East Coast (after about 1850), or were shipped through the Panama Canal (after 1914).

Here too might be noted other objects discovered with the jar, which could reveal that its purchaser, for example, was not a wealthy mine owner, but Thaddeus Cochran, a mechanic who fixed mining machinery and wagons—all going to prove how egalitarian were American tastes.

From just a few simple, non-technical observations and a very few minutes of recording, then, we've been able to place a little mustard jar into the context of American history. A distillation of similar reports by hundreds, maybe thousands of historians and collectors could result in whole new chapters in the history of commerce, glass manufacturing, and the American dinner table.

*   *   *

The method for ensuring that each and every artifact recovered is accompanied by a complete record of its discovery is surprisingly simple and costs almost nothing. We need just a few things:

A clipboard
Field report cards (shipping tags are good to use)
A pencil
Paper bags (various sizes)
A cardboard or wooden box to carry bagged finds

A full recording usually can't be completed at the site, so it's absolutely imperative that the artifact and its *field report* stay together at each and every step along the way. Here's a foolproof method of accomplishing that.

After uncovering a bottle, leave it in position until you've measured its depth and recorded this and the basic site location on a field report card. Then carefully remove the bottle—do not attempt to clean it at this point—and place it in a paper bag with its field report card attached if possible (which you can do, for example, if you use shipping tags for cards). Place the bag in your carrying box. Just repeat this step for each bottle you find, placing each bottle in its own bag.

If the bottle is broken, remove it embedded in its clump of soil, making sure you have all the pieces, and place the whole thing in a larger bag if necessary. Don't think that because a bottle is broken it is less valuable; it may be the one of a kind you've been hoping for.

If you've recovered a pile of bottles in a cellar or refuse pit, you may want to make a photographic record of the site before removing the bottle, especially if it is within or near an old foundation, the cellar walls, or perhaps is still on a dusty shelf. Again, photographs of the site could be valuable in determining the origin and use of the bottle. For example, after consulting an old map and photographs later, you may discover that what you thought to be just a refuse heap was actually the site of a drugstore or even a glasshouse. And whenever the site is to be destroyed or built over, photographic recording of the site is a must.

When your photographs are taken and your finds have been properly marked and bagged, take the artifacts home for inspection and cleaning. To make sure that bottle and description do not get separated, work with only one find at a time. Carefully inspect the bottle, noting if the glass is cracked or decaying. Cleaning bottles in good condition is usually just a matter of washing them under running water in a plastic dishpan (so you can't drop the bottle in the sink) and removing caked soil with a soft brush (an old toothbrush or fingernail brush works fine). Bottles found in salt water should be washed with particular thoroughness because any salts remaining will destroy the surface. If you suspect that the bottle is cracked,

---

GLASS BOTTLES. To be sold by *Jonathan Williams*, on the south-side of the Town Dock, near the Stamp Office; all sorts of Glass Bottles, by large or small quantities, Case and Pickle Bottles from one quart to a gallon; quart and pint Black Bottles by the Gross, Glasses for Chymists, and Window Glasses of different sizes. [*Boston Gazette*, August 23, 1756]

NEW JERSEY GLASS MANUFACTORY. The proprietors of the New-Jersey Manufactory have on hand for sale on reasonable terms, the following articles of Glass-Ware viz:

Retorts and receivers, tincture bottles, Snuff and mustard bottles, Pocket, quart and two quart farmers' bottles, Claret and lavender bottles, Vials assorted, from half ounce to 8 ounces. Orders received for any of the above kinds of Glass, by Levi Garret, no 120, Fourth Front-street, Philadelphia, and the proprietors Woodbury, Gloucester county, N. Jersey. Heston & Carpenter. [*Mercantile Advertiser*, December 6, 1799]

GREEN GLASS. — Imported by George Ball. . . .

Green Glass
Gallon square bottles,
Two quart ditto,
Pint ditto,
Pint and half pint flasks,
Ink bottles,
Blue, oval and round salt lining,
Ditto white   ditto
One penny per pound for broken white flint Glass. [*The New-York Journal or the General Advertiser*, August 3, 1775]

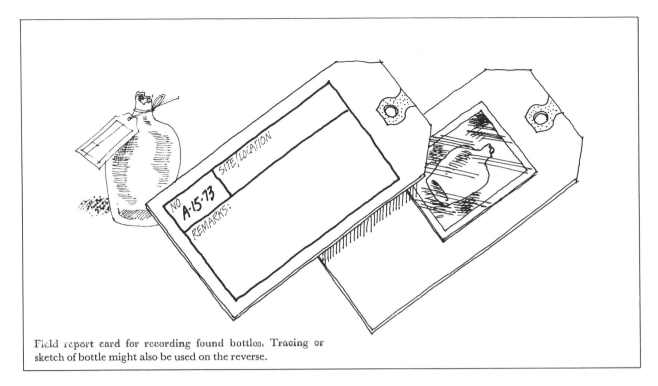

Field report card for recording found bottles. Tracing or sketch of bottle might also be used on the reverse.

place it in a strainer for washing. This way, if the dirt is actually holding the bottle together, you can catch the pieces as the dirt is washed away. Each piece, just like an intact bottle, should be dried and then, for safe keeping, returned to the bag.

Some bottles you find will not be in good condition. Bottles that have been submerged in water or exposed to the sun for a long time are often decayed. Decayed bottles flake and chip, or in advanced stages turn to powder, and must receive special attention. You begin, as always, with a careful washing. What you do next depends on the bottle's condition. Where decay is not too severe, the bottle should be upended on a peg and painted with clear epoxy varnish. In more advanced stages of decay, the bottle could require soaking in epoxy varnish or even in a laboratory preparation. If such a preparation is necessary you should consult more expert advice, perhaps from the preparator at a local museum. (If expert advice is not available, see "The Artifacts: Treatment, Study, and Storage," in Ivor Noël Hume's *Historical Archaeology*. Hume also offers valuable information on gluing together broken glass and pottery.)

After washing and, if necessary, varnishing, the next step is to number each bottle and to write the same number on the field report card. Once this is done, the bottle can be separated from its record card: the card can be filed, and the bottle can be moved about.

You can devise your own numbering system, or consult a local museum and see how the museum does it, but, in any case, the purpose of the number is simply to keep track of field reports and artifacts. One method consists of assigning a letter to each site and then numbering each bottle found there: A-1; A-2; A-3. Another is to add your initials and the year, A-1-DW75, indicating that this is bottle 1, from site A, excavated by DW (me, in this case) in '75.

This number is then inked onto the bottle with india ink and a fine quill pen, is allowed to dry, and is then covered with clear nail polish. If the surface of the bottle won't take the ink, cover a small area with clear nail polish, let it dry, and then ink on the number, finishing up with another coat of nail polish. For dark bottles you can use opaque white ink. Be sure to record the bottle number on the field report card.

Photographing Bottles

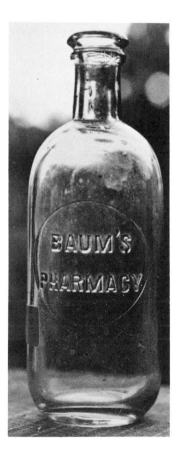

I found that the best way to photograph bottles that you've collected is to place them in a bright, sunny window, on the sill, or better yet on a little shelf, positioning each one so that the lettering and decorations show up clearly. Then get as close as you can to each bottle so that it is as large as can be in your finder and take the picture with the light coming through the glass. That's how I took these pictures.

Finally, bottles may be photographed, traced, drawn, and even "copied" on a Xerox machine as part of the recording process. A simple tracing on the back of the field report card can help you later to compare and classify bottles by shape or size. Photographs provide more information about color, patina, texture, and inscriptions; and small contact prints can be made inexpensively for gluing to the card. Getting the proper lighting for photographing bottles is tricky, and each specimen will require some experimentation, particularly to bring out raised or incised lettering on the bottle's surface. Generally, the lighting should come through the bottle either from behind and through the lettering or from below. Photographed in a dark or dim room with the bottle up against the window, the raised lettering will be sharply delineated. Opaque or dark bottles will have to be surface lighted, the light striking the bottle at an angle which best emphasizes the raised lettering. If none of this works because the lettering is worn, a simple rubbing using a dark crayon and ordinary paper can bring up the impressed or raised lettering.

Completed, the field report card becomes a valuable recording and research tool. Even though your fragile and bulky collection of bottles and jars can't be shipped around the country from collector to collector, the field report cards can be easily copied (six on an 8½-by-11-inch sheet) and made available to historians, collectors, and museums anywhere, thus allowing many people to examine and use the information.

*　　　*　　　*

How can you use these cards? You might, for example, want to classify your bottles, and cards are certainly easier than bottles to sort and classify. One way you might want to classify the bottles is by their contents—wines and whiskeys, medicines, foods, cosmetics, household items. Groupings of this sort will enable you to make some generalizations about the most popular uses of glass bottles and jars.

Collectors of bottles from mining camps, for example, have discovered that purchases of drugs and medicines far exceeded the purchase of liquor, revealing either real health problems in the camps or the existence of hypochondria as a trait in the early American character. Every kind of nostrum imaginable was bought by the thousands in mining towns.

For muscles:
HAMLIN'S WIZARD OIL
MEXICAN MUSTANG
DR. H. MCLEAN'S
KIKAPOO INDIAN OIL

For the stomach:
ENO'S FRUIT SALTS
LAXOL
NAU'S DISPEPSIA REMEDY
PEPTO-MANGIN
DR. D. JANES TONIC VERMIFUGE
MULFORD'S LAXATIVE SALTS OF FRUIT

For the lungs:
DR. SYKE'S CATARRH CURE
DR. JAYNE'S EXPECTORANT
GIRAFFE BRAND TONSILINE
DR. SETH ARNOLD'S COUGH KILLER
FORCE'S ASTH-MANNA
SCHLENK'S PULMONIC SYRUP
SHILOH'S CONSUMPTION CURE

For chills and fevers:
GROVE'S TASTELESS CHILL TONIC
FEVER AND AGUE ANTIDOTE
DR. KENNEDY'S RHEUMATIC DISSOLVANT
DR. MILES RHEUMATIC BLOOD PURIFYER
LORD'S OPODILLAC

For pain:
KING OF PAIN
BROMO-CAFFEINE
DR. MCMUNN'S ELIXER OF OPIUM
BURNETT'S COCAINE

For the kidneys and liver:
RADWAY'S READY RELIEF
EXTRACT OF SMARTWEED
DR. KILNER'S SWAMP ROOT LIVER REMEDY
LASH'S KIDNEY AND LIVER BITTERS
DR. SANFORD'S LIVER INVIGORATOR

For the eyes:
DR. THOMPSON'S EYE WATER
DR. DICKEY'S OLD RELIABLE EYE WATER

For the hair:
FRANK MILLER'S CROWN DRESSING
PARKER'S HAIR BALSAM
HASWELL'S WITCH HAZEL CREME
WILLIAM'S BRILLIANTINE HAIR VIGOR
BARRY'S TRICOPHEROUS FOR THE SKIN AND HAIR

Or, for that "rundown feeling":
BALSAM OF LIFE
GOLDEN MEDICAL DISCOVERY
LYDIA PINKHAM'S VEGETABLE COMPOUND
HERBINE
W. H. BULL'S HERBS AND IRON
CELERY COMPOUND
OREGON KIDNEY TEA
DR. SHOOP'S FAMILY MEDICINE

This wasn't a new quirk in the American mentality, this weakness for drugs and cures. It began long ago, as shown in an apothecary's notice in the *Virginia Gazette* for April 4, 1766, announcing to the apothecary's customers what he had just received from England.

. . . large and genuine assortment of DRUGS and MEDICINES, among which are fine Peruvian bark, ipecacuanha, India and Russia rhubarb, jalap, Glauber and Epsom salts, camphire, saffron, antimony, saltpeter, borax, calomel, red precipitate, quicksilver, crucus of antimony, Venice treacle and turpentine, gentian, orange peel, juniper berries, camomile flowers,

sarsaparilla, China root, aloes, Spanich flies, balsam capivi, lucatelli, Peru, tolu, sulphur, &c . . . Florence and palm oil, mercurial and other ointments, plaisters, Bateman's drops, Anderson's pills, British oil, Spuire's and Daffy's elixir, Godfrey's cordial, Stoughtone's bitters, Turlington's balsam of life . . .

This is a chapter on American life we didn't come across in school, and there are others that bottle history will help you discover for yourself. If you've done a good job of recording information on your field report cards, it should be possible to discover all manner of things about our past, particularly if you have an opportunity to share your finds with those of museums and other collectors. But regardless of how you decide to use the information you've found, these suggestions for recording will help you to get the most out of your collecting and turn just collecting into a valuable historical project.

*   *   *

Now that you've begun thinking about and looking at bottles and, perhaps, even begun collecting them, you're probably wondering if there's any way to tell the age of a particular vessel by looking at it. In some rare instances, the bottle will carry a date, but, unfortunately, such dates might refer to the date of the bottle, or to the date of its contents, or perhaps to the first year the contents were made. The date on a wine bottle is more than likely a vintage year.

One element that can help us to date wine bottles in particular is shape, and you might compare your bottle to the type series of bottles from 1660 to 1850 shown on page 133. The earliest bottles were of dark green glass, blown in the simple shape of a large bubble on a long neck and pushed in slightly at the base so that they would stand. The changes over the years are mainly in the shape of the bubble, the depth of the kick-up base, and the shape of the string rim at the top of the neck.

Dating by shape is not entirely dependable, however, because there is always the possibility that a bottle made in the 1880s was a copy of an earlier style. We do have a more dependable way of dating bottles, and it's also quite simple. We can usually determine the approximate age of a bottle by the manufacturing techniques used in its production. There is, of course, overlap, when the old technique was still being used at the same time that a new method was gaining in popularity, but we're interested in an approximate date anyway, so we shouldn't let things like that bother us.

The next page shows some of the steps in the evolution of bottlemaking, giving the dates when processes began to be used and when special features like stoppers and lettered panels first appeared. The most important single clue, particularly for old bottles, is the presence or absence and the position and number of mold marks on the bottle. When molten glass is blown inside a mold, it picks up the surface of the mold, including imperfections and the seams where the sections of the mold come together. On the glass, the seams become raised lines, called—for obvious reasons—mold marks. Any time molds are used to produce bottles, mold lines appear, and, conversely, if no lines or impressions appear on the bottle, then it must have been free blown, without a mold.

◆ ● ◆ ● ◆

How Old Is That Bottle?

Until ca. 1790. Free-blown bottles are asymmetrical and lopsided. The surface is smooth and shiny and without any impressed designs or lettering. Since no mold was used, such bottles have, of course, no mold marks, and any design would have to have been engraved or etched into their surface.

1790 to 1810. The first mold-made bottles. The body was formed in a one-piece dip mold and then the neck and shoulders were formed by hand, resulting in a horizontal mold mark around the bottle where the shoulders start. These bottles usually have a pontil mark, a spot of rough glass on the base indicating that a pontil rod had been attached there to hold the bottle while the blowpipe was struck off. The surface of such a bottle has a hammered-metal look.

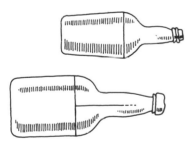

1810. Bottles blown in three-part molds—a one-piece body mold and a two-piece hinged mold for forming the shoulder and neck. The surface of this bottle, too, has a hammered-metal look. The lip of the bottle was hand-finished throughout the 1800s.

Also in 1810. Nicholas Appert discovered that the ferments that cause food spoilage could be neutralized by heating foods and packing them in glass jars and bottles with wired cork stoppers.

1815–1870. Hundreds of historical flasks were produced during this period; they can be grouped by the images stamped on them: (1) Masonic (the jars continued until only the 1830s); (2) designs and emblems depicting economic life; (3) portraits of national heroes with designs depicting their deeds; and (4) portraits of presidential candidates and the emblems and slogans of their political campaigns.

1825. Octagonal medicine bottles first appeared, with oval bottles appearing somewhat later.

Ca. 1850. Two-piece mold begins to replace three-piece bottle mold. The mold lines—two of them, one on each side—run vertically from the base of the bottle to the neck, where they fade out. This happens when the upper neck is reheated and more glass is added to form the lip. These bottles don't have the hammered metal look of the earlier bottles because they are made in a different kind of mold, a chilled iron mold. There is no pontil mark on the base from this time on because of the newly invented snap case which holds the bottle without leaving any marks. So, if the bottle has two-piece mold marks and a hand-finished lip but no pontil mark, it was made in a snap case.

1858. Mason jar patented. After this date, almost any domestic sites yielding bottle collections will certainly include one or more Mason jars with their zinc lids.

1860s. First glass kerosene lamps appear.

1867. Earliest appearance of square and rectangular bottles with recessed panels on one or more sides listing in raised letters the contents, the name of the manufacturer (Frank Miller's Crown Dressing), and sometimes the city and state where it was bottled. These bottles were used mostly for patent medicines. Sometimes the initials of the bottle manufacturer appear impressed on the base.

1860–1900. The time of the great bitters (patent medicine) fad promising cures for everything.

After 1868. **Period of the figure bottles, such as the one above.**

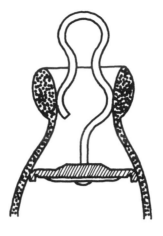

1872. Patent issued for the "pop" bottle closure, the Hutchinson stopper which sealed the bottle from the inside. To open the stopper the iron loop emerging from the bottle was struck, forcing the stopper down out of the neck into the bottle and producing a loud pop.

1881. The first semi-automatic bottle machine, producing bottles that can be identified by mold lines running vertically from the base up to the lip. Since the machine was not widely used there are comparatively few such bottles.

1882. The familiar lightning stopper with its rubber gasket and iron bail was patented in the United States by Henry Putnam. The stopper had earlier appeared in Europe.

1880s. First milk bottles.

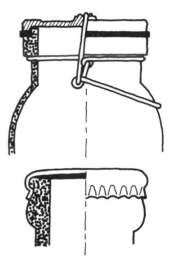

1892. Patent issued for crown bottle caps, which are still used today.

1903. Michael Owens awarded patent for the first fully automatic bottle machine, producing bottles recognizable by the continuous mold lines running up the sides and into the top of the lip.

Historical Flask Designs

Aggies, Alleys, Mibbs, and Immies

As children most of us were caught up in the romance of glass—in the world of purees, glassies, clayeys, and pee-wees—in the magic of marbles. Just when American children began playing marbles is uncertain, but by 1740 large numbers of marble and limestone marbles were being imported from Germany, then the only producer of marbles for export. Since that time at least, marbles have been a part of our childhood and like tops and skate keys can evoke waves of nostalgia at their very mention. Here's a brief history of marbles in America which also serves as a dating key to any that you might find underfoot:

1600s. Marbles produced in Holland and England probably came across the Atlantic with the first colonists.

1740s. First period of German marble exports to America. These marbles were of calcareous stone, such as limestone and marble, with diameters ranging from one centimeter to a little over three centimeters, usually brown, gray, and bluish-purple. Early marbles were smooth but often had small, flat facets probably resulting from the grinding operation.

1840s–1850s. Period of the crockery marble made of clay glazed light brown or blue. Marks in the glaze were caused by marbles touching one another and other things in the kiln while being fired. These marbles are sometimes referred to as "Bennington" marbles, the result of an early (incorrect) notion that they might have been produced at a Bennington, Vermont, stoneware company.

1860s–1880s. German agate marble production and export reached its peak during this period. Agates came in an infinite variety of natural colors and bands as well as in colors produced by artificial dyeing.

1884. First commercial production of clay marbles in America. These were usually a single opaque color—blue, pink, purple, green, white—and ranged from one centimeter to two and a half centimeters in diameter. Some white clay marbles with painted concentric rings have been dated to this period, and a few with mixed colors.

1880s. First commercially produced handmade glass marbles in the United States, manufactured in Iowa and Massachusetts. Handmade marbles will have two spots at opposite points on the surface where the finished marble was twisted and cut off from the glass rod on which it was made. American handmade glass marbles were clear, often with different colors of glass swirling and spiraling through the center. Glass marbles were also being imported from Germany during this period, and the marbles of the two countries are indistinguishable.

1901. First American marble-making machine.

1905. Large quantities of machine-made glass marbles produced in a vast array of designs and colors. Up to about 1926, marbles show evidence of grinding and cutting and were opaque, whereas handmade marbles were clear.

1926. Introduction of clear marbles containing images of comic strip characters against an opaque background, made by the Peltier Glass Company of Ottawa, Illinois. By now marble making had become something of an industry, with most of the marbles coming from plants in West Virginia where the ingredients—sand, soda ash, and natural gas for the firing ovens—were plentiful. Along with Peltier of Ottawa, Illinois, a host of companies in West Virginia—Champion Agate of Pennsboro; Heaton Agate of Cairo; Marble King of Paden City; Vitro-Agate of Parkersburg; and Master Glass of Clarksburg—produced marbles at the rate of about two hundred a minute, or three hundred and fifty million a year!

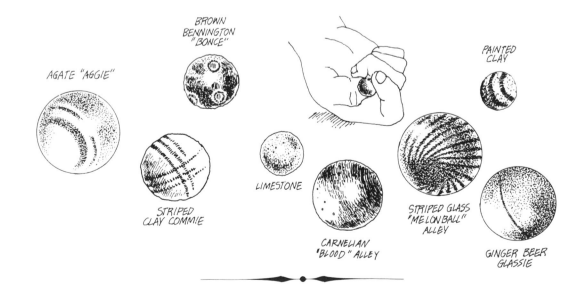

AGATE "AGGIE"

BROWN BENNINGTON "BONCE"

PAINTED CLAY

STRIPED CLAY COMMIE

LIMESTONE

CARNELIAN "BLOOD" ALLEY

STRIPED GLASS "MELON BALL" ALLEY

GINGER BEER GLASSIE

CHAPTER 8

Historical Buildings

This chapter, too, is about collecting and, in very small and personal ways, about preserving an architectural presence so familiar and so commonplace that we've perhaps no real idea of how much of our history and our essence is contained there. It's a kind of collecting that could conceivably take us anywhere in the country, to any one of thousands of cities, small towns, and rural settlements, and yet begin as close as our next look out our apartment window or the first step out the front door. Just outside my front door? Literally, but it is certainly understandable if you've not noticed what is out there. Architecture is not something we learn about through the usual channels of education in America. Buildings have been assigned a passive role in our history books; they are merely the settings, the inconspicuous props for historical events and personages. Nor are architects and builders made familiar to us, but are usually excluded from even those perfunctory chapters, those few pages conceded by most authors to inventors and craftsmen (local histories, though, are a notable exception). So we may not be really comfortable

with architecture, may never have learned to relate to buildings as we might have to art, or music, or automobile engines. We may have just relegated architecture to the realm of the mysterious and esoteric or, worse, the mundane. This chapter assumes, then, the need for some help in relating to buildings and offers some suggestions for approaching them, looking at them, seeing what it is about them that is unique and what is traditional. We'll begin with just seeing and becoming aware, collecting with our eyes, and go on to collecting with camera and pencils and paper and a few simple techniques—ready for the surprise that awaits us somewhere at the next turn of a corner.

Somewhere down the line, the ancestors of all of us came from someplace else, and nowhere is this story of America's cosmopolitan and immigrant beginnings told with more eloquence than on the faces of our buildings. The New England houses recalling medieval Europe and England, the Georgian and Revival mansions of the Old South, the solid brick apartments of Eastern and Midwestern cities mirroring the burgher dwellings of northern

Europe in the late nineteenth and early twentieth centuries, the Spanish overtones of the Southwest and California, the transplanted styles of the Mediterranean, and even China and Japan—tell the story of where Americans come from. And the wide variety of building materials—brick, stone, all kinds of woods, stucco, wood frame, steel and concrete, shingle, adobe, wattle, tile, plaster, marble, iron, glass —rare to be found all in one country—reveals a wealth in not only natural resources but in international talents and skills. The fact is that only a few cities around the world display the variety of architectural styles to be seen in almost any city in the United States.

And yet, for all the durability of architecture, no part of our heritage is more in danger of disappearing forever: old books and works of art we store with reverence in libraries and museums, but every year we let thousands of old buildings, each contributing in manifold ways to the color and texture of our lives, fall unnoticed before progress. Perhaps we need to recall once again how it all began and how much we are a part of the places and dwellings in which we've lived and how much they are part of us.

*   *   *

There was never really an American style of architecture. Even a visitor to the American colonies found a rich patchwork of building styles, in this case from all over continental Europe and the British Isles, that marks our cities and towns today. And these styles reflected the heritage of the people who made them.

The New England and Southern colonies from the very first (the early and mid-seventeenth century) were settled largely by the English, a fact reflected in the colonies' buildings, with their hanging upper stories, the angular roof lines, and thatch, all characteristic of medieval English architecture. Later, in the eighteenth century, public buildings and big houses were patterned after both the work of English architects like Inigo Jones, John Hawks, and Christopher Wren and the formal, balanced Georgian style which developed under the four Georges of England (who ruled from the early eighteenth century into the nineteenth).

In the Middle Atlantic colonies, on the other hand, the earliest traveler found a very different kind of architecture. To what is now New York, New Jersey, and Pennsylvania had come settlers of many nationalities—Dutch, German,

Swedish, French (and English), among others —who had each constructed buildings the way they knew how, in other words, in the way it was done in their homelands. As early as 1628 the traditional Dutch brick houses, like those seen in the old cities of the Netherlands today, began to appear along the Eastern coast, some even built of bricks imported from Holland. Swedish colonists settling in New Jersey and Pennsylvania, along the Delaware River, brought with them the house they knew best, one that also could be built from America's bountiful forests—the log cabin. Today we associate the log cabin with frontier life; it has become, to us, the symbol of the frontier spirit. The log cabin was so simple in construction that frontiersmen could build one as a house or barn in only a few days, and so it was an ideal architectural form for people moving westward through the thick forests and out onto the plains.

The simplicity and sturdiness of the first Colonial buildings are so pleasing to our eyes that we tend not to realize that they were built not by skilled specialists or architects but by the families who first lived in them. No one among the early arrivals at Jamestown was an architect, at least not in the sense that we use that word now. Some of these people learned how to build out of necessity or found building help among their townsfolk, for if a house was not built, there was just no other place in which to stay. Well, almost none—the obituary of Bartholomew Green, printer of the *Boston News-Letter*, reports that *his* father, Capt. Samuel Green, arrived in Charlestown in 1630 and "upon their first coming ashore both he and several others were for some time glad to lodge in empty casks to shelter them from the Weather, for want of Housing."

Practically speaking, then, everyone in the new American wilderness was both architect and builder, conceiving his (or her) own design, clearing the land, laying out the foundation, and hewing the timbers from the nearby forests. The earliest efforts of the architect-builders of New England reflect their principal concern, to gain protection as quickly as possible from the long New England winters. Aside from a carpenter, stonemason, or bricklayer who might be available, the work crew was composed of everyone in the community, children and adults, who all contributed to the task whatever skills each possessed. In a way, architects were not needed. These first New England houses of rough timbers, with walls

Mr. Zenger: I am a Carpenter by Trade and can read English, therefore I some Times borrow your paper. My fellow Trades Men say, that you are to print every Thing that is good and bad in the Country, and to reward all Men according to their Deserts. I hear that some Body has put a Clapper into the Fort Bell, and that it is to ring at Morning, Noon and Night, as in the old Times. I am heartily glad of it. It will produce a great Reformation. We shall breakfast, dine and sup, according to Rule and Compass, and know how to square our Work as in the Days of our Forefathers. I assure you, Mr. Zenger, that is a good deed, and ought not be slighted: Therefore I and the Rest of the Day Labourers in Town, intend very speedily to pay our Thanks to that worthy Artist, in a very Handsome address of which pray take Notice in your Papers. I am Bob Chizel. [The New-York Weekly Journal, January 7, 1733]

of wattle—interwoven twigs embedded in mud—and thatched roofs needed no designers or plans, for they were the very same kind of dwellings that had been built in England and Europe for centuries. The method of putting up such a building was common knowledge.

Eventually, however, there was some leisure and sufficient carpenters and craftsmen to enable those who wanted them to have houses in the new style—wood frame and clapboard. They hired a builder, but gave him no more information than the size and number of the rooms desired, plus anything special that might be needed in the way of a shop or storage place.

There were in America architects of sorts—that is, talented individuals who were skilled in the general techniques of the architect, though their training was informal. The usual way to become an architect was to return to continental Europe or England and work there for several years as an apprentice in the office of an architect or builder. Perhaps one's apprenticeship might even be with Christopher Wren, the Oxford professor of astronomy and the amateur architect who between 1670 and 1711 designed some of London's most beautiful buildings, including over fifty churches and numerous hospitals, libraries, theaters, and residences. (The work of Christopher Wren was so influential on early American architect-builders that one would almost think he had worked here.) The opportunity for training in the profession in America, however, was yet to come. In his *Notes on the State of Virginia* (1787) Thomas Jefferson spoke of architecture as being "one of the fine arts" and proposed the study of architecture as a part of the college curriculum. But this didn't take place for nearly another century, when the passage of the Morrill Land-Grant act made Jefferson's vision a reality and brought about America's first professional schools of architecture—Massachusetts Institute of Technology (1868), Cornell University (1870), and the University of Illinois (1871).

This informal architect-builder tradition of American architecture continued pretty much unchanged throughout the eighteenth and nineteenth centuries. Even the design and construction of large public buildings, like state

The drawings along the bottom of pages 147 through 169 comprise a brief history of American architecture from about 1680 to 1912, showing salient developments in construction and style. For dates and locations see the Table of Illustrations.

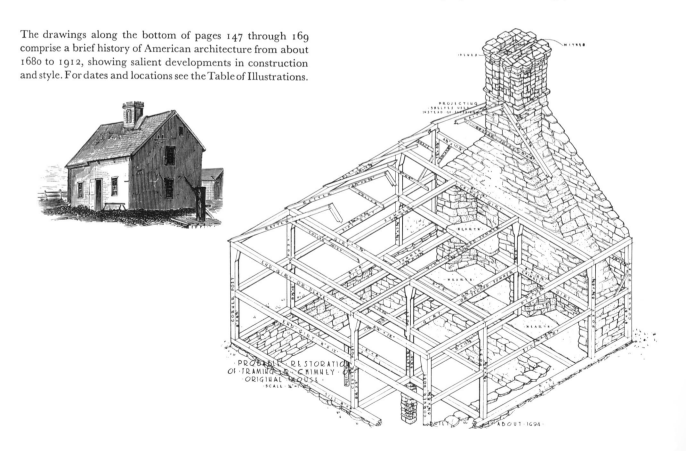

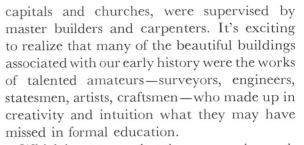

THE
Modern Builder's Assistant;
OR,
A CONCISE EPITOME
Of the Whole
SYSTEM of ARCHITECTURE;
IN WHICH
The various Branches of that excellent Study are efta-
blifh'd on the moft familiar Principles,
And rendered adequate to every Capacity ;
Being ufeful to the Proficient, and eafy to the Learner.
Divided into THREE PARTS.
CONTAINING
I. A Correct View of the FIVE ORDERS, explained in feveral Sheets
of Letter-Prefs.
II. Confifting of REGULAR PLANS, ELEVATIONS, and SECTIONS
of Houses, in the moft elegant and convenient Manner, either
for the Reception of Noblemen, Gentlemen or Tradefmen with
large or fmall Families, adapted to the Tafte of Town or Country.
To which PART is added,
A great Variety of other PLANS for Offices or Out-Houfes adjoining to
them of different Dimenfions for Domeftic Ufes ;
SUCH AS
KITCHENS, WASH-HOUSES, MALT-HOUSES, BAKE-HOUSES, BREW-HOUSES,
DAIRIES, VAULTS, STABLES, COACH-HOUSES, DOG-KENNELS, &c. &c.
Together with the
ESTIMATES of each DESIGN, and Proper INSTRUCTIONS
to the WORKMEN how to execute the fame.
III. Exhibiting (ornamental as well as plain) a Variety of CHIMNEY-
PIECES, WINDOWS, DOORS, SECTIONS of STAIR-CASES, ROOMS,
HALLS, SALOONS, &c. SKREENS for Rooms, alfo CIELINGS, PIERS,
and GATE-ROOFS, &c. &c.
The Whole beautifully Engraved on EIGHTY FIVE Folio Copper Plates,
From the DESIGNS of
William and *John Halfpenny,* Architects and Carpenters,
Robert Morris, Surveyor,
AND
T. Lightoler. Carver.

LONDON
Printed for JAMES RIVINGTON and J. FLETCHER in Pater-nofter Row, and
ROBERT SAYER oppofite Fetter-Lane, Fleet-Street.
MDCCLVII.

capitals and churches, were supervised by master builders and carpenters. It's exciting to realize that many of the beautiful buildings associated with our early history were the works of talented amateurs—surveyors, engineers, statesmen, artists, craftsmen—who made up in creativity and intuition what they may have missed in formal education.

Which is not to say that they were unlearned. Ideas for drawings, designs, and details were available to master builders in books fromEngland. Among the books advertised for sale by a printer in the May 13, 1760, edition of the *Boston News-Letter* as "importations in the last vessel from London" were Ware's *Paladio, or 4 Orders of Architecture,* Halfpenny's *Architecture,* Langley's *City and Country Builder's and Workman's Treasury of Designs, Twelve Designs for Country Houses,* and Price's *British Carpenter.* It's significant that these and many other European books on architecture were not exotic collectors' items in the American colonies but were available in large numbers and, what's more, were well known to builders and craftsmen.

*　　　　*　　　　*

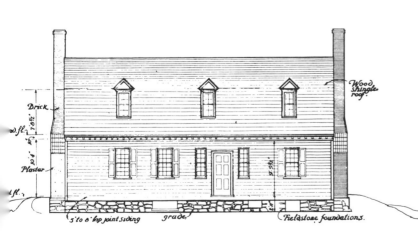

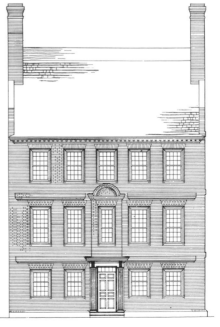

There's another source of information on early American building probably more readily available to the local historian who does not have access to a large library—the articles and particularly the advertisements in early newspapers and periodicals. Even the smallest library usually has back issues of local papers whose articles may include drawings and photographs of local buildings. From the ads come details of the life of early American craftsmen. This information, as we saw in an earlier chapter, is to be found in short, colorful autobiographies informing the reader of the craftsman's origin, his training, and even something of the circumstances of his arrival in America. Here's one story of a craftsman from Ireland:

The subscriber (with his wife) lately from Kilkenny in Ireland, and just arrived with Capt. Gifford from Bristol, by trade a bricklayer and mason, being indebted for his passage, to Capt. Gifford, £26 current money of New-York, is willing to enter into contract with any person who will pay the said money. . . . Patrick Blanchville [*New-York Journal or the General Advertiser*, June 2, 1768]

From other ads we get a detailed picture of all that went into a Colonial building—for example, this advertisement appearing in 1772:

WANTED, *For building a New Meeting-House in Brattle-Street, Boston, the materials following:*
Good stones for the Foundation and Cellar, Stones for two or three Courses above Ground, to be hammered to a good Face, each one Foot in height, and not less to go into the Wall. . . .

800 Thousand Bricks eight Inches long four wide and two thick, to be made of tough well-tempered Clay, and well burnt, one quarter Part of them to be struck in Sand for the outward Face of the Building.

Four Thousand Sand Bricks for outside Arches, nine Inches long four & half wide and two & half thick. . . .

Three hundred & thirty Hogsheads of the best Stone Lime.

Five Hundred Cart Loads of Sand of a good Grit and free from all Loom.

Oak Timber for the lower Floor of the proper Scantlings. . . .

Slate for the Roof.

Such Persons as incline to contract to supply the Materials abovementioned (all which must be such as shall be approved by the Committee and warranted good in their kind) are desired to write and seal up their Proposals (in which they are requested to describe the Quantity and Quality of the Articles they would supply them also the lowest Price for the Money) and deliver their Proposals at the Shop of Mr. Timothy Newell *in Dock Square, Boston, by the Eleventh Day of* March *next at farthest. . . .* [*Boston News-Letter*, February 20, 1772]

And we can even discover some of the very earliest of our building codes. Two ads, for example, from the 1770s describe what might be the earliest building materials codes on record.

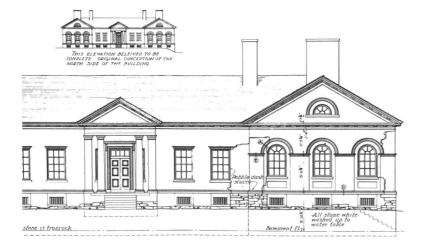

LUMBER INSPECTED—*Whereas a Law of the Corporation of the City of New York, has lately passed, to ascertain the Size, Dimensions, and Quality of Staves, Heading, Hoops, Boards, Timber, Shingles and Plank, which shall be brought to this City of New-York, for Sale, from and after the first Day of September, which will be in the Year 1770; Notice is hereby given, that we are appointed Measures and Inspectors of Timber, Plank, Boards, &c. and all Persons are desired to take Notice, that they are requir'd by the said Law, not to deliver to the Purchaser, any Plank, Timber, Boards or Shingles, before they are examined and measured. Isaac Chardavoyne, Francis Many, John Blank, Theop. Hardenbrook. [The New-York Journal or the General Advertiser, September 13, 1770]*

LAW FOR MAKING BRICKS—*We are desired to publish the following extract of a law of this colony, relative to the making of Bricks, passed the 19th June, in the year 1703; the regulation thereby directed, it is said, not being duly attended to.*

That no person or persons, shall make or suffer to [be] made, in any place or places within this colony, any bricks, or kiln of bricks, but such as shall be well and thoroughly burnt, and of the size and dimension following. That is to say, every brick to be and contain nine inches in length, four inches and one quarter of an inch in breadth, and two inches and one half inch in the thickness thereof, . . . [The New-York Gazette and the Weekly Mercury, April 6, 1772]

There is more in your own city's newspapers, but the most important record of the ingenuity of the early architect-builders is out there lining the streets of your town or city. They are works of art, folk art, and taken together they form a record of the country's changing architectural styles, the arrival in it of new immigrant populations, and the country's concepts of living spaces. History is where you find it, and for you it may begin the moment you step out your front door, go down the street a ways, and turn the corner.

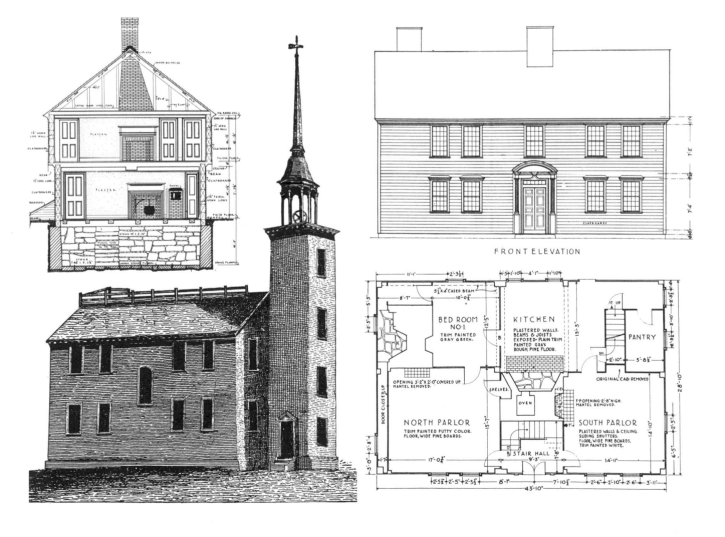

FRONT ELEVATION

Just becoming aware of the buildings around you for the first time gives you a sense of their being, for they are beings, you know—a sturdy, carefully fashioned barn; the Gothic Revival church down the street; apartments in an immigrant neighborhood whose rooms have heard dozens of languages; the school; an old spice mill—all have lives in memories and old photographs: the years before they were built (the land was pasture then), the work of their construction, the many businesses or families they sheltered, and their demise—all this clusters together as landmarks in a town's history and in the long memories of elder townsfolk. The Meetinghouse, Perry's Saloon, the public steam bath, Felix's Bakery ("good rolls and French bread"), the Hemingway house, the blacksmith's shop are the stage and sets on which a town's history has been played. They are "historical personages" as much as the mayor whose antics on the Fourth of July were the howl of 1906, the corner newspaper vendor, and the old folks who spent their days down at the bench on the courthouse lawn. Even after years of abandonment and abuse, the magic of an old building remains—and it is never stronger than when, as is happening more and more these days, it becomes the focus of a restoration project, which itself usually signals the rebirth of a community consciousness.

Houses and buildings are indeed very personal things, not at all the inanimate hulks we sometimes take them to be. They reflect in their design and materials the builder's craftsmanship and style as surely as does an old rocking chair or pewter candlestick. They reflect also an era of style, the work once done in the buildings, the size of the families which filled their rooms, even something of the aspirations, the dreams, and the flights of fancy of those who built them—all in a way very different from life today yet not difficult for us to understand.

You're probably not aware of it, but when a person walks down the street, particularly in the older downtown area, he or she seldom looks above street level. One's attention is usually fixed on the storefronts, doorways, and signs all along the street. Which is why architectural change usually occurs only at that level and why that is the location of the new things, the modern images of the city. But right above these new things is—the past.

Raising a Steeple

Ever lean way back to look up at an old church steeple or meeting-house spire and wonder just how its builders got it up there in the 1600s or 1700s? Steam power was unknown then, and the only motive power available was manpower or that of horses or oxen, yet they were able to lift heavy structural members thirty feet or more above the ground! Well, it appears that in Connecticut, at least, the method was to build the spire on the ground and then raise it in place. One eyewitness (1771) tells how "the steeple above the belfry was raised entire." Another tells us how the spire of Center Church on

New Haven Green was "built within the tower and then raised by windlass and tackle. I was a schoolboy at the time. It took about two hours, and went up beautifully." Although the exact details are not certain, here is an illustration and description of a method using "shears."

From the apex of the shears, guy lines "X" and "Z," extending to the ground, held it in position. The lower end of line "X," passed through the snatch block, was wound around a snubbing post. The lower end of "Z," after passing through a snatch-block, was fastened to a capstan. The spire, resting upon the ground, was

suspended at a point above its center of gravity, by means of a tackle and falls attached to the apex of the shears. This tackle was, as shown, connected with a windlass anchored to the ground. Now, by operating the windlass, the spire was raised from position "A" to "B." Then by operating the capstan, line "Z" was taken up, and "X" paid out, elevating the shears and spire to position "C." It was then a simple matter to lower the spire into place. [J. Frederick Kelly, "Raising Connecticut Meeting Houses," in *Old-Time New England*, July 1936]

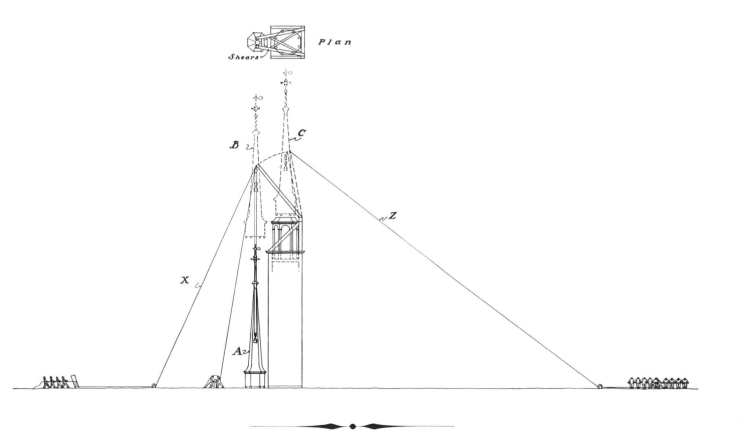

Nailing Down a Date

Dating well-preserved old buildings may require some detective work, but dating the few foundation stones and rotted timbers which are often all that remains of a timeworn structure requires the eye of an archaeologist. Though it might seem hopeless at first, clues to the age of a ramshackle farmhouse, barn, or cabin usually survive weathering and fire and even human carelessness. The most important of these possible clues are nails. Once hand-wrought and now machine-produced by the millions, the different ways that nails have been made over the years provide us with a guide to making some fairly accurate guesses as to when they were used.

First, you should be aware that there are three kinds of nails: wrought nails, cut nails, and wire nails. Wrought nails were handmade from rectangular strips of soft iron—called nail rods—which were about a quarter of an inch thick and several feet long. The flat sides of wrought nails and their uneven heads were rough, showing the nailer's and smithy's hammer blows. (This "imperfection," by the way, gave these old nails a strong clench.) They were used in house construction up until about 1800, when they were replaced by machine-cut nails. This was about ten years after Jacob Perkins of Newburyport, Massachusetts, was granted a patent for a machine that cut and put a head on nails in one operation.

After 1800, houses were built with cut nails. These were also rectangular but formed in a cutter which sliced off slivers from a piece of iron plate, the tapered cut producing both the shank and the point of the nail. If you look closely you'll be able to tell the difference between wrought nails and these earliest cut nails and, thus, the age of the structure in which you found them. Wrought nails taper toward a point on all four sides, while cut nails are tapered on two opposite sides, the two parallel sides being part of the surfaces of the plate from which the nail was cut. Also, instead of hammered surfaces, cut nails have smooth sides which, upon closer inspection, show the striations caused by the downward slice of the blade. After the establishment of two cut nail factories in Philadelphia in 1797 the cheaper cut nail replaced the hand-wrought nail completely.

Cut nails also come in two kinds, from two distinct periods of nail manufacture. Cut nails manufactured from the late 1790s until about 1825 have very irregular heads, with several uneven surfaces which are actually facets formed by the blows of a hammer. But if you find a cut nail with a level top showing none of the crudeness of a hammered head, then it was made after 1825 when machinery was perfected to head nails with a single blow. (Note: cut nails are still manufactured today, but have slightly rounded heads.)

Wire nails—so called because they are cut from spooled lengths of wire—first appeared around the middle of the nineteenth century and soon replaced the flat-sided cut nail, allowing us to set the earliest date of a house built during the 1800s.

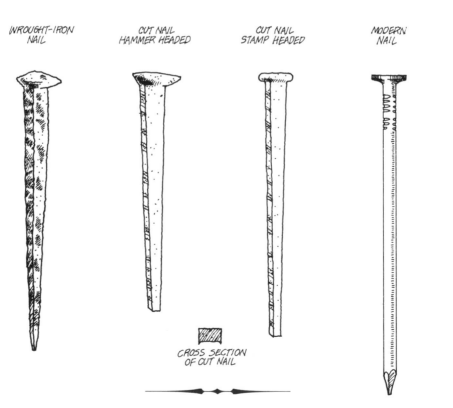

WROUGHT-IRON NAIL   CUT NAIL HAMMER HEADED   CUT NAIL STAMP HEADED   MODERN NAIL

CROSS SECTION OF CUT NAIL

The next time you go out for a walk, look up. Ignore what is happening on the street and concentrate on the upper parts of the buildings from about the second story up to the roof. My guess is that you'll be surprised, for here above street level will be another world, a view of the street you are on and the buildings you are looking at as they would have appeared thirty years, fifty years, even a century ago! You'll see until-then unnoticed ornamentation, tiles, a variety of brick and stone patterns, elegant windows, cornices.

Just recently I looked up at a building I had walked past almost daily for twelve years, vaguely aware of its ordinary aluminum and glass front. What I saw now was a building put up some time in the thirties in the Moderne style with all its geometric designs and with some of the most elegant iron work I had ever seen on a building. I became almost dangerous to my fellow pedestrians as I continued to wander around with my eyes on the upper stories of the buildings around me. Later, I began photographing these upper stories with something of the feeling that I was in a time warp, projected out of the present into the 1930s or, in some cases, the early 1900s. And then it happened: just a few steps off of the main business street I found myself in the last century gazing at the date 1887.

Recording such buildings—like the other forms of recording we discuss in this book—is another step in the work of keeping something of the past so that we may better understand whence we've come. Photographs and drawings and sketches of buildings, just like the pictures of our family and ancestors, allow us glimpses into the past that really are unattainable any other way. The visual depiction of the form and style of old buildings, their character, their setting in or near the city or on a farm, the interplay of textures on old and weathered materials, the intricate architectural details, the many origins of American architecture provide a background for the words of oral and written histories. Pictures of the buildings that served as the backdrop to our ancestors' daily life make our perception of that life just that much clearer.

There are sometimes more compelling reasons for photographing buildings. We may want to "preserve" something from the past that is about to fall before the wrecking ball and bulldozer. Sadly, photographs can be all we have left of entire eras in a town's life. Or we may need a "before" or "as is" record of a structure about to enjoy restoration, but which will be significantly altered in the process. For example, the structure might need to be changed—so interior details like beautiful but rickety old staircases must go. Or perhaps exposed construction and engineering details (plumbing or old gas fixtures) will be covered. More technically, photographs provide a convenient and accurate way to measure dimensions that we cannot reach from the ground. In the past buildings were "scaled" from measured drawings—that is, architectural scale

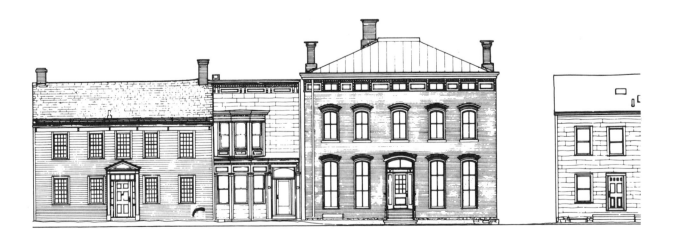

drawings made to record exact dimensions. But if scale drawings are not already available, photographs may be used instead (the dimensions are marked off on the print with an architect's scale or proportional dividers).

We could also use another kind of image, historical images—the snapshots or official photographs made at the dedication or opening (you know the picture: the mayor in his handlebar mustache cutting a ribbon or digging the first shovelful), as well as the architect's photographs and drawings. A photograph recording the laying of a church's cornerstone will help pin down elusive dates or may even help identify the oldest building in town.

The photographic recording of buildings, then, is an important part of what we have set out to do, and here's how such recordings are made.

*   *   *

The photographic recording of historical buildings requires above all else considerable care and attention to detail. Just as in copying photographs, a simple, inexpensive camera can usually do the job, especially if we make the most of its possibilities. As far as I can tell there is no correlation between the price of one's camera and the aesthetic quality of one's pic-

tures, but there are some technical operations that the simple camera, with its single shutter speed and lens aperture, just cannot perform. Most buildings, it is true, are easy enough to photograph with a simple camera—they're always outside, they don't move a lot, and if the day is too cloudy when you want to take the picture, you can always come back. But it is also true that a camera with a wider range of adjustments is sometimes preferable for architectural photography. All of the suggestions in this section, whether for a simple or a more complex camera, can help you understand the basics of recording historical buildings, even if you do your recording with pencil or watercolor sketches.

Although the basic principles of photography—concerning camera operation, film, and exposure—apply here as elsewhere, architectural photography, like copying work, presents some special problems and considerations, particularly if you intend to produce enlargements for local history groups and museums (or you want to record a local building officially with the Historic American Buildings Survey).

The aim of the photographer-historian is no different from that of any other historian—to

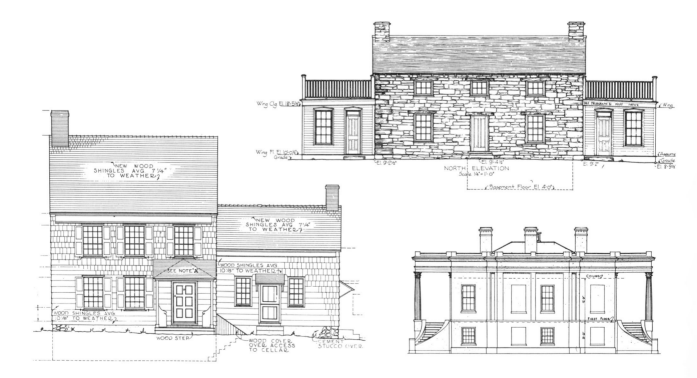

achieve the clearest and most accurate images possible. The bases of good architectural photography are a keen eye and some feeling for structures, style, and materials. Architectural images (1) should be free of distortion; (2) should render architectural details and textures clearly and with the utmost acuteness; and (3) should make the experience of viewing the prints or slides as much like actually seeing, walking around, and being inside the structure as possible. As an inducement to be as accurate as possible, it sometimes helps to assume (alas, the assumption in certain cases soon becomes a reality) that the building you are photographing will be destroyed moments after you've taken your last photograph. When the building is leveled, all anyone will know about the structure is what is on your negatives! In any case, structures eventually will be destroyed, if not deliberately, then by time along with the elements, and the recorder of buildings no less than the recorder of human beings has a tremendous responsibility.

THE NEGATIVE

It all begins with producing high-quality negatives. What's more, this is *all* you need to concern yourself with at this point. Don't worry about what you'll do with the negatives after you have them; it is only important that you indeed have them. We seldom set about photographing historical subjects knowing exactly how the pictures will be used. Perhaps they will just remain negatives, or little images on proof sheets, or will be used to make prints no larger than a post card. Then again, they may ultimately make 8-by-10, or 11-by-14, or 16-by-20 prints, or even wall murals several feet on a side for a museum display. *But what is essential now is that you produce negatives capable of doing any or all of these things a month or fifty years from now.* Just remember: it costs no more to produce a good negative than a bad one! Moreover, all you need in order to preserve a beautiful old house or store forever is within any budget—a few rolls or sheets of film, some inexpensive chemicals, and a very few simple pieces of darkroom equipment (most or all of which is right there in your kitchen).

A good negative is a good negative, of course, but a good negative of a building involves some special considerations, among them perspective control, scale, definition, and selecting of views. We'll take a close look at each and at a few other general considerations (keeping records of your exposures, developing the film to standards of archival permanence) and some special problems.

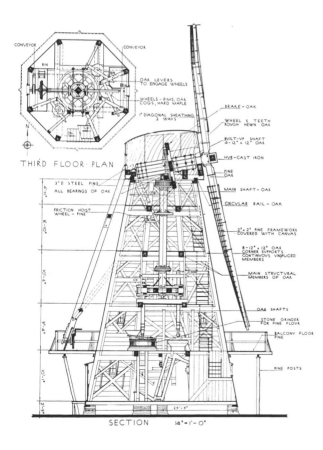

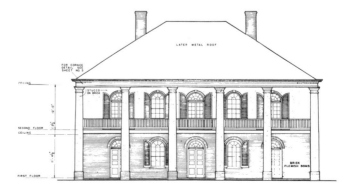

PERSPECTIVE

Distortion in architectural photography usually results from the illusion that parallel lines
appear to converge as they recede from the
viewer. Let's look at a problem of trying to
photograph a tall structure close up—that
beautiful two-story Victorian building over
there across the street. You raise your camera
to your eye, align the bottom of the finder with
the sidewalk or curb, and . . . wait a minute,
the top's not there. What happened to the
gingerbread trim around the eaves? So you
deftly take one step back and fall over backward into the hedges. (It happens.) Upright
again, you position the camera so that the
gingerbread shows. But now the stairs and
lower story are not in the picture. So you turn
the camera ninety degrees, the frame is now
vertical, the whole building is in, all you have
to do is tilt the camera slightly upward, and
you have the picture—almost. That last little
adjustment, tilting the camera back, caused
the camera to "look up" at the house; the verti-
cals converge, and so you've introduced perspective distortion into the picture. And that's
serious. Not only do the sides of the building
appear to converge, but so do all the other vertical lines—the window frames, doors, siding,
porch columns, everything that was vertical
and parallel. Windows and features of the upper floor look smaller than those of similar

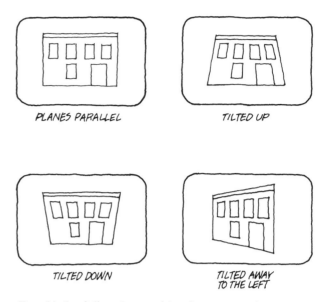

PLANES PARALLEL   TILTED UP

TILTED DOWN   TILTED AWAY
                      TO THE LEFT

Four kinds of distortion resulting from perspective as seen
through the camera viewfinder.

dimensions on the lower story. The whole picture has been distorted.

Fortunately, the problem is not difficult to
solve, providing you plan ahead and think
about what you're going to do. You even have
some choice in the way you solve it. All of these
solutions and any others you might think up
are based on one important principle: the film
plane must be "flat," or parallel to the plane of
the elevation being photographed.

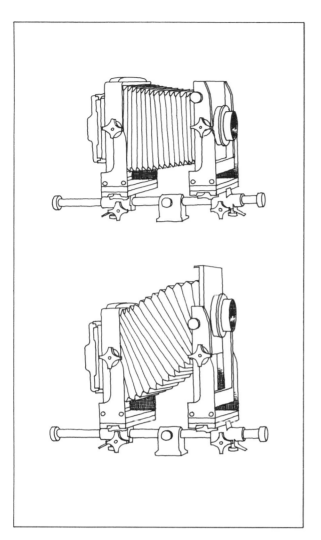

PERSPECTIVE: THE VIEW CAMERA

There used to be only one answer to the problem of perspective control, the so-called view camera, considered by professionals a must for their own architectural photography, and they were probably right. There's no doubt that the 4-by-5, 5-by-7, or 8-by-10 view camera, with its sliding, tilting, swinging back and its lens board, gives the architectural photographer-historian optimum flexibility and control.

As you can see from the illustrations, the camera is designed so that the front or lens board can be kept parallel to the plane of the building elevation, then raised to include the upper part of the building, and still remain parallel to the film plane. Even if the camera must be pointed upward or downward, the film plane and lens board can be adjusted so that they're parallel to each other and so that both are parallel to the plane of the building elevation. All of this can be viewed on the ground glass, and final adjustments can be made before inserting the film holder and making the exposure.

But don't get carried away with all this freedom. Correcting for perspective in this way results in other kinds of distortions. The best course with a view camera, or any other camera for that matter, is to plan your setup carefully so that camera adjustments are held to a minimum.

There are a few other difficulties with view cameras. The cameras come in all sizes, but some problems grow in proportion to the size. Bigger cameras are heavier, requiring a more substantial tripod or support and, particularly in the case of 8-by-10s, incredible muscular feats. Larger film is more expensive, increasing the cost of experimentation and of remedying inevitable error, but this disadvantage is compensated for somewhat by the fact that with the larger film you don't have to have an enlarger and can make contact prints. This large film size, by the way, allows you to make mammoth enlargements, to cover whole walls if you like, with little loss of definition.

All in all, if the view camera is the way you decide to go, the 4-by-5 is the best choice, combining portability (remember not all those buildings you'll want to record are at the roadside!) and all the flexibility you could want. A final point. Sheet film for the 4-by-5 is available in a greater variety of emulsions than for other sizes, though this variety, particularly for the beginner, is less of a blessing than film manufacturers suppose.

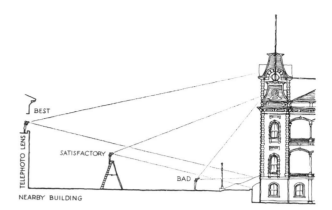

Going higher to attain perspective control.

PERSPECTIVE: 35MM

It is now possible to obtain some of the image control of the view camera—the rising front—through the use of special lenses designed for 35mm single lens reflexes. Two lenses currently available, the Perspective Control Nikkor and the Leitz PA-Curtagon-R, are actually wide-angle lenses in mounts designed to allow lateral movement of the lens. Unlike the view camera, the optics of these systems can be displaced

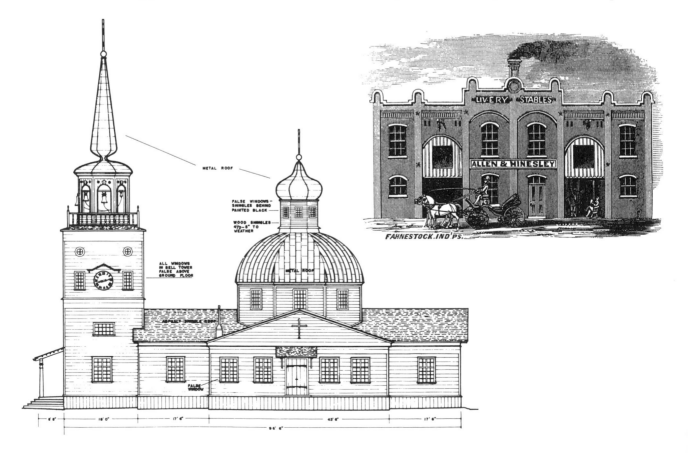

only a small distance, but as the diagram shows, this small displacement combined with the wide-angle lens makes it possible to keep the film and subject planes parallel even for tall structures. The mounts can also be rotated about the optical axis so that the lens may be displaced sideways as well as vertically, allowing for correction where the film plane must be swung back to the right or left as, for example, in a narrow street.

PERSPECTIVE: GOING HIGHER

For most of us, view cameras and special lenses are pretty exotic equipment, and very expensive. Besides, neither piece of equipment helps the photographer who is using a camera with a rangefinder/viewfinder. But there is an alternative method of photographing tall buildings—the step ladder. Right, all you really need is a step ladder about half as tall as the structure you're recording—obviously not a useful approach for photographing old skyscrapers in downtown New York City, but nevertheless satisfactory in a surprising number of cases.

If standing atop a sixteen-foot ladder in a brisk wind while you try to focus and shoot your 8-by-10 handheld view camera makes you wish you had stuck to oral history, there are still other options. You may find a tall building nearby that affords an excellent view from the roof or upper story. If the building seems too far away, you can use a telephoto lens. Or you can stand on the top of your car or a truck. Or you may be able just to walk across the street and set up on a front porch (also lifting you above the parked cars and traffic). Out in the country where none of the above applies you might even use a tree limb of convenient height. It doesn't matter what you stand on; the point is that you want to get about midway between the ground and the top of the structure so that the camera doesn't have to be tilted up or down, when you-know-what happens. All photographs on page 165 were made with a 35mm single lens reflex without any special lenses and using one of the above options.

PERSPECTIVE: IN THE DARKROOM

If distortion is only minor and if nothing else works, you can control perspective at the enlarging easel. This means simply raising one edge of the casel and inclining the paper in such a way that the visually converging or diverging parallels become parallel again. In effect, this adjustment is similar to that made by the view camera and, as with the view camera, can introduce other kinds of distortion elsewhere. When you use this approach, the enlarger lens should be stopped down to its smallest aperture so that the entire image remains in focus.

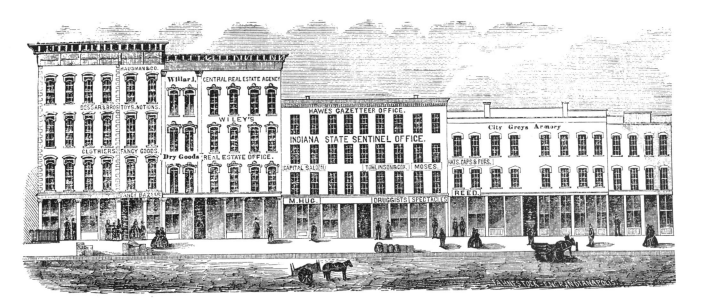

SCALE

Scale is a fairly technical matter. Still, since we don't know how our photographs will be used, we should know something about it. We usually determine the scale of an object in a photograph in one of two ways, either by knowing its actual size through experience or by comparing it to other objects nearby whose size we know. We determine scale by direct comparison, then, and scale becomes a problem only when we have no experience with the object (or when we have no understanding of the object's function, often the case with photographs of artifacts which do not include a scale).

Because photographs of houses and buildings (though not necessarily other structures) usually include doors and windows, or even people and other clues to scale, they often present us with little problem. However, common clues like doors and windows (but usually not bricks and siding) can vary enough that scale may not be obvious from the photograph. The photographer-historian can avoid this problem in any number of ways. First, several photographs in any series should show the structure in its surroundings, so that trees, other buildings, streets, and sidewalks provide the scale.

If more accuracy is required, particularly if the photograph may be used for photogrammetric measurement, then the photograph of each elevation should include a meter stick, or a tape measure hung from a nail, or, better, a surveyor's leveling rod (8-foot) in good condition with dark numerals against a white background marked at 1-inch and 1-foot intervals. A measuring device is especially important when the building is about to be destroyed, for we must usually assume that no measured drawings are extant.

FILM AND LIGHT

After distortion our next concern in architectural photography is definition, the precise rendering of fine textures and architectural details. Here film and light work together. The film must be of fine enough grain to record even the smallest detail and hold it for large prints. And the lighting must be of a quality and must strike the surface being photographed at an angle that together brings details out in relief.

Though it is hard to generalize here, flat lighting usually destroys detail—wood grain, bricks, carving, inscriptions, trim, shingles can

all disappear in bright flat lighting. Waiting just an hour or so to take your pictures when the light strikes the same surface obliquely makes all the difference in capturing detail. Before photographing a structure, it is important, if possible, to visit it at different times of the day to note the best hour to photograph each of the several elevations. Usually, you will have to plan at least two or three sessions at different times of day to get the elevation in its best light.

Film choice can be reduced to a simple rule and a half—use the finest grain film available and one within your technical abilities. Fine grain films can be classified into two categories. First, there are the old standards, easily available to amateurs, fine grained, and capable of considerable enlargement with a minimum of darkroom wizardry: Kodak Panatomic X, Ilford Pan F, Adox KB-14. Properly exposed —that is, minimum exposure—and developed with care, these films can yield good enlargements and, assuming that you don't want to make photomurals of them, can yield negatives with all the resolution you could want.

The second group of fine grained films includes what you might call sophisticated films

that, though they are by no means difficult to use, require considerably more care (bracketed exposures, focusing series, and strict development controls, for example) and so should be considered only by more experienced amateurs: Kodak High Contrast Copy Film 5069, Fuji HR, Ilford Micro Negative Pan, H & W VTE Pan (for *Very Thin Emulsion*). This last one, again depending on the care in exposure and development, is capable of enlargements exceeding 125x and makes 8-by-10 enlargements of the quality of contact prints from a view camera plate. In short, the technology exists to produce big, big enlargements with 35mm film, but if your needs are simpler, Kodak Panatomic-X and other fine grain films in the first group do extremely well.

IT'S A QUESTION OF BALANCE

The agony of the photographer-historian would seem to be choosing between aesthetics and accurate historical recording, between "re-creating a feeling" or the "straight shot." Beautiful old buildings (even lovable, ugly old buildings), like colorful historical personalities, excite our most romantic instincts and often cloud what for the historian must be a very real

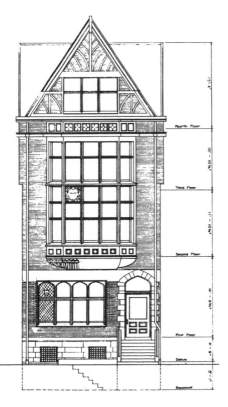

distinction between expressing a personal, stylized impression or rendering a precise record. Some people cannot make the distinction and wrongly regard the one as the other; others see the choices as mutually exclusive alternatives.

In fact, we need not make a strict choice of one or the other. Rather, the question is one of balance. In reaching this balance, the photographer-historian is no different from the historian who records and writes history and seeks the proper balance between poetry and historiography. Just as good written history is a mixture of fact and subjectivity, so is good historical photography. Rather than a whether-or-not question it is really a question of where each is most effective.

Another balance needs to be struck between context and detail too. Like a historical personality, a building withers if taken from its surroundings. But if the photographer-historian records life only through "wide-angle" vision, producing broad panoramas, the results will be as superficial as the work of the historian whose wide-angle mind can never close in sufficiently for us to see the details. Conversely, given only the intricacies and the details, it is impossible for us to see the broad outlines and setting.

So we must allow for both, aesthetics and accuracy, context and detail. But we must not attempt to do them in the same frame. Some pictures should be realistic, accurate, precise; others can be interpretive, subjective, even romantic.

THE RECORDING SHEET

Once we have our photographs, we need to go one more step and note what we have done on a recording sheet. The recording sheet is essential for several reasons. It gives you information about your subject weeks, or months, or years later, when you've photographed so many buildings that the particulars all seem to run together, and allows you to turn over your negatives and photographs to either a museum, the local or county historical society, or an architect (who perhaps will take photogrammetric measurements) and be sure that the recipients, too, know something about each view. And recording sheets help you to keep negatives, contact proof sheets, and prints together.

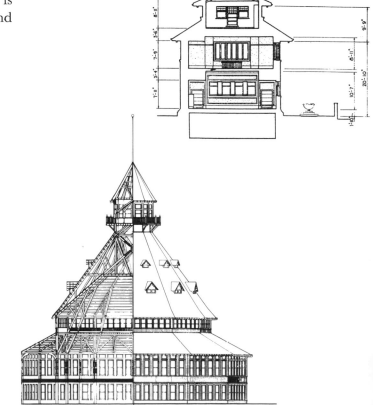

Contact proofsheet of general exterior views and details of the
Atherton House, San Francisco, California, 1881. The recording sheet is on the next page.

Atherton House (1881)
1919 California St. (SW corner Octavia)
San Francisco

April 10, 1976   Pan-X   ASA 32

№ 14A
Exterior general
views & details

1	South elevation – general view	**19**	NW corner
2	Portico columns, roof & dormer	**20**	Window grill – ground floor (west)
3	Wood trim, roof, gable & window detail (SE section)	**21**	Portico & dormer (east)
4	Oriel (SW corner)	**22**	Side entrance (east) & passageway to
5	Oriel (west elevation)	**23**	adjoining building
6	Rear (north elevation)	**24**	Portico roof & dormer detail
7	Detail of eaves and wooden numbers "1881"	**25**	Siding & brackets (west elevation)
8	Detail of eaves, cornice, coping & corner tower (west)	**26**	Leaded window & carved panel (west)
9	Portico columns & soffit main (south) entrance	**27**	Oriel window detail (SW corner)
10	North & west view	**28**	Carved frieze &
11	Rear (north) gable and wood trim	**29**	window sill detail (nw corner)
12	General views (SW corner)	**30**	Gable & battlement (north)
13		**31**	Gable, roof & cornice (north)
14	Main stairway & iron handrail	**32**	Portico column & soffit
15	Window grill – ground floor (west)	**33**	2nd floor windows (south)
16	Ventilator grill – ground floor (west)	**34**	South gable
17	Window grill – ground floor (west)	**35**	Corner tower conical roof
18	Partial rear (north) view	**36**	

Recording sheet describing photographic record of the Atherton House. Note that the facing direction of elevations and architectural details is given in each entry.

The first step in coordinating negatives and a recording sheet is to make sure the negatives and recording sheets can't get separated from each other. The simplest way to do this is to number the rolls of film you take consecutively and assign the number of each roll to a corresponding recording sheet. There are at least a couple of ways to mark negatives with a number. One way is to write the number and other information with a technical pen and india ink on the blank space or leader of each roll of film. You'll find that the emulsion (dull) side takes opaque ink well, but make sure the ink is permanent and waterproof. But a better way is to record this information photographically right on the first frame. Just write it out in dark felt-tip pen on a piece of white paper, move up as close as you can with your camera, and photograph the number and subject of the roll. Record this number on the recording sheet and repeat the process for each roll you take. You might use a number for each job and then a letter for each roll taken of that subject.

The illustration provides some specific examples of recording sheet entries, but in all the examples there are some basic guidelines to be kept in mind. Be as brief and specific as possible. Compass direction as well as view should be given—for example, "south (rear) elevation" or "doorway on west (side) elevation." The same applies to interior details and general views. You should also note whether it is an interior or exterior view, but only where it is not obvious from the picture.

DOING IT

Just how many pictures you take of a building will be determined by the size and complexity of the structure, and after recording a few buildings you'll soon be able to make the decision yourself. If your subject is a simple little miner's shack or a circa 1880 tannery sandwiched between two huge skyscrapers downtown with only its front elevation visible, a roll of thirty-six exposures will probably do. But faced with a beautiful old stone church or a block of Victorian row houses, you'll need lots more. You need to be somewhat systematic, of course, so here's a checklist of photographs that should be included in any survey: (1) wide-angle views showing the entire structure, its setting, and its relationship to other buildings around it; (2) exterior general views; (3) exterior details; (4) interior general views; and (5) interior details.

And here is the way your first recording session might go. Assuming you've had enough time to visit the building (maybe you walk by it on the way to work every day) and to decide what time(s) of day would be best to do your

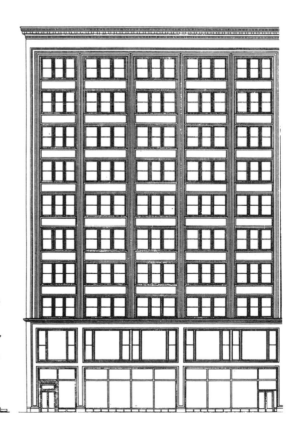

recording, you've arrived ready to take your photographs. You should have plenty of film (the more you look at a building through the finder of your camera, the more you'll see what deserves recording), your camera, a normal (50mm) lens, and a telephoto (135mm to 250mm) lens. You'll also want a clipboard with a recording sheet so you can write down information about each frame. Position your range pole or tape measure hung from a nail at one edge of the structure where it will record on the film.

With the normal lens on your camera you set up and take the exterior general views, including the front elevation, the two sides, and the rear. (Don't forget the rear. It may not be beautiful but it often says as much about the building as its front.) In cities, particularly, the front and back elevations may be the only ones accessible, the sides also being the sides of something else. Then you may want to record some major feature of the building—a huge doorway, the steps, a small structure attached

to the back, a chimney, or a garden. As you take each picture, you or a helper makes notes on the recording sheet. Remember that it's a good idea to take too many pictures rather than risk ending up with too few.

Then you'll want to move in more closely to get the exterior details, switching sometimes to your telephoto lens to get details high off the ground. Some of the things you'll want to include in your record of details are doorways, porches, ornamental woodwork, dormer windows, cupolas, ornate fire escapes, balconies, railings, stone and wood trim, anything, in fact, that catches your eye. These details are valuable to the historian, not only because they allow you to date a building whose origins are obscure, but they may even allow an experienced architect to make at least a good guess at the building's architect or builder.

With the exterior details completed, you'll spend some time inside, photographing both general interior views and details. Unless the building is of considerable interest, demanding

extensive recording, you'll probably just want pictures of one or two typical rooms and some of the interesting details like staircases, fireplaces, sculptured ceilings, woodwork, wallpaper patterns, lighting and heating fixtures, and other ornamental features. Don't forget to look into kitchens and bathrooms, as they are often more reflective than other rooms of the builder's creativity and ingenuity.

Interior views demand your close attention to lighting patterns. Old rooms particularly look best in their natural illumination and should be photographed that way unless significant details are obscured by shadows. Old office buildings, high-windowed Victorian buildings, and even factories and warehouses were designed to be illuminated by daylight, so they generally present some interesting naturally lit interior shots for the photographer.

It may be that at first you're having trouble relating to buildings and knowing just what to photograph. But the nice thing about architectural photography is that it also provides an excuse and something of a system for looking at buildings. It's very much like the new things we discover about photographs we're copying,

though we've seen the photographs dozens of times before. The finder of the camera helps us to see architecture in a different way; with a telephoto lens, we'll see even more than we saw before. Very likely the excitement you felt when you looked close-up at that old daguerreotype of your great-great-grandfather will happen again as you discover an expressive little stone carving high up on that plain old warehouse down the street.

The Historic American Buildings Survey

The recording and preservation of historical buildings is usually the work of state and community historical associations, architectural heritage groups, and city landmark preservation commissions. But what happens if your community has none of these groups and during your historical amblings around town you've discovered a building you think deserves special attention? You might consider starting your own group or petitioning the city council to establish a commission, or you could begin working on recording the building yourself, right now. If you've acquired just a few of the local historian's skills, you can take the vital step that might mean survival for that structure, at least on film.

Since the 1930s the Historic American Buildings Survey—a cooperative effort of the National Park Service, the Library of Congress, and the American Institute of Architects—has collected drawings, sketches, photographs, copies of plans, and written data on historical buildings and assembled them into a national architectural archive. Not all of the buildings recorded have survived, but what's important is that at least they have been preserved on paper and film. Much of this work has been done by concerned amateur historians.

Your introduction to the Historic American Buildings Survey is a free booklet, *Documenting a Legacy* (Government Printing Office, 1973), which contains twenty-eight pages of photographs and drawings of structures from almost every period and style of American architecture.

If you're interested in the work of recording local buildings and registering them with HABS, you can begin with the suggestions and techniques in this chapter. But you'll need to know more about HABS requirements and criteria, and while the registration procedures are not difficult there is a required format. All of this is explained in Harley J. McKee's *Recording Historic Buildings* (1970), available from the U.S. Government Printing Office by mail or from GPO bookstores in larger cities. The book gives directions for completing a HABS project, including organizing your survey, measuring, documentation, and recording techniques, and also offers a brief pictorial and photographic history of American architectural styles.

If you are interested in looking at buildings but do not want to get involved in photographic recording there is still a lot in the HABS archives that will interest you. Photographs and drawings for over fifteen thousand American buildings are available by mail from the Library of Congress photoduplication service at reasonable price (which is how many of the illustrations for this chapter were acquired). There's even a guide to the thirty thousand measured drawings, forty-five thousand photographs, and twenty-two thousand pages of historical data: the *Historic American Buildings Survey Catalog* (1941) and its several supplements. Also available are state and regional catalogs, for example *The Architecture of Cleveland, Twelve Buildings, 1836–1912*, or *Records of Buildings in Charleston and the South Carolina Low Country*. To find out just what is available write the Office of Archaeology and Historic Preservation, National Park Service, Department of the Interior, Washington, D.C. 20240, and ask for a publications list.

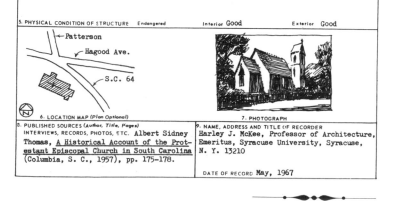

| 1. STATE **South Carolina** | HISTORIC AMERICAN BUILDINGS SURVEY |
| COUNTY **Barnwell** | INVENTORY |

1. STATE **South Carolina**
COUNTY **Barnwell**
TOWN **Barnwell**   VICINITY
STREET NO. **Hagood Ave. & Patterson (on S.C. Rt. 64, SE. of business district)**
ORIGINAL OWNER **Episcopal Church**
ORIGINAL USE **Church**
PRESENT OWNER **Episcopal Church**
PRESENT USE **Church**
WALL CONSTRUCTION **Wd. frame; board & batten.**
NO. OF STORIES **One; gallery   ten.**

HISTORIC AMERICAN BUILDINGS SURVEY
INVENTORY

2. NAME **Church of the Holy Apostles (Episcopal)**
DATE OR PERIOD **1856; consecrated 1857**
STYLE **Gothic Revival**
ARCHITECT **Barbot & Seyle of Charleston**
BUILDER **—**

3. FOR IBRARY OF CONGRESS USE

4. NOTABLE FEATURES, HISTORICAL SIGNIFICANCE AND DESCRIPTION   OPEN TO PUBLIC **Yes**

This congregation was established Nov. 18, 1848. In 1856 the Rev. E. A. Wagner set aside 1 1/8 acres of land for the building of this church: a Gothic structure with a nave 25' x 50', vestry 8' x 9', and tower 8' square. It was built at a cost of $3,500. The building was seriously damaged during the Civil War. Repairs were made and a new organ installed in 1867. The building was vacant in 1883. A new organ was installed in 1925, a new altar and heating plant in 1946. The building was renovated in 1948.

This attractive small wooden church, which is oriented in the traditional manner, has a gabled tower projecting from the north side of the second bay, its lower story being the entrance vestibule. The walls are covered with vertical boards and rather heavy closely-spaced battens; bays are marked by wooden buttresses. Windows on the sides are arched (two-centered, pointed) and trimmed with hoodmoulds. A larger single window at each end is ogee-arched and ornamented with a finial. The roof is gabled.

The nave consists of five unaisled bays. Over the west end is a gallery; a two-centered pointed arch at the east end opens to the chancel, from the west side of which projects a gabled vestry. The nave has an open-timber roof of scissors trusses; there is a plaster cornice with cove.

A cast-iron fence encloses the church yard, in which is a cemetery. The tower is seen to advantage looking south along Patterson St.

5. PHYSICAL CONDITION OF STRUCTURE **Endangered**   Interior **Good**   Exterior **Good**

6. LOCATION MAP *(Plan Optional)*
←Patterson
Hagood Ave.
S.C. 64
N

7. PHOTOGRAPH

8. PUBLISHED SOURCES *(Author, Title, Pages)*
INTERVIEWS, RECORDS, PHOTOS, ETC. **Albert Sidney Thomas, A Historical Account of the Protestant Episcopal Church in South Carolina (Columbia, S. C., 1957), pp. 175-178.**

9. NAME, ADDRESS AND TITLE OF RECORDER
Harley J. McKee, Professor of Architecture, Emeritus, Syracuse University, Syracuse, N. Y. 13210

DATE OF RECORD **May, 1967**

A Glossary of Some of the More Common Architectural Details

bargeboard

shed roof

broached spire

cupola

bell roof

saltbox

hip roof

gambrel roof

mansard roof

curb roof

plancier

roof with curved gables

hammerbeam roof

flat arch

gauged arch

colonial panel door

fanlight

double-hung window

louvered door

dormer window

lancet window

French window

coupled windows

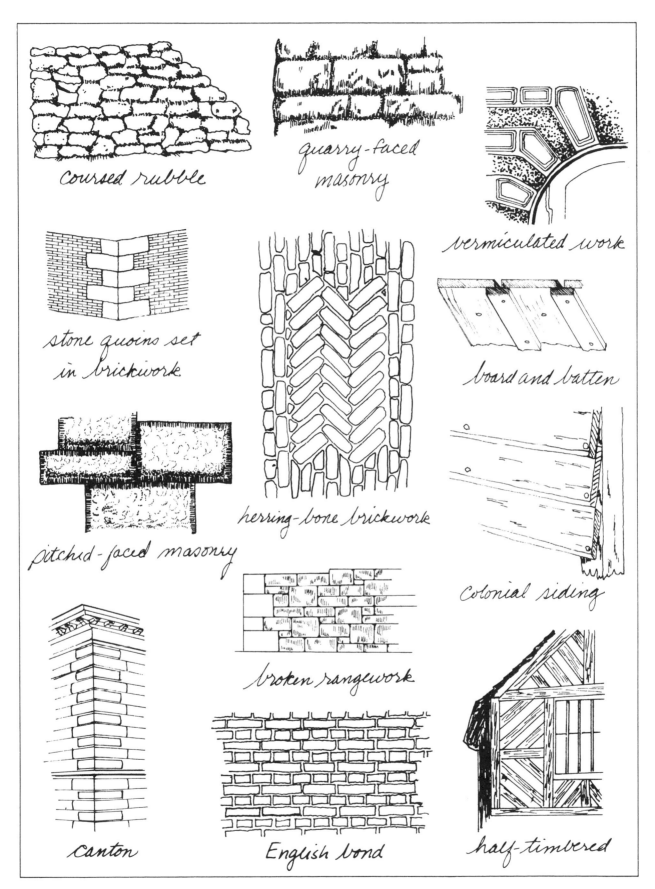

coursed rubble

quarry-faced masonry

vermiculated work

stone quoins set in brickwork

herring-bone brickwork

board and batten

pitched-faced masonry

colonial siding

broken rangework

canton

English bond

half-timbered

JOURNAL OF HENRY EDGAR—1863.

NOTE:—The following contribution was transcribed by Mr. Israel Clem (Representative from Meagher County in the Seventh Session of the Montana Territorial Legislature) from the original journal of Henry Edgar, and is of interest not only in showing the dangers of the early prospecting expeditions, but particularly because on this trip the first discovery of gold was made in Alder Gulch. The notes to the text were made by Mr. Clem, except where otherwise designated.

Feb. 4th, 1863:—We left Bannack. There were eight of us. Lew Simmons, Bill Fairweather, Barney Hughes, Tom Cover, George Orr, Mike Sweeney, Harry Rodgers and your humble servant, Henry Edgar. We arrived at *LaBarge City to trade for horses needed on the trip.

La Barge City was a small place, but a wild one, where the strong hand keeps his own. We want to meet the Flathead Indians as they come back from their hunting over on the east side of the mountains. We have five gallons of alcohol with us and the fact becoming known, we find it hard to keep. Some one will ask for "some of the stuff" and be refused.

A Mr. Skinner came to the camp and said he came for some of "that stuff" pointing to the keg and would have it. Bill pulled his rifle and Simmons his rifle. Tom Riley, a man by the name of Moore and a man by the name of Powell got in between Skinner and Bill Fairweather and the trouble quieted down. Well it was for Skinner, for in another minute he would have been filled full of holes. He was told never to come to the camp on such an errand again.

---

* LaBarge City was named for Capt. LaBarge, steamboat Capt. of early days. The Historical Society has the original town plat of LaBarge City or Deer Lodge.—(Ed.)

CHAPTER 9

Library Archaeology

History books are for some a joy and for others a torment. It may be that history just isn't for everybody, but if that is true, how can we explain the universality of recalling history and lore in the family and village circle? No, I suspect that it has more to do with the concept of history we acquired in childhood and whether or not we've had happy experiences with history books and history teachers than with history itself. Attitudes toward history are probably also affected by the matter of human differences and how we've each learned to deal with life, at a distance or always deeply and personally involved close up. Depending on which one of these oversimplified types we are, we might like a history of civilization (the view from afar) or history embodied in the life of one person (the individual as history). In other words, there are different kinds of people, so why not different kinds of history? The popularity of biographies and autobiographies and "people" magazines suggests that not only are readers aware that history is supposed to be about people, but they also measure books on the basis of the books' humanness, their ability

to reconstruct and portray a life in such a way that a relationship can be formed between character and reader. This chapter will attempt to help you approach your history through the people who made it, for it suggests a return to the library, this time to look through biographies and autobiographies of people in your own family and community and through books of local and family history. You may find your own name in one of these books, or the exploits of some distant ancestor, and you may find a kind of history you never thought existed.

Libraries often contain forgotten treasures of historical archaeology. The particular part of the library I'm thinking of is the least frequented—it's the very depths of the stacks with its dimly lit shelves of gold-stamped, leather-bound, now brittle and yellow-paged tomes which are hidden there like fossils. There's a chance they might not be there, possibly having been wrapped and boxed and stuck away somewhere else. Even worse, they may have been sold off for five cents each at last year's friends-of-the-library bookstall sale. These are the library's first and oldest books, some of them (particularly in New England communities) going back to a time when, as the colophon of a book's English publisher will suggest, there were no printers and publishers in the New World. In the stacks with these books you may also find volume upon volume chronicling the proceedings of the state legislature a century ago, the hand-bound numbers of the community's first historical association, or nothing more—and yet nothing more moving—than a little hand-written diary of a rural farm child.

Don't be discouraged by the darkness of the stacks, the dust, and uninspiring titles like *Antiquarian and Natural History Society of the State of Arkansas, Mecklenburg Centennial and Monumental Association,* or *Philomathic Club.* Reach out in the dimness to take a book off the shelf and flip through the pages. As the old typefaces, photographs, whimsical drawings, and woodcuts pass before your eyes you'll reach for the next volume and the next, and soon you'll be feeling for a comfortable spot on the floor, and the minutes will become hours. Out from the pages will come a procession of bonneted and sideburned faces, engravings of high-steepled churches and backwoods log cabins, architects' plans, maps, candlesticks, quilts, Shaker boxes, Indian blankets, old Dutch clay pipes, recipes, advertisements, coffee grinders, copper foot warmers, and a fire engine or two. The dreary surroundings of the stacks will be forgotten as you're transported back to Maine, or Kansas, or Colorado, or Oregon in the 1880s. You'll feel like taking the books home, every last one if you can carry them all—and there on the little blue charge slip on the inside front cover you may discover that the last reader returned your favorite volume on December 12, 1916!

The kind of armchair archaeology one does at the library is not in the least secondary to searching for and collecting at a real site. For the historical archaeologist the printed word, the picture, the description of a pasture now buried beneath concrete and asphalt, the inscription on a tombstone are finds. But you will discover that you need no more of an excuse to search through these old volumes than the pleasure derived from wandering through pages from the past. If mere browsing seems somehow too passive, not meaningful enough, then think of it this way. Librarians often put in storage or dispose of old books that haven't been checked out for several years to make room for new books, and if you check out an old book today, you'll not only ensure its continued stay on the shelf (it may be the first time the librarian's ever seen it), thus saving it for future generations of library archaeologists, but you'll also find yourself in the new role of protector of antiquities. You might want to suggest to the librarian that the old local history section be dusted off, moved to a more accessible location, and even displayed.

As a dividend for the armchair archaeologist, sometimes libraries are housed in historical buildings. One example is the wooden Victorian structure in which you'll find the writings of Greenville, Mississippi's native authors (and journals by local chapters of the Mississippi Valley Historical Association going back for generations) and even the shelves of books that were in the house before it was a library. There is a real feeling of peace inside, an old quiet. Few experiences can match settling deep into the library's worn chairs, browsing through reminiscences of a little Southern town on the Mississippi levee, the room bright with sunlight from the eight-foot-high windows—and recalling that Mark Twain too has been here.

*　　　　　*　　　　　*

Libraries are wonderful rainy day havens, particularly for car-weary travelers and curious historians. Perhaps while on a long trip you've stopped in a little town like Ware, Massachusetts—once known as Ware Village—and, out of curiosity, visited the library. Visiting an old library is in itself enjoyable, even if you're not searching, but in this instance, if you did search, you would be rewarded by finding Arthur Chase's *History of Ware Massachusetts,* gold-embossed green binding, yellow deckle-edged paper, and all. Its frontispiece is an engraving, a view of Ware in the 1830s, which is a long time ago, but even then Ware was over one hundred years old. The earliest recorded survey of the area is dated 1714, and by 1725 the first settlement appeared in the wilderness. Just four months after the battle of Lexington and a few weeks after George Washington assumed command of the Continental forces, Ware officially became a town. According to local lore, the name derives from the Indian word given to the river flowing through the village, Nenameseck or "fishing weir" (pronounced *ware*). The favorite fishing spot of the Indians was the falls, which later provided power to the village mills.

There is something of interest to almost anyone who would pick up this old book, for Ware, like any little town as old, is America in microcosm. Of course Ware is not as old as more famous towns like Jamestown or Salem, but imagine a village whose history spans the French and Indian Wars, the Revolution, the War of 1812, the Civil War, and continues right up to the present day. Amidst the muster roles and military payrolls, for example, the reader finds the following order by the selectman purchasing supplies for the Ware detachment early in the nineteenth century:

Oct. 24, 1814:

Simeon Cummings for a cartridge box . . . . . *$ 1.00*
Nathan Snell for a gun *11.00*
Calvin Morse, beef for the soldiers *8.16*
James Cargill, baking for the soldiers *2.65*
James Cargill, for carrying the baggage . . . *18.00*
Joseph Cummings for onions and baking
  bread for the soldiers *2.50*
Nov. 14, 1814:
John Osborn, making cartridges *2.10*
Jan. 2, 1815:
James Brakenridge, beef for the soldiers . . . *5.50*
Feb. 15, 1815:
Eli Snow, for goods for soldiers *2.19*

We then learn from the town records that at a March meeting in 1815 it was "voted that $4.00 per man be given the Militia that were detached and did serve in defense of the state from this town last fall." From these items, we get a sense of the military life of the early nineteenth century.

The *History* contains lots more: accounts of building and construction projects, new roads, schools, and churches; the buying and selling of property; stories about Ware's families over the years; information about cemeteries and records of burials—all this illustrated with little engravings and, later, by some of the first photographs.

I myself was struck by the mention of mills by the falls in the Ware River, and if you'll indulge me in my interest in old buildings—particularly old industrial sites—we might concentrate on the mills and find out what we can of early industries in Ware. The reference to mills in the *History*, incidentally, is a good example of the value of library research. In the search for old mills, it often happens that the usual sources of information we've explored in this book just don't work. None of the old-timers around remember anything about the mills, and even the town clerk has lost track of the mills because they haven't appeared on the tax rolls for years (maybe centuries). Mills sometimes seem just to drop out of current memory. This is where a little library archaeology helps. Often just a sentence in an early history of the town or a notation on a map provides everything you need. In the case of Ware, we fortunately have not only historical records but also maps and pictures.

Our historian's intuition originally led us to expect industry in a town which has grown beside a river, which itself, moreover, contains a falls, so that we are not too surprised to come upon this passage that immediately confirms our hunch:

Saw and grist mills were established at the falls on Ware River soon after 1729 by Jabez Omstead. These are believed to have been the earliest mills within Ware territory.

An iron furnace, in which the smelting was done with charcoal, was built on the west bank of the river near the Otis Company's dam in the first quarter of the last century. A machine shop was established at the same time near the South Street bridge. The map of 1830 shows the furnace, machine shop, cotton, woolen and grist mills grouped about the falls at the village.

On Muddy Brook stood Judah Marsh's mills, of which record is made as early as 1752. They were afterwards known as Harding's Mills. The grist-mill is shown on the map of 1830, and a saw-mill on the same spot is indicated on the map of 1854.

The artificial pond just north of Aspen Grove Cemetery has furnished power for many years. In 1828 a road is laid out from near the East meeting-house past "Greenleaf's works, so called." Two years later the same establishment is referred to as tan works. Greenleaf's Tannery stood at the north of the pond. Stephen P. Bailey ran a grist-mill near the same place before 1850. Snow's Mills have occupied the site for the past sixty years. Marsh's Mills were in 1826 known as Newcome's Mills.

The list of Ware's industries over the years is long, and it includes a tannery, a fulling mill for homespun linen, gristmills, John Pepper's Saw Mill, brickyards, and a paper company. This last leaves behind an interesting footnote to Ware's history and shows something of how small towns live and die.

In 1883 the West Ware Paper Co. was incorporated, and a mill was built on the east side of the river, but it was unfortunately destroyed by fire in April, 1905. As the mill was not rebuilt, West Ware, once a flourishing little settlement, has dwindled away.

Still other industries are listed in Chase's *History of Ware*—stone quarries, cotton mills (which during the season 1849–50 consumed 3,000 gallons of whale oil for lighting), manufacturers of flannel, broadcloth, and straw goods (said by Chase to be a most important industry), an apple orchard that produced "fifty to a hundred casks of cider a year," makers of boots and shoes (62,490 pairs in 1837), and a flourishing business in wood-boring tools—Snell's augers:

The one unique business of a former generation was the manufacture of augers. Thomas Snell, son of Polycarpus Snell, removed to Ware from Bridgewater about 1700. He acquired a farm of 135 acres in the Flat Brook Valley, but his special business was blacksmithing. It is claimed that he was the first to manufacture twisted augers in America, and the first to make "bight" augers in any country. He was at any rate a mechanical genius, and undoubtedly originated his own method of manufacture. It is related on the authority of his son, Deacon Thomas Snell, Jr., that he made augers in Ware soon after 1790. These early augers were made of iron with just enough steel welded to the end to make the cutting part. They were called steel-cut augers. The shank was long and left in the rough and the implement was known as a "tanged" auger.

Thomas Snell, Sen., and Susanna his wife had a large family. Seventeen children were born to them, the first in 1792, the last in 1819. Among them were Thomas, Jr., born in 1798, and Melville, born in 1804. It was probably not until these two were grown that the business assumed very considerable proportions. The shops were located on Flat Brook about a mile above the meeting-house, and at their best employed twenty men. The augers were taken to Boston to be sold, a load of steel, iron and supplies being brought back in exchange.

A series of town maps, the earliest from 1733, and old engravings and photographs of the mills as well as many other aspects of life in Ware help our imaginations to go on from where the words leave off.

*   *   *

Looking upon the photographs and painted portraits of people in towns like Ware leave me wondering about what the people must have been like, their voices, how they might have talked, what they would say. It's impossible to know, of course, the invention of recording being so comparatively recent. And yet, for the persistent and diligent historian a great deal is possible, even the re-creation of the speech of two hundred years ago.

It is true that the experienced library archaeologist soon becomes aware of differences in the written language, as well as of obsolete spellings and grammatical constructions, but only occasionally do we acquire something of the spoken language of the past. Diaries, reminiscences, and memoirs, for example, sometimes provide glimpses of regional dialects. But if these materials have been published in book form, they have been edited to conform with standard English, as were early school books and primers. Besides, if you are interested in the ways ordinary folks talked, books help little because ordinary folks in those days seldom wrote books, and if they did, it probably wouldn't be in dialect. No, if we want to learn something about ordinary speech in the days of our ancestors, we're going to have to do some digging.

Digging will lead us to finds like Frank Whitcomb Tarr's little piece, "Quaint Speech and Lore of Sandy Bay now Rockport," reported in the July, 1934 issue of *Old-Time New England*, the journal of the Society for the Preservation of New England Antiquities.

When I was a small boy and spent considerable time around the stove in my father's grocery store, one of the expressions in common use was "going to the leeward" (pronounced leward). I have not heard this for many years but well remember when one of our friends was failing in health, the Rockporters said that they were "going to the leward."

A person being ill or poor was said to be "bad off," and, if not bad off, would be called "peaked," or else they were rather "slim." When in moderate health they were "fair to middling." When recovering they were "coming to."

Married women were not called Mrs., but always "Miss." When a word ended with the letter g, it was never sounded, but pronounced as follows: doin', goin', nothin', aimin', singin', havin', etc.

The surnames of Rockporters were pronounced as follows: Norwood, Norrerd; Thurston, Thusten; Parsons, Passons; Marshall, Mashall; Choate, Chot; Butman, Bootman; Morse, Moss; Cunningham, Kinnikum; which in Nova Scotia, I am told, was Kunnikum, Hannah was Hunner.

By several old men, a clerk was called a "clark," a reminder of English usage. An animal instead of being called a creature, was a "critter." A horse was a "hoss," and an Indian was an "Injun."

The old-fashioned rye and Indian johnnycake, according to the records a relic of the Puritans, seemed to pass away with my father's generation, and was always called "rye and Injun johnny cake." My father could not eat stewed beans without a "rye and Injun johnny cake," which I believe was one-third rye and two-thirds yellow corn meal.

A grandfather was called "grandsir" and old Capt. Charles Tarr, who lived in a very old house on Cove Hill, now the "Blue Sails" tea house, and died over fifty years ago at the age of about ninety-five years, was called Sir. Tarr by his family and neighbors. I could never ascertain the reason for this distinction. . . . He was Captain of the Sea Fensibles in the War of 1812 as well as Captain of fishing boats and coasters.

— ◆ ◆ —

JULIUS CAESAR, POPE GREGORY XIII, AND GEORGE WASHINGTON'S BIRTHDAY

February 22 is one of those magical dates, like October 12, November 11, February 12, and the last Thursday in November, remembered and cherished by American school children and adults alike as school holidays. Now February 22, 1732, was, as mostly everyone knows, George Washington's birthday. Yet if you could find the first President's birth certificate, you'd discover that his birthday is actually recorded as February 11, 1731. That kind of discrepancy could also show up in your own search of family papers, public records, and gravestones. The source of the discrepancy goes back to 1582, to Rome, and to Pope Gregory XIII who, in that year, established a new calendar. It seems that the calendar in use before this date, the Julian calendar (so named because it was established by Julius Caesar), was based on a 365-day year that was eleven minutes longer than the solar year. By 1582 this error amounted to ten days, and the vernal equinox instead of occurring on the customary date of March 21 was now occurring on March 11, affecting the calculations for the date of Easter. Pope Gregory ordered, then, that ten days be dropped out of the calendar and that a new calendar — now known as the Gregorian calendar — be used which, though also 365 days, now included leap years to keep the calendar and the sun together. Catholic countries all over the world, except for one, went on the new calendar. The exception was England, whose queen, Elizabeth I, like her father, Henry VIII, before her, was, shall we say, in difficulties with the Church of Rome and not about to accept the Pope's calendar even if it was more scientific. So it was not until almost two centuries later, in 1752, that Parliament finally relented and passed an act adopting the Gregorian calendar in England and the colonies.

By this time, however, there was an eleven-day difference between the English calendar and the Gregorian calendar, which by 1752 had been in use in Europe for a hundred and seventy years, during which time the new year in England began on March 25. To complicate matters further for the historian, many people in the colonies, particularly those who had immigrated from the continent, had been using the Gregorian calendar well before it became official. This gave rise to the practice of double-dating during the period between the Gregorian new year (January 1) and the English new year (March 25) until 1752. Double-dates appear on public documents, records, tombstones, and newspapers dated anytime from January to March. Thus a tombstone or a genealogical entry in a family Bible or a newspaper might read 12 March 1720/21 which indicates that while it is still officially 1720 (New Year's Day would come on March 25), it was already 1721 in the minds of those using the new calendar. If you are recording dates in your family history before 1752, you may use the old style (O.S.) calendar or convert the dates to the new style (N.S.), but in either case be sure to indicate what you've done. To convert a date from the old style calendar to the new style you need only remember to add eleven days.

Now you can understand why Washington's birthday was changed from February 11, 1731, O.S. to February 22, 1732, N.S. — and you can still have faith in your grammar school history teacher (who wasn't simply misinforming you all those years) and in those traditional school holidays.

A small boat properly called a dory was called a "wherry," sauce was spoken of as "sass," garden vegetables were called "garden sass," and "apple sass" was always a popular dish.

The cranberry marsh was the mash. *Inclement weather for a few days was spoken of as* a spell of weather. *Curious was* curis. *The word attach was called* teach, *and this is illustrated by the following story.*

A local fisherman was in debt to a certain man in town and could not be induced to make any kind of an attempt to pay; in fact he was said to be a "dead beat," so when the fisherman came in one day and landed his dory-load of fish on the beach, the creditor was there to meet him and said, "In the name of the Commonwealth of Massachusetts, I hereby teach these fish," whereupon the debtor assisted him to load the fish on a hand barrow and take them to the creditor's fishhouse. Later, the debtor told one of his friends, that he did not think Mr. So and So would go so far as to "teach" his fish.

Modern ways, higher education and correct speech, did not find their way to Sandy Bay, located on the extreme end of Cape Ann, as early as in more accessible locations. My father used to tell me of a trip he took as a sailor in a Rockport schooner, to New York City, in 1838. When he and one of his shipmates went on shore to see the city, they overheard two Frenchmen in conversation and as they had never before heard a foreign language spoken, they followed them about a mile and were greatly amused and entertained. I believe at that time there was no person of foreign birth in Rockport with the exception of one Irishman.

So as not to spoil your pleasure (and likely surprise) I'll not continue, but Tarr's anecdotes and homespun yarns do go on for several pages and include the town shoemaker whose usual greeting was "Ho-hum! I'm glad I'm going to die pretty soon," as well as the story about two "highly respected, stout maiden ladies" named Fiducia and Fidora and a story about the fire department's Johnson pump that threw onto the blaze a stream of water "a little smaller than a lead pencil."

*   *   *

Now that you've gotten this far, I think I should warn you that, by nature, the work of library archaeology cannot be very systematic —which is also much of the fun. University libraries and some larger libraries around the country will have specialized bibliographies and indexes to help you find specific topics in state historical journals and quarterlies, and some journals put out their own indexes (though publication of these is usually erratic). But in general, there is just no easy way to find material on a specific subject that interests you, so the library archaeologist must depend pretty much on the technique of searching the stacks and browsing.

Much of what you will find—and this is what is so intriguing—is virtually unknown, often even to scholars (stop for a moment to remember when it was that you or anyone you know last checked a state historical journal out of the library). This state of affairs is also true with regard to collections of papers, personal journals, business records, and letters donated to or purchased by libraries, for few have been thoroughly studied and indexed and most remain to be opened and browsed through for the first time. Maybe you'll have the excitement of going through a collection for the first time. With growing public interest in state historical publications and collections of unpublished documents, the materials will become more and more accessible. But for now each visit to the library begins with considerable uncertainty and is therefore likely to end in the unexpected.

Some rules do apply. The best place to look for old books on local history is in older libraries —the older the better—and in main libraries rather than in branches. It is in the main library that you're most likely to find complete or nearly complete collections of state historical journals, local histories, town records, maps and surveys, business directories, and family documents.

But of course don't discount your neighborhood library. Remember that what are now neighborhoods in large cities may once have been little villages or towns a long journey from the city a century or two ago, a situation recalled in the names by which some neighborhoods around large cities are still known. Here, in any case, in your neighborhood library, you might find non-books such as handwritten diaries, loose family papers in cardboard files, photo albums, and genealogies, as well as photographs or paintings from the days the library first opened. Many small libraries have become sort of neighborhood museums, containing not only books but furniture, artwork, and family portraits collected by librarians over the years or donated by old families and patrons. (For me, there was the serendipitous discovery of Taos, New Mexico's little library, hidden on a back street and revealing in its comfortable little sitting rooms not only some first editions, furniture, and memorabilia associated with D. H. Lawrence's life there in Taos but some of his paintings too.)

But the main rule is: browse, browse, browse —and not in the card catalog but on the shelves. In a spirit of confession, I now admit that I use the card catalog principally as a means of finding the section of the stacks where I want to begin my browsing. There are some legitimate reasons for this. First, I am constantly finding books in libraries all over the country that simply have escaped the catalogers' attention. (Or, I think, that the catalogers never knew about—this is not just a Richard Brautigan fantasy; people actually do put their own books, books from other libraries, all kinds of books on the shelves.) Even more intriguing is the fact that the books I find this way, by means of this unfocused, unacademic browsing, are usually more interesting than the ones in the card catalog! (Strange? Books, old books particularly, and their cards sometimes get separated.) Another reason for treating the card catalog lightly: titles of books usually offer little information about what's really in them, and the description of the book's contents on the author-subject card is minimal and conveys nothing of the style and feel of the book. Another reason: seldom do we approach a subject knowing the names of the relevant authors, particularly in local history. Subject catalogs can help us find the right section in the stacks, at least, and maybe a few of the books we're looking for, but the basic reason is really the first—all the surprises there in the stacks.

One of my rewards for shelf browsing came in a soft, well-thumbed black leather binding, shaped with rounded corners to fit into a car's glove compartment—the *Official Automobile Blue*

Book: Standard Road Guide to America, 1920. It's a joy. One page shows a pastoral scene crossed by a smooth but rutted dirt road protected, where the shoulders fall away, by a wooden guard rail. The caption reads, "typical California highway." The back section includes an abstract of state motor laws warning that in California the speed should be "reasonable and proper," but that in any case it "shall never exceed 35 miles per hour" (30 miles per hour in Oregon). At the heart of the guide are trip itineraries with specific driving instructions ("end of road at flagpole, turn left"; or "end of road at blacksmith shop; turn right, cross dry creek"), where to find garages and accommodations, and road conditions.

Irregular 4-corners; bear left with pavement across stone bridge.

End of road; turn left, passing small school on left. Cross numerous bridges over irrigation ditches.

Cross narrow gauge RRs.

Left-hand road, blacksmith shop on far left; turn left with travel.

3-corners at stone fence; bear left, following road thru lava beds.

Keep straight ahead thru deep sand.

Fork, just beyond gate; bear left downgrade. Thru gate. Avoid left-hand road at house.

Left-hand diagonal road at foot of grade; bear left across bridge, going thru lumber yard.

End of road; bear right along phone line.

Fork, edge of big meadow; keep left. Thru 4-corners.

Irregular 4-corners; bear left upgrade. Pass spring (drinking water) on left.

3-corners; bear right. Caution for timber chute.

Fork; keep left, crossing alkali flat just beyond.

Fork; bear left. Enter New Pass, following along wash.

Cherry Creek, at hotel. Reset odometer to 0.0 in front of P. O. and go east with poles.

3-corners at fence corner; bear left upgrade. Pass water trough on left 30.7. Avoid right-hand road at abandoned cabin.

Fork, water-trough in center; bear right.

Left-hand diagonal road, log cabin and corral on right; bear left.

*　　　*　　　*

Maps can provide the historical archaeologist and local historian with all kinds of leads on the location of building sites, old mills and shops, small burying grounds, barns, ghost towns, bridges, and historical markers. These maps are readily available and inexpensive, even free if your local library maintains a collection of maps for the area. Some of the most helpful maps are also the most common: survey maps, hand-drawn maps inserted in old editions of local histories, topographic maps, and Sanborn maps. Each has a special value to the historian.

If it's information on family lands, homes, and farmsteads you want, then the best place to start is in the office of the county surveyor or assessor. Here you'll find maps and surveys which may go back several hundred centuries. And here too you might find an old hand-drawn survey map showing the boundaries of your great-grandparents' farm before they divided it up among their children, who may then have divided it again for your parents. Survey maps may help you find old roads, sites where barns and farmhouses once stood, or family burial grounds hidden away in a small stand of trees. In the same office you might also be able to search and read old wills and deeds, which often describe features of the land and vanished structures.

Larger in scale, and more helpful in other ways, are topographic maps, which show very small sections of the earth in relief and, with color and symbols, physiographic features such as woodlands, orchards, marshes, vineyards, dunes, and water courses. Of particular interest to historians, though, are the manmade features of the landscape like bridges, dams, roads, and structures that also show up on topographic maps. You'll want to obtain the largest-scale map you can for the area, preferably a *7½-minute* map (which means that the map covers a square or quadrangle seven and a half minutes latitude by seven and a half minutes longitude). One inch on this map equals about two thousand feet on the ground and is of large enough scale that you might discover an abandoned narrow-gauge railway, a blacksmith

Maps to the Past

shop, an old mining site, a pioneer cemetery, or the quarry from which your ancestors took stone for their houses. Symbols also show the locations of schools and churches, small masonry dams (an old mill site?), mine dumps, windmills, footbridges, and village sites.

Topographic maps are available from government map stores in larger cities, wilderness camping equipment shops, or by mail from the Map Information Office, U.S. Geological Survey, Washington, D.C. 20242. You might begin by requesting a free index map for your state, showing which maps are available, their names, and whether they are in the 7½-minute or 15-minute series. And while you're at it, request a copy of *Topographic Maps*, a little booklet explaining map scale, the different series, and topographic map symbols.

For historical searches in cities there are Sanborn maps, some going back to the 1850s. Sanborn large-scale maps (one inch on the map will equal fifty to four hundred feet on the ground, depending on the scale) show with color and symbols all kinds of details. Buildings are shown to scale and are color coded to indicate type of construction — adobe, stone, brick, iron, wood frame, or concrete block — with symbols to record particular details such as lofts, skylights, water tanks, and door con-

struction. On one of these maps of your city you might find a historical church, a row of sheds along an alley once housing a machine shop, a stable now being used as a garage, a wagon shed, or a long-forgotten walkway. Older maps will show cemeteries, which may be only vacant lots now, or a row of old wood frame buildings dating back to the last century. Maps from successive surveys will show the growth of city limits and how it happened that your great-great-grandparents' orchard is now right in the middle of Detroit. Sanborn has mapped most of the communities in the United States with a population of twenty-five hundred or more and sells its maps to city, county, and state offices, as well as to libraries. If maps are not available to you at one of these sources and you'd like to know when and if your community has been mapped, then write to Sanborn Map Company, 629 Fifth Avenue, Pelham, New York 10803.

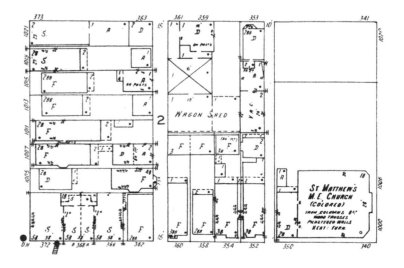

Digging through old newspapers just can't be surpassed as a rewarding and downright entertaining library activity. Any historian, professional or amateur, who ventures just once among the newsy, informal pages of the *Pennsylvania Gazette, Georgia Gazette and Weekly Mercury, Dubuque Visitor, Telegraph and Texas Register, St. Louis Post-Dispatch*, or *Alta California* sooner or later succumbs to the lure of history on newsprint. Here indeed is the realm of the adventurous, those who would be transported all the way back to Colonial times, day by day, or at least week by week, by sheets of soft yellowed paper, to experience events reported only days or hours after they happened, by men and women who were there! Remember what happened the last time you came upon an old newspaper used as packing or somehow stuffed into the old wall you're removing for the new bedroom: work stopped, the world seemed to stand still, and you lost yourself on each crumbling page. Contemporary events and personages great and trivial described with spontaneity, freshness, and often considerable humor—for this characteristic alone newspapers are not only one of the local historian's most valuable resources but the most direct touch with the past.

Anything this good, you would expect, must be scarce, hard to find, or costly. But that's the surprise of it. Newspapers are everywhere—almost any town of any size in this country has had a newspaper sometime in its history—and they have been in America since almost the very beginning. The American newspaper really began on September 25, 1690, when the governor of Massachusetts censored and suppressed the first and only issue of Benjamin Harris' *Publick Occurrences Both Foreign and Domestick*. Harris, who had to flee England after his imprisonment for publishing a seditious pamphlet, had struck again. But it was a prophetic beginning for American journalism. Harris had promised the readers of that first issue that he would keep them informed, that the little three-page paper (a fourth page was left blank for notes and letters), only 6 by 9½ inches when folded in half, would be "furnished once a month (or if any Glut of Occurrences happen, oftener)."

Fortunately, Americans considered newspapers more indispensable than did their Colonial governors. Our familiarity with, indeed what might be a national preference for, newspaper journalism marks us as a nation of newspaper readers—as if all the jokes and cartoons about Americans and their morning newspapers at the breakfast table could leave any doubt. And it's always been this way with Americans. The familiar names of Peter Zenger, Benjamin Franklin, Joseph Pulitzer, Mary Baker Eddy, and William Randolph Hearst remind us of the journalist's role in American history. Even those of us who don't spend much time with books have read some of the large metropolitan dailies.

But there's another, even more important element to newspaper history, the abiding tradition of community weeklies. In these little papers, operating for years on a shoestring and usually walking the tightrope of solvency, is the stuff of local history. It may come as a surprise to generations of Americans alive today, who look upon their neighborhood weekly as just a "supplement" to their reading in the big city papers, but little weeklies are deeply rooted in the American past (with branches right into the present) and once brought the news to rural and small towns where most Americans lived. It's hard to believe in this day and age, when the *New York Times* (or a paper from anywhere in the world, for that matter) appears on California newsstands hours after it comes off the press, but once smalltown America depended on its local presses, indeed the big dailies were looked upon with suspicion as outsiders, city slickers whose big city interests not only made no allowance for but were actually detrimental to the values of rural America. Throughout most of our history, during the 1700s and 1800s and into this century, the community newspaper—weekly, semimonthly, or whatever—carried the important news, the news closest to you and your neighbors.

The big newspapers are the johnny-come-latelys. Actually, the metropolitan dailies began their rise to importance only about one hundred years ago, just after the Civil War, when the industrial revolution in America caused large shifts in population from the farms and small towns to the cities that had jobs and the exciting life. But even then community papers grew in numbers, until in their heyday, around 1914, there were 14,500 such papers around the country. And they were a varied lot too. Many were foreign language papers (in 1860 almost 10 percent of the newspapers sold in America were foreign language papers) in French, Dutch, Italian, Spanish, Norwegian, Swedish, even Welsh, and there was a German language newspaper in almost every state. Before the Civil War, over twenty Negro newspapers decried slavery and spoke for black Americans; the first, *Freedom's Journal*, appeared in New York in 1827. There have been countless other underground papers throughout our history, and even today, after decades of consolidations, chains, and falling revenues, something over ten thousand little papers still hang on. Perhaps the new momentum in America back to smalltown life will also signal a renaissance of the community weekly.

There's something about little newspapers, even today, that sets them apart from their big city cousins. Smaller staffs (usually part-time and more often than not volunteer) are writing about their neighbors, individuals not among millions but only a few hundred. You just write differently about people you know, who share your interests, whom you might run into tomorrow. It is this smallness, simplicity, and neighborliness that prompted the editor of the *Ware Gazette* back in 1850 (having just recently changed the paper's name from the *Village Gazette*) to inform his readers that "all subscribers may consider themselves contributors." (A subscription cost only 37½ cents a year.)

The first of the *Gazette's* four 12-by-16-inch pages carries the paper's motto: "A Record of the busy World, Its Clouds and Sunshine, Smiles and tears"—leaving the reader to meditate on the editor's decision not to capitalize that last noun. The pages of the *Gazette* are covered with local and national news, literary notes, humorous anecdotes, and the presidential election news of 1848 ("Good news for the Whigs"), including the vote cast in Ware: Whig 218, Democrat 124, and Free Soil 151. And among the advertisements were these:

S. Newbour & Brother have just taken over the Old Company Store.

S. F. Pepper, Variety Store. Muffs etc. Wood. Patent Medicines. "Pepper's burning fluid, or chemical oil, 75 cts. per gallon." Daguerreotypes taken.

L. Hilton, Oyster Room.

LIGHTNING *The Subscriber has recently set up one of those recently invented batteries for the purpose of Gold and Silver plating. L. Babcock.*

FOR SALE *The Carpet in Pew No. 101, Congregational Church, 2 hymn books, and various small articles including a mouse trap. Addison Stanford.*

Little glimpses of life in America await the newspaper browser. Here is a sampling. First, an item that includes a personal demographic footnote:

FIRST *Girl born in the Massachusetts Bay Colony, Salem. On the 14th Current there died at Beverly,* Elizabeth Patch, *Aged 86 years; she was the first born English Female of this Town, and of all that part of the Province formerly call'd the Massachusetts-Colony.* [Boston News-Letter, January 16–23, 1715/16]

The obscure notice of the arrival of a soon-to-be-famous visitor:

COLONEL *Washington. Last Friday came to this Town from Virginia, the Hon. Col. Washington, a Gentleman who has deservedly a high Reputation for Military Skill, Integrity and Valor; tho' success has not always attended his Undertakings.* [Boston Gazette, March 1, 1756]

An early census concluding with a note of social commentary:

POPULATION *of Boston in 1742. The selectmen having appointed a number of suitable Persons to go through the several wards of the Town. . . . They reported on oath as follows, viz. 16,382 souls, including 1374 Negroes, 1719 Houses, 166 Warehouses, 418 Horses, and 141 Cows. In the Almshouse are 110 Persons supported by the Town, and 36 in the Work-House. There are also in the Town at least 1200 Widows, and 1000 of them in very low circumstances.* [Boston News-Letter, December 23, 1742]

A bizarre end to Robert Hunt, lime seller of Boston:

Robert Hunt, a lime seller of Boston, differing with a man, drew a sword and made two or three passes at him, upon which the man seized the sword and broke it and went for a warrant to apprehend Hunt who at once shut himself up in his house with a loaded gun and two pistols beside him. When the officers appeared he fired out of the window several times and wounded two boys but at last was taken and committed to prison where three days later he committed suicide by hanging "with an old single Garter." The same afternoon his body "was carried thro' the Town in a Cart, and buried near the Gallows, having a stake first drove thro' it." [*Boston Gazette*, April 18, 1749]

And, of course, problems with the mail:

These are to give Notice, That the Bag of Letters designed for England *by the Briganteen* Experiment, *Jonathan Evans, Master, that was Stranded at Hampton, are now in the Post Office at Boston; And any Person that wants their Letters again may have them.* [*Boston News-Letter*, November 4–11, 1706]

America, it would seem, has always faced traffic problems:

By laws were adopted by the Town of Boston in 1727, Trucks and Carts and were in force in 1744, providing that no truck should be driven through the streets and lanes, "whose Sides exceed the length of Sixteen Feet"; nor "with more than Two Horses at a Time"; nor carrying "more than One Tun weight at a Load"; and every driver should "go by the side of the Thilhorse, with his Halter in his Hand." [*Boston News-Letter*, March 22, 1744]

But advertisements were once very different from what they are now:

Any Person that has a mind to take a walk in the Garden at the Bottom of the Common, to eat Currants, shall be Kindly Welcome for Six Pence a piece. [*Boston News-Letter*, July 10–17, 1735]

All the little newspapers and big dailies of such long standing are at once the joy and the agony of the historian, presenting a dilemma of too much information too widely dispersed, rather than too little. If state and local historical journals lack consistent and comprehensive indexing, alas, newspapers are much worse. With the exception of the largest dailies—the *New York Times* is the prime example of a newspaper that publishes an almost universally accessible index—newspaper indexes are all but non-existent. (Even the indexing of books is only a fairly recent development—to the consternation of anyone who has tried to find a specific reference in a book printed in the nineteenth century or even from the early years of this century.) I suppose it's even possible that newspapers, at least in the beginning, never really considered themselves of historical interest and eschewed any commitment to posterity in the rush to get news out while it was news. Yet the very qualities that made newspapers appealing to their immediate audience make them even more interesting to the historian.

There are other difficulties in using old newspapers, like the matter of continuity or, rather, the lack of it. Some newspapers have been publishing for a long time; many which appeared in the seventeenth, eighteenth, and nineteenth centuries ceased publication somewhere along the way many years ago; others have appeared, historically speaking, only very recently. As for papers that have been around for a century, they sometimes have undergone changes in name and ownership, not just once but several times. The *New-York Journal*, for example, during its nine-year history, 1784 to 1793, went through seven variants of its name:

The New-York Journal and State Gazette
The New-York Journal and General Advertiser
The New-York Journal, or the Weekly Register
The New-York Journal and Weekly Register
The New-York Journal and Daily Patriotic Register
The New-York Journal and Weekly Register
The New-York Journal & Patriotic Register

Some newspaper editors with a sense of history (and infinite storage space somewhere) have kept every issue since No. 1; others keep only the last five or ten years on file; but happily many others have turned their collections over to museums, libraries, and local and state historical societies.

* * *

The qualities of American newspaper publishing that we've been discussing often present a real headache to historians. But as chaotic as the situation at large appears, the files of the local newspaper offer an exciting, and quite manageable, focus for the work of the local historian who can spend perhaps no more than an hour or two a week with them.

State historical societies and amateur local historians have made something of a start compiling excerpts and indexing newspaper articles, particularly from the Colonial period. Two most notable examples (which incidentally offer fascinating browsing) are Rita Susswein Gottesman's two-volume work for the New York Historical Society, *The Arts and Crafts of New York* (New York: 1938, 1954), and George Francis Dow's *The Arts & Crafts in New England, 1704–1775: Gleanings from Boston Newspapers Relating to Painting, Engraving, Silversmiths, Pewterers, Clockmakers, Furniture, Pottery, Old Houses, Costume, Trades and Occupations &c. &c. &c. &c. &c.* (Topsfield, Mass.: The Wayside Press, 1927). Gottesman's survey of the newspapers published in New York during most of the eighteenth century, 1726 to 1790, is a model for the amateur local historian, culling advertisements and news items that describe the fantastic range of goods and services available to New Yorkers, from balloons to waxworks. The Dow volume is better illustrated (though both works are disappointing on this account) and makes a nice companion to the Gottesman volumes. Both works are helpful in illuminating a task that will require many years of work by many historians.

You should keep in mind that there are sources for the newspaper browser-historian other than public libraries. Back copies of newspapers may also be found in newspaper offices, museums, collections of the local historical society, and even elementary and high school libraries (don't forget school yearbooks and student newspapers).

*   *   *

While some libraries maintain a separate periodical file showing which numbers are in their collection, the main card catalog will serve as a quick check as to which newspapers are in the library. Healthful exercise is one of the many benefits of browsing through old newspapers, for a six-month collection or a complete volume of bound newspapers, replete with Sunday sup-

plements, weighs a lot, especially when it's five shelves up and underneath two or three other bound volumes.

But it may happen that just as you've readied yourself to wrestle six months of the *Boston Transcript* down from the top shelf, the librarian might hand you a little cardboard box about three inches square! Inside will be a plastic spool of microfilm containing a little transparency of every page of every issue for several months, all of which, with a little practice, can be read easily on a microfilm reader. Some newspapers might be on heavy white cards (known as microfiche), which are read in a somewhat different reader, but in either case, transparency or white card, they allow libraries not only to store a lot of newspapers in a space perhaps no bigger than a file cabinet but also to acquire collections of rare newspapers and others long out of print. One final note on all this helpful technology. Larger libraries have special copy machines that enable you to make paper copies, frame by frame, from the microfilm, the copies producing a newspaper page reduced to 11 by 14 inches.

In any case, whether at a newspaper office or a library, you'll next need to decide what it is you have the time and energy to do. Indexing and excerpting is sometimes tedious and is very demanding work. If you've got lots of help (an entire high school history class, for example), then you might try a general index. If you're working alone, then stick to a subject that interests you and make a special subject index. Almost any topic will be of interest to someone somewhere, but here are some suggestions to get you started:

WEDDINGS AND PARTIES	WOMEN IN LOCAL HISTORY
SPORTS	SCHOOLS
AUTOMOBILES	TRADES AND OCCUPATIONS
INDUSTRY AND COMMERCE	ARTS AND CRAFTS
RAILROADS	RECIPES
POLITICS AND VOTING	WEATHER
CHURCHES AND CHURCH	EDITORIALS
NEWS	TOWN FIRSTS
FARMING	TOWN PLANNING
ARCHITECTURE	

Whether you intend to produce a general index or an index to a subject that interests you, the procedure is the same. You'll need a quantity of 3-by-5 cards or scrap paper (save a tree by cutting up paper that's been printed only on one side) and a box of some sort with dividers that will serve as an alphabetical file and help keep everything organized, particularly if you have to move around from home to library, or if several people are working together. It won't take long before you'll have more cards than you know what to do with, so it's a good idea to be organized right from the start.

If the number of cards under one title becomes numerous, you'll want to set up subheadings for the index:

RAILROADS	RECIPES
Cotton Belt	*Baked goods*
Diesel power	*Casseroles*
Freight	*Drinks*
Maintenance shops	*Fondues*

You'll need to create new subject headings as the project progresses, but keep a list of them (pasted on the inside of your file box cover) so everyone working on the project knows what the headings are.

Once completed, your newspaper index becomes a valuable community resource and may in fact be put to use by local historians who have heard that the project is underway. You might just leave your index on cards— useful and easy to supplement—to be kept with the back issues of the newspaper. Or you might think of publishing it in some form. If there's enough interest in the community, your neighbors might be willing to subscribe to a limited edition. Issuing an index to back issues illustrated with excerpts and old woodcuts and photographs is a great way for the community and its newspaper to celebrate an anniversary.

The mere presence of a resource like an index can cause all kinds of nice things to happen, for an index not only makes it easier but actually encourages local history projects. Individuals with both the time and a sense of history might compile their own collections of excerpts, even their own town histories, replete with recipes (menus from old-time restaurants), local characters, stories, local customs, and memorabilia. Still another outcome of your efforts might be a fifty-years-ago-today column in the neighborhood weekly, or a history series. If you make note of illustrations on your index cards, you will help photographers find old cuts and photographs which can be copied for local history exhibits.

So the possibilities for community awareness are endless, and all this for little expense, except many hours of enjoyable browsing. An accurate index, even one that's not yet completed, will at least reawaken the young and new members of the community to the many interesting years that have gone before and could be the focus of a whole new local history movement which is helped by and in turn gives a new impetus to the neighborhood weekly.

———— • •◆• • ————

One of the many joys awaiting those with the patience and curiosity to browse through local and state historical journals is the discovery of some fine old recipes. In a copy of the historical quarterly Annals of Iowa *I found a couple of treats from a little book called the* Falcon Cook Book, *apparently published sometime between 1893 and 1917, the years the Des Moines Roller Mills produced Falcon flour.*

JOHNNIE CAKE

Three tablespoons Falcon flour, three tablespoons sugar, one-half cup shortening, two eggs, salt, one pint sour milk, one teaspoon soda, corn meal to make good batter, not too stiff. Bake in a shallow pan.

OYSTER SHORTCAKE

Crust: Two cups Falcon flour, two teaspoons baking-powder, one-half teaspoon salt, two teaspoons butter, three-fourths cup milk. Mix very soft and bake in two layers buttering between. When baked split open and pour over it as follows: One-half pint oysters, one and one-half cups milk and three tablespoons butter, three tablespoons of Falcon flour. Scald the oysters. Make a white sauce of butter, flour and milk and liquor from the oysters. Add to the scalded oysters, salt and pepper. [*Annals of Iowa*, Fall, 1966, p. 479]

MOLASSES GINGERBREAD

One table spoon of cinnamon one spoonful ginger, some coriander or al-spice, put to four tea spoons pearlash, dissolved in half pint of water, four pound flour, one quart molasses, six ounces butter, (if in summer rub in the butter, if in the winter, warm the butter and molasses and pour to the spiced flour) knead well till stiff, the more the better, the lighter and whiter it will be; bake brisk fifteen minutes: don't scorch; before it is put in, wash it with whites and sugar beat together.
[*Old-Time New England*, Fall, 1966]

Selected Bibliography

CHAPTER 1

Willa K. Baum. *Oral History for the Local Historical Society*. Nashville, Tenn.: American Association for State and Local History, 1974.

CHAPTER 2

Ansel Adams. "Copying Techniques With Artificial Light." *Artificial-Light Photography*. New York: Morgan & Morgan, 1968.

Time-Life Books. *Caring for Photographs*. New York: Time-Life Books, 1975.

CHAPTER 3

Gilbert H. Doane. *Searching for Your Ancestors*. New York: Bantam Books, 1974.

CHAPTER 4

James Deetz and Edwin S. Dethlefsen. "Death's Head, Cherub, Urn and Willow." *Natural History* (March, 1967).

Harriette Merrifield Forbes. *Gravestones of Early New England and the Men Who Made Them, 1653-1800*. Boston: Houghton Mifflin, 1927.

Andrew Kull. *New England Cemeteries: A Collector's Guide*. Brattleboro, Vt.: The Stephen Greene Press, 1975.

Allan I. Ludwig. *Graven Images: New England Stone Carving and its Symbols, 1615-1815*. Middletown, Conn.: Wesleyan University Press, 1966.

CHAPTER 5

America the Beautiful Fund. *Old Glory, A Pictorial Report on the Grass Roots History Movement and The First Hometown History Primer*. New York: Warner Paperback Library, 1973.

Ivor Noël Hume. *Here Lies Virginia*. New York: Alfred A. Knopf, 1963.

————. *Historical Archaeology*. New York: Alfred A. Knopf, 1969.

CHAPTER 6

Clarence S. Brigham. *History and Bibliography of American Newspapers, 1690-1820*. Worcester, Mass.: American Antiquarian Society, 1947.

George Francis Dow. *The Arts & Crafts in New England, 1704-1775*. Topsfield, Mass.: The Wayside Press, 1927.

Rita Susswein Gottesman. *The Arts and Crafts in New England, 1726-1776*. New York: New-York Historical Society, 1938.

————. *The Arts and Crafts in New England, 1777-1779*. New York: New-York Historical Society, 1954.

CHAPTER 7

J. C. Harrington. *Glassmaking at Jamestown*. Richmond, Va.: Glass Crafts of America, 1952.

CHAPTER 8

Ansel Adams. *Camera and Lens*. New York: Morgan & Morgan, 1970.

————. "Architecture and Industry." *Natural-Light Photography*. New York: Morgan & Morgan, 1968.

Jerry Katz and Sidney Fogel. "Ultrasharp Black-and-White Photography with High Contrast Films." *The Leica Manual*. New York: Morgan & Morgan, 1973.

Harley J. McKee. *Recording Historic Buildings*. Washington, D.C.: U.S. Department of the Interior, National Park Service, Historic American Buildings Survey, 1970.

CHAPTER 9

Directory of Historical Societies and Agencies in the United States and Canada. Nashville, Tenn.: American Association for State and Local History, 1974.

Index

Acknowledgements
and Picture Credits

The author is grateful to the following people and institutions for material which appears throughout the book: Daniel M. Lohnes and the Society for the Preservation of New England Antiquities for permission to use excerpts from "Kim's Store: Reminiscences of Sarah Endicott Ober," Augustus Peabody Loring (ed.); Frank Whitcomb Tarr's "Quaint Speech and Lore of Sandy Bay now Rockport"; and "Raising Connecticut Meeting Houses" by J. Frederick Kelly, from *Old-Time New England*. The Iowa State Department of History and Archives for permission to reprint excerpts from Rae McGrady Booth's "Memoirs of an Iowa Farm Girl" and Don Buchan's "Pioneer Tales" from *Annals of Iowa*. The Arkansas Historical Association for permission to use excerpts from "Arkansas Boyhood Long Ago" by Boyce House and E. A. Holcombe's "Spring Mill" from *The Arkansas Historical Quarterly*. Alex Haley for use of excerpts from "My Furthest Back Person—The African," Copyright © 1972 by Alex Haley and reprinted by permission of Paul R. Reynolds, Inc. The Minnesota Historical Society for permission to include excerpts from Esther Jerabek, "Letters to Bohemia: A Czech Settler Writes from Owatonna, 1856-1858," in *Minnesota History*, 43:137-138 (Winter, 1972). Hilda Dischinger Morhart for permission to use "The Autobiography of John Sturm" from her book *The Zoar Story*. The University of Chicago Press for permission to use excerpts from B. A. Botkin (ed.), *Lay My Burden Down: A Folk History of Slavery*, © 1945, The University of Chicago Press. Ellen C. Masters for her permission to reprint "The Hill" from Edgar Lee Masters' *Spoon River Anthology*, Copyright © 1962 by The Crowell-Collier Publishing Company. Columbia University Press for permission to use excerpts from Vance Randolph, *Ozark Superstitions*, Copyright © 1947 by Columbia University Press. The *Round Valley News* for permission to reprint the article "Grain Mill Set in Motion Again" (August 8, 1975).

The author would also like to thank the people who made available the illustrations and photographs which appear on the following pages:
30, 32, 34—Eastman Kodak Company. 50—Courtesy of The Bancroft Library. 58, 69, 126 —Courtesy of The Society for the Preservation of New England Antiquities. 87, 88, 89—from *Early New England Gravestone Rubbings* by Edmund Vincent Gillon, Jr. Copyright © 1966 by Dover Publications, Inc. 92, 94, 95—Alden Robertson. 142—illustrations from *The Primer of American Antiquities* by Carl W. Drepperd. Copyright 1944 by Carl W. Drepperd. Reproduced by permission of Doubleday & Company, Inc. 96—The Library of Congress. 148-152, 155-160, 162-164, 167-169—Historic American Buildings Survey.